T0402480

Property Law in the Society of Equals

OXFORD PRIVATE LAW THEORY

Oxford Private Law Theory publishes leading work in private law theory. It commissions and solicits monographs and edited collections in general private law theory as well as specific fields, including the theoretical analysis of tort law, property law, contract law, fiduciary law, trust law, remedies and restitution, and the law of equity. The series is open to diverse theoretical approaches, including those informed by philosophy, economics, history, and political theory. Oxford Private Law Theory sets the standard for rigorous and original work in private law theory.

ALSO PUBLISHED IN THIS SERIES

Wrongs, Harms, and Compensation
Paying for our Mistakes
Adam Slavny

Standing in Private Law
Powers of Enforcement in the Law of Obligations and Trusts
Edited by Timothy Liau

Private Law and Practical Reason
Essays on John Gardner's Private Law Theory
Edited by Haris Psarras and Sandy Steel

Rights, Wrongs, and Injustices
The Structure of Remedial Law
Stephen A. Smith

Civil Wrongs and Justice in Private Law
Edited by Paul B. Miller and John Oberdiek

Property Law in the Society of Equals

CHRISTOPHER ESSERT

Oxford University Press is a department of the University of Oxford. It furthers the University's objective of excellence in research, scholarship, and education by publishing worldwide. Oxford is a registered trade mark of Oxford University Press in the UK and certain other countries.

Published in the United States of America by Oxford University Press
198 Madison Avenue, New York, NY 10016, United States of America.

Library of Congress Cataloging-in-Publication Data
Names: Essert, Christopher, author.
Title: Property law in the society of equals / Christopher Essert.
Description: New York : Oxford University Press, 2024. |
Series: Oxford studies in private law theory | Includes bibliographical references and index.
Identifiers: LCCN 2023048126 (print) | LCCN 2023048127 (ebook) |
ISBN 9780197768952 (hardback) | ISBN 9780197768976 (updf)|
ISBN 9780197768969 (epub) | ISBN 9780197768983 (digital-online)
Subjects: LCSH: Property. | Equality—Sociological aspects. | Government property.
Classification: LCC K720 .E87 2024 (print) | LCC K720 (ebook) |
DDC 346.04—dc23/eng/20231012
LC record available at https://lccn.loc.gov/2023048126
LC ebook record available at https://lccn.loc.gov/2023048127

DOI: 10.1093/oso/9780197768952.001.0001

Printed by Integrated Books International, United States of America

Note to Readers

To Ginny, Arlo, and Sam

Contents

Acknowledgments

In the course of writing this book I was lucky to incur many debts.

I'm grateful to Paul Miller and John Oberdiek, as editors of the Oxford Studies in Private Law Theory series of which this book is a part, for their early and enthusiastic support. And I am grateful also to everyone at OUP and to the book's reviewers.

The Faculty of Law at the University of Toronto remains an unparalleled environment to engage in the sort of legal theory of which this book is (I hope) an example. I am grateful to all of my colleagues for their engagement with my work and to the two deans during my time here, Ed Iacobucci and Jutta Brunnée for their support. I conceived of this book and began work on it while I was a member of the faculty at Queen's Law, and I am thankful to my colleagues there and to then-Dean Bill Flanagan for their early support of the project.

The work on the project has been supported throughout by the Social Sciences and Humanities Research Council of Canada, which support I hereby gratefully acknowledge.

For participation in presentations of various parts of (sometimes quite) earlier versions of the material, I am grateful to audiences at (or in internet video calls hosted by) Binghamton University, Dartmouth University, Harvard Law School, King's College London, the London School of Economics, Northeastern University, Osgoode Hall Law School, Oxford University, Rutgers Law School, Stanford University, Tel Aviv University, the University of California at Berkeley, the UCLA School of Law, the University of Michigan, the University of Pennsylvania, the University of Surrey, the University of Toronto, the University of Southern California, and Western University.

At those sessions and on other occasions formal and informal, for comments, questions, discussions, suggestions, and expressions of mild skepticism and outright disbelief, I am grateful to Ben Alarie, Dominic Alford-Duguid, Haim Abraham, Hrafn Asgeirsson, Steve Bero, John Borrows, Andrew Botterell, Molly Brady, Alan Brudner, Jutta Brunnée, Sarah Buss, Bruce Chapman, Eric Claeys, Josh Cohen, Bob Cooter, Nico Cornell, Hanoch Dagan, Yasmin Dawood, Avihay Dorfman, Daniela Dover, Abraham Drassinower, David Dyzenhaus, Ken Ehrenberg, Blake Emerson, Kim Ferzan, Sarah Fine, Allan Gibbard, Maytal Gilboa, Jonathan Gingerich, John Goldberg, Kate Greasley, David Grewal, Jeff Helmreich, Barbara Herman, Scott Hershovitz, Desmond Jagmohan, Zoë Johnson King, Renée Jorgensen, Larissa Katz, Greg Keating, Emily Kidd White,

Dennis Klimchuk, James Krier, Nadia Lambek, Joanna Langille, Michael Law-Smith, James Lee, Elly Leggatt, Ira Lindsay, S M Love, Tim Macklem, Paul MacMahon, Daniel Markovits, Gabe Mendlow, David Miller, Alex Mogyros, Ezequiel Monti, Russ Muirhead, Stephen Munzer, Jen Nadler, Chris Newman, Jason Neyers, Alissa North, John Oberdiek, David Owens, Manish Oza, Herlinde Pauer-Studer, David Plunkett, Dan Priel, Daniel Putnam, Jon Quong, Tony Reeves, Massimo Renzo, Arthur Ripstein, Veronica Rodriguez-Blanco, Arie Rosen, Luke Rostill, Becca Rothfeld, Nick Sage, Wendy Salkin, Irit Samet, Alex Sarch, Tim Scanlon, Margo Schlanger, Amy Sepinwall, Chris Serkin, Scott Shapiro, Seana Shiffrin, Zoë Sinel, Matthew Noah Smith, Henry Smith, Lionel Smith, the late Stephen Smith, Sandy Steel, Hamish Stewart, Annie Stilz, Becca Stone, Martin Stone, Andy Summers, William Swadling, Victor Tadros, John Tasioulas, Jean Thomas, Malcolm Thorburn, Kevin Toh, Sabine Tsuruda, Manuel Vargas, Gerry Vildostegui, Konstanze von Schutz, Emmanuel Voyiakis, Jordan Wallace-Wolf, R Jay Wallace, Gary Watson, Charlie Webb, Grégoire Webber, Arnold Weinrib, Ernie Weinrib, Jacob Weinrib, Daniel Wodak, Ekow Yankah, Andy Yu, and Ben Zipursky.

I mentioned the benefits of working on this book at the University of Toronto Faculty of Law. Two of them merit detailed mention. First are our fantastic students. For their attention and patience and questions, I owe a lot to the students in the Property and Tort Law courses I taught over the course of writing this book, as well as those in several seminars that covered some of the book's material. I am very grateful to Joie Chow, Jasmit Kaur, Michael Law-Smith, Adrian Ling, Olivia O'Connor, Amit Singh, and in particular Ben Zolf (who read and closely edited two drafts of the entire manuscript) for research assistance, to Megan Pfiffer for an essential final proof read, and to Hannah Rosenberg for preparing the index. Second is the Faculty's Legal Theory Reading Group, which has been meeting weekly since the year that I was born (although I have not been attending the whole time). The members of the group graciously agreed to work through the entire manuscript of this book over weekly meetings for the academic year 2021–22. For their participation in those sessions and copious amounts of incredibly valuable feedback—really, a depth of sympathetic but critical engagement that was a true model of the very best of the academic endeavor—I am extraordinarily thankful.

At one point or another, I had a discussion with each of Barbara Herman, Sophia Moreau, Martin Stone, and Jacob Weinrib that probably seemed to them to be just another chat but which, in each case, had an enormous impact on my thinking in this book. So in each case I owe them thanks.

I owe particular thanks to three colleagues: Arthur Ripstein, Ernie Weinrib, and Abraham Drassinower. Over a number of years, Arthur patiently helped me to work through Kant's views and his views, and, in so doing, to figure out my own. Although I never took a class with Arthur, there is nobody from whom I have learned more. In my first year of law school, I had the extremely fortunate and incredibly formative experience of taking Torts with Ernie and Property with Abraham (or, as I then styled them, Professor Weinrib and Professor Drassinower). Since then, Ernie has inspired me with dedication to the scholarly endeavor. His engagement with the manuscript of this book was incredible in its focus and depth, and improved it immensely. Finally, it would not be too much to say that the seed of this book was planted in my head in that first-year Property small group where Abraham was my teacher. In the years since, I have learned so much from him and benefited from his unflagging support, encouragement, and friendship.

My greatest debt is to my family. Each of them, in their own way, inspired some part of this book's contents. But that is the least of what they did and do. So it is to them that this book is dedicated.

Introduction

Property law is an essential constituent of a society of equals. Only when we can have things as yours or mine can we relate to one another on terms of equality, with none superior or inferior to any other. An institution of property realizes what I will call the idea of yours and mine, and in doing so makes it possible for us to interact with respect to spaces, objects, and other parts of the social world in a way that is consistent with our relating on terms of equality. We are required by our most basic moral commitments to have an institution of property law, the law of yours and mine. Property's role in our lives is constituted by and regulated according to its capacity to solve a problem about equality. It is in the nature of property that any institution of property, as the realization of a kind of egalitarian relation, must aim to ensure that none of its subjects be subordinated with respect to its subject matter. So a demand that the institution not be allowed to generate its own forms of subordination, including in particular a demand that no member of the society be homeless, is internal to property. Property is, and should be, an egalitarian institution.

That, in a very few words, is the account of property that I defend in this book. I will justify those abstract claims and show that they provide us with a way of thinking about property that is not only attractive from the point of view of political morality but also illuminating of a wide variety of legal questions about property law. That is, I will show that, if we think about property as the realization of the idea of yours and mine, we can better understand the basic common law of property, including rules about trespass, nuisance, acquisition, transfer, and so on; we can understand how to think about ownership of intangibles and more broadly about what can be owned; and we can understand the differences and commonalities between property rights, personal rights, and contract rights. I will also show that by conceiving property in this way, we can see how property is subject to a regulative ideal that demands that each subject of an institution of property be given sufficient property of their own—that there be no homelessness—and that the use of property may be constrained as a matter of both private and public law to more fully strive towards the realization of its egalitarian basis and its essential place in a society of equals.

Before we get to all of that, I want to spend some time in this Introduction talking in more general terms about property and equality, about the relation

Property Law in the Society of Equals. Christopher Essert, Oxford University Press. © Oxford University Press 2024.
DOI: 10.1093/oso/9780197768952.003.0001

between them, and about how a certain conception of that relation provides the basis for the approach I take to the subject matter of this book.

I.1 Two Egalitarian Challenges

Nothing is naturally anyone's, but almost everything belongs to someone. How could this be okay? One common answer, with a pedigree that traces back almost to the very beginning of philosophy, is that nothing could make it okay. Nothing could justify property: property is "theft" or a kind of "bondage." This sort of answer comes in different flavors, with different emphases. But at least one important subset of these answers—offered by great philosophers and by thoughtful citizens—locates the core of the case against property in its connection to equality, or, perhaps better put, inequality. I mean: look around. We are living in times of almost unprecedented inequality of wealth, and things do not seem to be getting better. Quite the contrary. As Leonard Cohen put it, the poor stay poor and the rich get rich. And it is natural to lay the blame for this state of affairs at property's feet. Poverty and wealth seem to be grounded on property: when individual private persons are allowed to have things as their own—when they are allowed to own them—it seems that the stage is set for an inevitable progression toward an unequal allocation of a society's resources, as some accumulate a great deal and others are left with little, or nothing.

As I said, this worry is easy enough to see. It is often offered by a character whom we might name the "Everyday Marxist," a character who observes an intuitive connection between private ownership of property and inequality and concludes that we ought to eliminate property altogether. A recent (as I write) article in a magazine at least nominally aimed at teenagers, for instance, begins by noting the widespread demands for relaxation of residential tenants' obligations to pay rent during the COVID-19 pandemic and the attendant economic collapse and concludes with a call for a "rejection of the construct that any one person should own this earth's land." The line of thinking runs like this. The divide between rich and poor rests on the institution of property, since the richness of the rich is grounded on their legal entitlements in their wealth. So to eliminate the inequality, we need to eliminate property, and presumably replace it with some kind of communism of the sort associated with Marx and in particular with his and Engels' *Communist Manifesto*, whose single most famous line tells us that "the theory of the Communists may be summed up in the single sentence: Abolition of private property." Hence "Everyday Marxism."[1]

[1] This character is inspired by Liam Murphy and Thomas Nagel's discussion of property and taxation in The Myth of Ownership (2002), which takes as its interlocutor the converse character, the "everyday libertarian."

Marx's own views on this question are, of course, significantly more complicated than the Everyday Marxist's, and saying any more about them would require a different book than this one. But there is a different philosopher whose treatment—or, as it will turn out to be more accurate to say, treatments—of the relation between property and equality is both clearer and more helpful here. The first sentence of this section may have tipped my hand: the philosopher I have in is mind Jean-Jacques Rousseau. Rousseau's *Discourse on the Origin and the Foundations of Inequality among Men* (which, following common practice, I will call the "Second Discourse") contains an important and influential discussion of the connection that is our current target, referring to it at one point even as "the Law of property and inequality."[2]

Rousseau, in his discussion of inequality, makes two importantly different kinds of arguments about the relation between it and property, employing two importantly different conceptions of that relation. One of them—the one that seems more prominent in the Second Discourse and often invoked by the Everyday Marxist—is causal or, if you like, genealogical. It is an argument about how institutions of property tend to lead (or perhaps always lead) to inequalities of wealth, roughly because of the urge of the rich to always have more. The thought is that inequality is something that accumulates over time, though, as Rousseau says, "a slow succession of events."[3] Again, the poor stay poor and the rich *get* rich. It is the getting that is the issue on this causal reading, because property creates the conditions in which inequality is able to take root and to grow: once people can own things, they want to own more things, and, through hard work or good luck or exploitation of others, they come to do so, and are protected in these unequal holdings by property and its rules. So property makes possible this slow succession of events whose eventual outcome is significant inequality. This critique of property was also Proudhon's. He thought that property "resting necessarily on equality, contradicts its own rationale," because "the perpetual and absolute right of retaining one's patrimony . . . involves the right to alienate, to sell, to give, to acquire, and to lose it; and [it] tends, consequently, to nothing less than the destruction of that equality for which it had been established."[4] We can call the thought that property leads, through a slow succession of events, to an unequal distribution of resources, the first egalitarian challenge

[2] Rousseau, Discourse on the Origin and the Foundations of Inequality among Men II.33 [OC III, 178] (1754). All Rousseau quotes are taken from the Cambridge University Press versions of the texts, translated by Victor Gourevitch, except in one case indicated below.

[3] Rousseau, Second Discourse II.1. Paragraph 27 is a good illustration of this idea. In that paragraph, Rousseau talks about human qualities being "set in action," about *amour propre*'s capacity to make us "become" different than we were, about how things were "previously," and then "finally." All these are constructions indicating a process leading toward inequality.

[4] Pierre-Joseph Proudhon, What Is Property? 63, 65 (Donald R Kelley and Bonnie G Smith eds., 1840/1994).

to property. In what follows I spend some time talking about this challenge, but it is not, in my view, where our investigation should begin.

To see why, note that Rousseau also invokes quite a different conception of the connection between property and equality, on which there is some kind of internal or constitutive connection between property and inequality. The idea here is not that property causes inequality, but that property and inequality are "inseparable," so that there was a "moment" when "equality disappeared [and] property appeared."[5] Rousseau indicates the centrality of this idea, in fact, in his Introduction, when he describes his subject "precisely" as "the *moment* when, Right replacing Violence, Nature was subjected to Law."[6] This idea that there is some moment at which we can locate the origin of the inequality that property gives rise to rests on an understanding of property and inequality that is quite a bit different, quite a bit more sophisticated, and, crucially, quite a bit more challenging than the causal story of the first egalitarian challenge. In that story, the slide from property to inequality is complex and takes time and therefore (in principle at least) could be avoided. But here, the problem of inequality arises at once, upon the initiative of "the first person who, having enclosed a piece of land, thought to say 'This is Mine.' "[7] In other words, we might find inequality of a sort that we should be worried about in the very instant at which someone took something for their own. According to this view, if I were to somehow invent property by grabbing something—an avocado, perhaps—and calling it mine, I would have created a kind of inequality between us. But surely this is not the idea that there is a problem of inequality where the poor have more than the rich. It would be an odd and unusual understanding of the idea of a divide between rich and poor that committed us to saying that a single avocado could make me rich and you poor. What notion of equality could be at play here?

To answer, notice first that, according to an intuitive and familiar understanding of property—which is also, it is worth saying even here in this Introduction, the law's actual legal understanding—because the avocado is mine, it *is up to me rather than you* whether and in what circumstances you can interact with it. If I want to use the avocado to make and eat guacamole myself, that is my decision; if I want to lend or give it to you, that is also my decision. My decision determines what you are and are not permitted to do with respect to the avocado. So I have a kind of power or control over you. Before the avocado was mine, none of that was true: you were free to do whatever you wanted to do with it (short of using it to harm me, but we can set that aside). When it became mine, I gained

[5] Rousseau, Second Discourse II.27, 19 [OC III 175,171].

[6] Rousseau, Second Discourse, Introduction para. 4 [OC III, 131] (my emphasis).

[7] Rousseau, Second Discourse II.1 [OC III, 164]. This is the place where I depart from Gourevitch's translation. The French text of that sentence fragment is as follows: "Le premier qui ayant enclos un terrain, s'avisa de dire, ceci est à moi."

a claim of a right over you, and thus the capacity to determine what you are and are not permitted to do, at least with respect to the avocado. And the very moment that it became possible for me to say "this is mine" was the moment when I gained this power over you, this power that disrupts a kind of equality between us that seemed to exist absent property. Let me explain. If neither of us could have things as yours or mine—if there were no property—then the kind of power over others that property gives rise to would be impossible (or, more strongly even, inconceivable[8]). You would have your rights over your person and I would have my rights over mine, and neither of us could have a kind of right that the other did not. So we would be in that way equal. Property seems in its very conception at odds with this notion of equality, Rousseau is telling us, because the very idea brings with it a kind of power over another in a way that seems in tension with a very basic and intuitive moral idea, that none of us is naturally the superior or inferior of any other, that we are, in that way, one another's equals. The same point was put in slightly different language by Gerrard Winstanley, a Digger (a kind of seventeenth-century English opponent of private ownership), when he referred to property as a "coming in of Bondage," that is unjust insofar as it involves the idea that "one branch of mankind should rule over another"[9] Property, on this telling, constitutes inequality rather than just causing it. Or, as Proudhon famously put it, property *is* theft.

We should be clear that this line of thought rests on a different idea of equality, according to which equality is not about a comparison of how much stuff we have but instead about the relations in which we stand vis-à-vis one another. We are equals, on this conception of equality, when neither of us is the superior or inferior of the other. I will say much more about this idea in what follows, but it is most easily understood by way of contrast: the slave and master are not equals, because the slave is, as of right, subject to, inferior to, subordinated to, dominated by the master. When you and I relate as equals we relate precisely not in that way. Like others, I take such a conception of equality to be the basic notion, or among the basic notions, of political philosophy, and take it to structure much of our thinking about legal and political institutions.[10] The second line of thinking about property and equality that is present in Rousseau's discussion suggests that

[8] Without property, if I said, "don't touch that avocado, it's mine," you could reply, "what are you talking about?" or, "I don't see why you would think that uttering words like that would give me any reason in respect of that avocado."

[9] Gerrard Winstanley, "The True Levellers' Standard Advanced: Or, the State of Community Opened, and Presented to the Sons of Men" (1649). For detailed and insightful discussion of Winstanley's views, see Dennis Klimchuk, "Property and Necessity" in James Penner and Henry E Smith eds, Philosophical Foundations of Property Law 47 (2013).

[10] With me here are, I think, Rousseau and Kant, republicans such as Philip Pettit, relational egalitarians like Elizabeth Anderson and Samuel Scheffler, Niko Kolodny, arguably John Rawls, and others. I'll have more to say about many of these folks, their views, and the relations among those views at various points in what follows.

property is in tension with this notion of equality, and necessarily so, because the power that property gives to owners is precisely the kind of power that is inconsistent with this basic equality. When I can make the avocado mine, I gain power over you that you do not have over me and thus, at least with respect to that avocado, I am your superior. Applied to a broader and more pressing set of cases, Rousseau's thought is that property is in its very conception inconsistent with our standing as equals.

Call this the second egalitarian challenge to property. I indicated that I view the second challenge as more pressing than the first. We can now see what I meant by that. The first challenge claims that inequality arises through a slow succession of events: we begin with equality, add property, and then slowly watch the latter crowd out the former. The second challenge is sharper because it denies that any causal process is necessary: the very instant that property is instituted, it says, equality disappears. So it presses the challenge much more directly, and denies that property can be consistent with equality even in its conception. On this basis, my primary target will be the second challenge, although, as we will see, confronting the second will give us the means to better understand the first.

I.2 Flipping the Script

I think Rousseau himself offers among the most compelling replies to the second challenge—his own challenge—in the brief treatment of property that he offers in the *Social Contract*, written some years after the Second Discourse.

The *Social Contract* has a claim to be one of the most important works in the history of political philosophy and I have no plan to give it any detailed analysis. Suffice it to say that Rousseau is clearly concerned, in his defense of an account of political legitimacy, with at least an inchoate idea of equality along the lines of the one I gestured to earlier. He tells us at one point that "no man has a natural authority over his fellow-man," and grounds the basic idea of the social contract, in part, on the fact that each party to it enters on the same terms as each other—"since each gives himself entirely, the condition is equal for all"—so that there is none "over whom one does not acquire the same right as one grants over himself."[11] When Rousseau comes, then, to his brief discussion of property, he must confront the question of how property can be consistent with this idea of equality. The details of how Rousseau does this are complicated, but ultimately he comes to the view that, under the social contract, each member is able to gain a "genuine right" in property that would be unavailable outside the social contract, where any possession would be "usurpation." His thought, basically, is that,

[11] Rousseau, Of the Social Contract I.4.1, I.6.6–8 [OC III 355, 361–62] (1762).

outside the social contract, we can have only illegitimate (physical) possession but inside, our possession can become legitimate, a matter of right.[12] The explanation that Rousseau offers for this is absolutely crucial. He calls "the basis of the entire social system" the idea that

> the fundamental pact, rather than destroying natural equality, on the contrary substitutes a moral and legitimate equality for whatever physical inequality nature may have placed between men, and that while they may be unequal in force or in genius, they all become equal by convention and by right.[13]

This is tightly compressed, but we can expand it in light of what I have said so far. If we assume, as I think Rousseau does, that we all stand as equals as a moral (or more broadly normative) matter, we can ask how things might be for us with respect to the stuff of property law. Absent an institution of property—or in Rousseau's terms, outside the social contract—Rousseau seems to be saying that, with respect to land, objects, and so on, we could not relate on terms of equality at all: we could only relate, as he puts it, through "whatever physical inequality nature may have placed between us." If you were stronger than me—superior in "force or genius"—you would be advantaged, in that you could get your hands on whatever you want and keep my hands off it: if you were able to snatch the avocado I picked while I look away, you could do so, and I could not stop you. Absent an institution of property, there would be nothing wrong with that as such, since it would be impossible to say (or think) the avocado was mine rather than yours. So without property we could not relate as equals. By creating an institution of property, Rousseau is hinting, we would be able to "substitute a moral and legitimate equality" for the inequality that would obtain in its absence.

Take a step back here: the second egalitarian challenge, which I ascribed earlier to the Rousseau of the Second Discourse, claimed that property was in its nature inconsistent with equality. But the reply from the Rousseau of the *Social Contract* is that the *apparent* equality that would obtain absent property was only *illusory*, that naturally we would be unable to relate as equals, and that we need an institution of property specifically to enable us to have relations of "moral and legitimate equality." This strategy, I want to note, responds to the second egalitarian challenge precisely by flipping that challenge on its head: it argues that the idea of equality that is at the heart of the challenge, properly understood, reveals that equal relations are actually impossible absent property, and that equality itself demands an institution of property. Equality, far from proscribing property, actually requires it.

12 Rousseau, Social Contract I.9.6 [OC III 367].
13 Rousseau, Social Contract I.9.8 [OC III 367].

It is crucial to see here that the claim is not that property automatically or inevitably assuages any worries about equality. That would be absurd. Rousseau himself says as much in a note to the passage I just quoted. He writes, "under bad governments, this equality is only apparent and illusory; it serves only to maintain the poor in his misery and the rich in his usurpation."[14] I think the way to read Rousseau here is to understand him to be saying that the equality that he calls the "basis of the entire social system" is the point of the institution. In the language that I employ throughout this book, we can say that, absent property, we would have a problem, a problem that we would be unable to relate to each other in the way that we ought to do, that is, as equals. The point of property, its constitutive role in our social world, is to solve that problem, to allow us to relate as equals with respect to its subject matter. That—of course—does not commit us to thinking that every institution of property does its job fully or correctly. But it does commit us, I think, to the view that an institution is failing on its own terms—that it is, in Rousseau's crisp construction, a "bad" institution—if its subjects are not relating as equals. Moreover, we can now bring the first egalitarian challenge back into the picture: if the property institutions we have now have resulted, through a slow succession of events, in material inequality among their subjects, we might want to say that they are failing on their own terms and that we ought to reform them in the light of that. But even though equality might require much by way of such reform, the Everyday Marxist's challenge fails. Equality requires property, so the proposal that we eliminate it entirely must be rejected on the very egalitarian grounds that it purports to rest.[15]

This is all very schematic. But pause here and look at how this presentation of some of Rousseau's ideas sets a kind of framework for thinking about property. It is this framework, I bet you guessed, around which this book is constructed. In short, a careful examination of how the social world would look in the absence of any institution of property reveals that in those circumstances we would be unable to relate to one another on terms of equality with respect to spaces, objects, and the subject matter of property more generally. We would have a problem, a problem that only property can solve. Instituting property to solve that problem presents us with a related but distinct problem: while property makes it possible to relate as equals, it does not guarantee that none of its subjects is subordinated with respect to its subject matter. So property institutions must be regulated according to the degree to which they actually eliminate such subordination,

[14] Rousseau, Social Contract I.9.8, [OC III, 367]. Again Leonard Cohen might be thought to agree: in his telling, the explanation for inequality is that "the fight was fixed." In a fight that is fixed, the equality of the competitors is only illusory.

[15] Rousseau saw this point, too: "What, then? Must we destroy our societies, annihilate yours and mine, and return to live in the forests with the bears? A conclusion in the style of my adversaries, which I would like to prevent rather than to leave them the shame of drawing." See Rousseau, Second Discourse Note IX, [14] [OC III, 207].

and must strive toward a fuller realization of the ideal of equal relations and antisubordination to ensure property law's place in a society of equals.

Importantly, this regulative ideal is itself derived from the very same normative considerations that called for the creation of an institution of property in the first place, which is to say that it is internal to the idea of property. This is the basis of the answer to the second egalitarian challenge and, in its way, to the first as well: a system of property that allows for too great a divide between rich and poor—perhaps one that fails to ensure that "no citizen be so very rich that he can buy another, and none so poor that he is compelled to sell himself"[16]—is failing on its own terms, it is a bad institution of property *qua* institution of property. Of course, this means that I am very sympathetic to the common thought that things have gone deeply wrong in our current institutions of property,[17] and that fundamental and important changes are required if these institutions can have any claim to be just constituents of a society of equals. Indeed, that common thought is among the motivations for this entire endeavor, and I say a great deal in this book about what reform I think is called for. But notice that the structure of the account will constrain what I say in the following way: as unjust as our current property institutions are, we cannot do without property. So the right response to the calls for radical reform of our institutions is just that: radical reform, not abolition. The point of property is to allow us to relate as equals, so we should strive constantly to ensure that our property institutions create, foster, and protect such relations and prevent any of their subjects from being subordinated to any others.

I.3 Plan of the Book

My plan in this book is to elaborate this way of thinking about property. The book as a whole has seven chapters, but it is meant to flow as a single sustained argument; much of what happens in later chapters will depend on arguments made in earlier chapters.

Part I presents the argument in abstract philosophical terms through a specific sequence of thoughts. I first explain the problem to which property is a

[16] Rousseau, Social Contract II.10.2 [OC III 391–92].

[17] In using the expression "common thought" in the text, I mean to indicate an awareness that one reaction you might have to what I've said is that, in the end, it ends up being extensionally equivalent to a relatively familiar liberal egalitarian intuition about property. The intuition, roughly, is that property is an important part of a democratic constitutional order, but one that requires significant reform in order to be just or justified or what have you. If you share that intuition, then you can understand the account I offer here as an attempt to provide a robust justificatory explanation of your own view. (In this way, the book is an exercise in philosophy in the sense that it is an attempt to make sense of, illuminate, and articulate a coherent account of something that others find obvious.)

solution, then present the idea that property just is whatever solves that problem, and finally show how that conception of property brings with it an internal regulative ideal according to which inegalitarian property institutions are bad in a specific sense.

In chapter 1, I introduce some of the central ideas of the book. The first is what I call the *idea of yours and mine*, which is the abstract idea that is required to think or talk about something being yours or mine (or someone else's). It is, in short, the basic thought we need in order to have any system of property. I begin by imagining what the world would be like without that idea and, thus, a fortiori, without any institution of property. I rely on the abstract idea to avoid prejudging the question of what does or does not count as an institution of property. I then show how, in a world without the idea of yours and mine, we would be unable to live together on terms of equality, since there is a wide and important part of the social world—doing things in space, using objects, sharing with others, and so on—participation as equals in which is constituted by the idea of yours and mine. But I assume (and suggest some reasons to think) that we are required by a *basic commitment to equality* to live together as equals, which is to say to create, arrange, and maintain our social and political institutions to ensure that we interact with and relate to each other on terms of equality, with none superior or inferior to any other. This basic commitment means that we cannot accept or endorse life without the idea of yours and mine. I name this situation the *Problem of Yours and Mine*, or, for short, the *Problem*. This Problem, I argue, is the problem that we need property to solve.

In chapter 2, I show how property solves the Problem, and suggest that we think about property as *the law of yours and mine*. I first defend the idea that an institution of property just is whatever solves the Problem of Yours and Mine. The argument here begins by seeing that the idea of yours and mine is abstract and indeterminate. Its abstract nature means that we need to create an institution to realize it, to make it real in the world. But its indeterminate nature means that it provides no detailed blueprint for such an institution, and that a wide range of institutions could count as realizing it. (This allows me to show that many calls to eliminate property are better understood as calls to reform one kind of property institution into another.) I then argue both sides of a biconditional that something counts as an institution of property if and only if it can solve the Problem. I first show that a range of familiar institutions of property, including importantly the common law of property and familiar kinds of socialism, can count as realizations of the idea of yours and mine. And I show how purported counterexamples to the second half of the biconditional fail, by showing that seemingly non-property institutions that seemingly solve the Problem all, upon closer inspection, turn out either to be institutions of property after all or else turn out to fail to meet the demands of the basic commitment.

In chapter 3, I confront the fact that many (if not all) real institutions of property seem not to be egalitarian at all, in that they allow for familiar and pressing forms of subordination, like homelessness. I show that the argument from chapter 2 that property is required to allow equal relations with respect to its subject matter means that property institutions are subject to an internal regulative ideal according to which such forms of subordination should be eliminated. Importantly, this means that we cannot properly understand the problem of the inegalitarian institutions we have unless we understand that the whole point of the institution is to enable equal relations. (Until we know what the point of property is, we cannot know why a given system is a good or bad instance of its kind.) I show, though, that there is an important difference between the form of interpersonal subordination that would obtain in a world without the idea of yours and mine and the form of structural subordination that best describes the inequalities we see within existing institutions. The fact that homelessness (among other forms of inequality) is a form of structural subordination, the result of the accumulated effects of individuals' nonsubordinating choices, means that a systemic solution is required, which is to say that the solution is a matter of public law and, in particular, state obligations to provide housing and constrain the exercise of private rights in various ways. With this view in mind, I try to disentangle some egalitarian complaints about our existing institutions and locate their various natures and the associated form of solution.

Part II of the book is about the private law of property, or roughly speaking, "property law" as common lawyers traditionally understand that term. The overarching idea throughout this part is that my account of property as the realization of the idea of yours and mine provides an attractive and illuminating perspective on the core questions of property law and theory. That is, we can gain insight into some familiar doctrines and doctrinal-theoretical questions by thinking about how the idea of yours and mine applies (or, in some cases, does not apply) to various kinds of interactions between private persons. The leitmotif throughout will be a development of the idea that property allows us to relate to one another on terms of equality by relating through the idea of yours and mine.

This second part begins with chapter 4, which is about the core of the law of property in land and tangible objects as it is taught in most English, American, and Canadian law schools. The thought here is not that property law needs to look the way it does, but rather that we can understand the law that we do have as one among many permissible realizations of the idea of yours and mine, and so see its various doctrines through the lens of that idea. First, I show how my account of property allows us to understand the contours of the law of trespass and the relation between trespass and licensed entries, as well as the law of nuisance, the law of acquisition and the role of possession in the law of property, the alienation of property, certain kinds of shared ownership including tenancy, and servitudes. I argue that this set of doctrines makes up the core of the law of property, in the sense that each doctrine responds to one of a set of questions that immediately confront us when we think about realizing the idea of yours and mine, questions about what it means when something is yours or mine, how something becomes yours or mine, how I can make something that was mine yours, how you and I can share something, and so on.

In chapter 5, I turn to a more theoretical question about what makes a property right a *property* right. I begin with a relatively common set of ideas about the form of property rights, in particular that property rights are *in rem* and alienable. I show how these ideas fit with the idea of yours and mine and allow us to draw lines between property rights and personal rights and between property rights and contract rights. I then show how these two formal features can be understood as connected to the justificatory account of property in terms of the idea of yours and mine and that we can helpfully explicate that connection by saying that a property right needs to be a right to a res, which is just to say that the idea of yours and mine requires, in its legal realization, that there be some subject matter to which it can apply, some "this" about which I can say "this is mine." But I go on to show how this idea of a res should be understood as fundamentally legal rather than empirical and should therefore not be confused with our nonlegal notion of a thing. This last point leads into an examination of some cases of intangible property, cases where the law recognizes a property right, a right to a res, but where the res is entirely a legal entity, where, that is, there is no pre-legal "thing" that is the subject matter of the right. There are two slightly different versions of this idea of the purely legal res. The first involves cases of intangible property, and it is here that I discuss the question of whether trademarks are a form of property and the famous *INS v AP* decision. The second set of cases is slightly more complicated. These are cases where certain kinds of in personam rights, like contract rights and debts, need, for reasons involving the systematic relation of all subjects of a legal system, to be recognized as generating a kind of a res, so that the in personam right is protected, as I will say, by a distinct *in rem* right. This abstract structure can be used to show why we talk about property in trusts, in debts, and in shares, and it can also be applied to the tort of inducing breach of contract.

Part III of the book is about property and public law. One divide in property theory, although one that is not much written about, is between those—libertarians, old-fashioned doctrinalists—who think that property is entirely a matter of private law, with any regulation of property rights comprehensible only as externally imposed and those—Realists, perhaps some adherents of so-called Progressive Property theory—who think the private law of property, like all private law, is merely public law in disguise. I reject both sides of this divide, because I think the subject matter known as "property law," which is to say the subject matter of this book, spans the divide between private and public law. As the argument earlier makes clear, I think we begin, in an important conceptual sense, with the private law of property, because we have property in the first place as a solution to a problem about private subordination: we need property to allow individuals to relate to one another as equals with respect to spaces, objects, and so on. But the very structure of the private law of property, we will see, turns out to set the stage for a variety of problems that have the form of what I will call structural subordination. In short, the idea is that the effects of individuals acting rightly, consistent with their own obligations to relate to one another as equals, can accumulate to make it the case that some are subordinated without anyone having subordinated them. Since none is subordinating, private law solutions are inadequate. But since some are subordinated, a legal solution is required, and one that recognizes that the subordination, being caused as it is on a systematic or structural level, is in an important respect the collective responsibility of every participant in the system. Thus the legal mechanisms that respond to structural subordination are public law mechanisms, involving state regulation and provision.

This part begins with chapter 6, which elaborates that set of ideas in some detail and then discusses what I think is the most important upshot of them, namely, the claim (already introduced in chapter 3) that the same considerations that require us to have property also require us to ensure that none is without property of their own, that is, that an institution of property requires that the state ensure that none of its subjects is homeless. I show how the nature and wrong of homelessness is uniquely comprehensible through an account of property of the sort I provide here and how the correct understanding of homelessness conditions the form of state response that is required. I argue that states are obligated to provide housing to their subjects that is adequate both physically (in terms of its size, location, physical condition, and so on) and legally (in terms of security of tenure). I show how these notions of adequacy are themselves egalitarian and comprehensible from the point of view of my account of property. I then turn to what this account tells us about some ways in which the rights of the housed might better be protected to avoid housing insecurity.

Finally, in chapter 7, I turn to a different set of questions about the relationship between property and the public, in particular questions about public property—that is, property that is held by the public. I show how private property as I understand it is necessarily inadequate to allow us to pursue certain kinds of essential public purposes, and therefore that we need public property. Here I discuss the nature of public roads and public parks and the tort of public nuisance. But I also suggest that these ideas give us reason to think that the private law idea of trespass should not apply to property that is held by the state, and that we need a different way to think about such cases.

The conclusion concludes by asking what the question "is property justified?" means, and providing some suggestions about how it can and cannot be answered. After it, there is a short appendix which probes in a little more depth some of the philosophical details of the claims made in the early sections about the nature of the Problem of Yours and Mine and (what is the same thing) why we need property, and who or what the "we" in that formulation is.

PART I
THE THEORY

1

The Problem of Yours and Mine

1.1 Setup

The organizing idea of this book is *the idea of yours and mine*.

It is a familiar idea. It is the central idea of the law of property, to be sure. But we also employ it all the time in a wide variety of situations. It is the idea that we use when we say "come over to my house tonight for dinner" or "would you like to share my guacamole" or "I think you left your watch in the kitchen." When something is yours or mine, it is *up to* you or me what others may do with it. In other words, you or I get to determine whether and under what circumstances others may perform a variety of actions that involve it: you may not enter my house without my say-so, I may not wear your watch unless you let me, and so on. Moreover, others take the fact that something is mine or yours as a reason to act in certain ways: they understand, that is, that they should not enter my house or take your watch just because it is mine or yours.

As we saw in the Introduction, it is intuitively plausible to worry that the idea of yours and mine is in some way in tension with a *basic commitment to equality*. This is the familiar thought, defensible on a variety of grounds, that we are one another's equals in the sense that none is naturally the superior or inferior of any other. The worry arises because when something is mine, it looks suspiciously like I am your superior and you my inferior, at least with respect to that thing, because it is up to me how you may act with respect to it: if I say you may not touch it, you (therefore) may not touch it. How can the idea of yours and mine be consistent with our standing as equals? I am going to argue, contrary to this worry, that in fact we need the idea of yours and mine in order to live together as equals in the way that we are required to do by the basic commitment to equality, and that in particular we need to create an institution to realize the idea—make it real—in order to live together in a society of equals. The name of that institution is "property." So I will show that we cannot do without property, that property is an essential constituent in a society of equals.

As those last sentences might indicate, you can think about the central claim of this book as one that turns onto its head a familiar worry that sees property as a fundamentally inegalitarian institution. According to the view I am going to defend, it will turn out that the opposite is true. Property is an egalitarian institution, in that *the very point of property is to allow us to relate as equals*. We need

Property Law in the Society of Equals. Christopher Essert, Oxford University Press. © Oxford University Press 2024.
DOI: 10.1093/oso/9780197768952.003.0002

property to solve a problem about equality, a problem about how equal relations would be impossible with respect to a wide and important set of activities and interactions that are indispensable for creatures like us. Equality does not proscribe property. Equality requires property. Of course, our present institutions of property contribute to and support inequalities that must be addressed. This means that they are defective as institutions of property. But understanding those inequalities, what is wrong with them, and what would count as addressing them requires an understanding of a more basic relation between property and equality, a relation of the sort I just described. So we will begin, in this chapter, with the idea that property solves a problem about equality.

We will adopt a familiar strategy: we will try to imagine what the social world would look like without property. And to be sure we are not prejudging the important question of what property is—a question we will return to later—we will imagine a world without the idea of yours and mine, on the assumption that the abstract idea of yours and mine is importantly enough implicated in our notion of property that a world without the idea of yours and mine is necessarily a world without property.

So what would a world without yours and mine be like? While nothing seems naturally to be anyone's, as it is, almost everything is someone's. Any time I am on or near the surface of the earth and pretty much any time I am holding or touching a physical object, I am in contact with something about which someone can say "that is mine," and exercise the sort of control we are interested in. It might be me; it might be you; it might be someone else. A social world without the idea of yours and mine would be a social world without any of that and would be really quite different than our own. Imagining such a world will take some work. Without the idea of yours and mine, we would not be able to think or talk about or relate in any of the familiar contexts that involve the idea. So I would be unable to ask or demand that you put down that avocado because it is *mine*; you would be unable to tell me to leave *your* home; I would be unable to invite you to share *my* guacamole; and you would be unable to invite me to stay in *your* guestroom.

It is true that in this imagined world—and we should be clear that this is an act of imagination, a tool for thinking, an idea of reason, and that I am not pretending that there ever was or could be a world like this one[1]—we would

[1] The phrase "idea of reason" here is Kant's: see "On the common saying: this may be true in theory but it does not apply in practice": 8:297 (1793). [Throughout this book, I will cite to Kant's works using the Prussian Academy pagination, rather than to any specific translation, and specific quotes will be from the Cambridge translations by Mary Gregor.] The essential thought is that by no means is any of the discussion of a world without yours or mine meant to implicate any claims that such a world has or even could exist but rather to provide us with a way of thinking about the relevant moral considerations. To the same effect is Rousseau's reminder, in the introduction to the Second Discourse, that "The Inquiries that may be pursued regarding this Subject ought not to be taken for historical truths, but only for hypothetical and conditional reasonings; better suited to elucidate

still have rights over our bodies,[2] which we can call "personal rights," so that I could demand that you not touch me or consent to your doing so. And sometimes these personal rights could extend to cover the space in which we stood or the object we held: moving me out of this space or taking the avocado from my hand would interfere with my body. But once I moved out of the space or put the avocado down I could have no control over what you could do with them, since, again, they would not—could not—be mine. Here we see a distinction that is central to our understanding, although sometimes latent in our everyday thought and talk: the distinction is between *holding* and *having*, between rights over the things that we are presently in physical possession of and rights over the things that are yours or mine even though we are not in possession of them.[3] My personal rights encompass objects or spaces that I hold, but without the idea of yours and mine I cannot have objects or spaces as my own, so they are free for the taking once I put them down. In our actual social world, having in this sense is central, since when something is yours or mine we take ourselves to have it and to have rights over it, even (or precisely) when we are not holding it. The difference between holding and having is closely bound up with the idea of yours and mine. When we imagine a world without the idea of yours and mine we can still imagine ourselves with personal rights and rights to the stuff we are holding, but we are imagining a world in which we cannot have things in that second sense.

Let us now notice another feature of this world that is importantly relevant to the overall inquiry. In the world without the idea of yours and mine, it would be true of each person that they would have personal rights.[4] I would get to determine what you could do with respect to my person—when you could touch it, what risks of harm to it you could impose—and you would get to determine precisely the same things for my actions with respect to your person. This suggests—although the details are subtle, we will explore some of them in what follows—that our relations would be in an important sense egalitarian: I would not be your superior or inferior and you would not be mine. But the possibility of having, of spaces and objects being yours or mine, seems to introduce a source of inequality. If something is mine, its being so gives me a degree of control over

the Nature of things than to show their genuine origin." Rousseau, Discourse on the Origin and the Foundations of Inequality among Men [OC III, 133] (1754).

[2] If you think (wrongly, sorry) that when you say "my hand," you're invoking the idea of yours and mine, see §5.2.

[3] Again, the distinction is Kant's: see The Metaphysics of Morals 6:253 (1797). For a treatment that reaches the same conclusion from a different direction, see C B MacPherson ed, Property: Mainstream and Critical Positions 3 (1978).To save words, although it is somewhat unidiomatic, I sometimes use the word "holding" so that standing on a spot will count as holding a location, making it exhaustive of the rights we have in spaces or objects that rest on our bodily contact with them.

[4] In this book, I use the word "they" as a singular gender-neutral pronoun, especially in examples or in constructions like the one in the text referring to some abstract, unnamed person.

you beyond that control grounded on my right to my own person. Thus the idea of yours and mine seems to introduce the possibility of unequal relations that would not exist in a world where all we had was personal rights. It is this possibility on which the egalitarian challenge to which this book is a reply—the one we called in the Introduction the second egalitarian challenge—rests. Before we begin that reply, we need to take a slight detour to clarify the notion of equality that is invoked in this challenge.

1.2 The Basic Commitment

Call *the basic commitment* to equality the claim that we must create, arrange, and maintain our social and political institutions to ensure that we interact with and relate to each other on terms of equality, that is, as equals rather than as superiors and inferiors. The basic commitment is constitutive of a familiar and attractive version of egalitarianism, one that takes the overarching goal of social and political life to be to create a society of equals. Now, "egalitarianism" is a big word, and not just in letters. It plays an important role in a wide-ranging set of positions in social and political philosophy as well as in law and politics more generally, and there are few who do not want at least to have the option to appeal, in defense of their own view, to some notion of equality.[5] Given this importance, there is also an extensive literature devoted to arguing about what equality is, about whether or not it sets constraints on the distribution of some stuff and, if so, what stuff; about whether or not it is instead a matter of the form of social relations among persons; about what it is in virtue of which persons or citizens ought to be treated equally or as equals, and many other related questions.[6] But this is not a book about equality, and wading into these debates would take us too far from our central object of concern. So I will say just a bit about two questions that are up for debate and about the approaches to those two questions that I take in this book. One question is about what the relevant notion of equality is, that is, about the substance of the basic commitment. I deal with that second. The other is about the basic commitment's grounds, about why it is that we ought to think about political morality in terms of equality. Answering this question

[5] For trenchant critique of this consensus, see Joseph Raz, The Morality of Freedom 217–44 (1986). Raz argues against a different conception of egalitarianism than the one I employ here.

[6] For some important works on the first set of questions, see Ronald Dworkin, "What Is Equality? Part 1: Equality of Welfare" 10 Philosophy & Public Affairs 185 (1981), Ronald Dworkin, "What Is Equality? Part 2: Equality of Resources" 10 Philosophy & Public Affairs 283 (1981), G A Cohen, "On the Currency of Egalitarian Justice" 99 Ethics 906 (1989). On the second, see Elizabeth Anderson, "What Is the Point of Equality?" 109 Ethics 287 (1999), Samuel Scheffler, "What Is Egalitarianism?" 31 Philosophy & Public Affairs 5 (2003), Elizabeth Anderson, "The Fundamental Disagreement between Luck Egalitarians and Relational Egalitarians" 40S1 Canadian Journal of Philosophy 1 (2010). On the third, see Jeremy Waldron, One Another's Equals: The Basis of Human Equality (2017).

would need a digression into a contentious set of debates in political and moral philosophy, metaethics, and metaphysics, which are not, I suspect, what you are looking for in this book. It is to avoid such a digression that I am employing the idea of a basic commitment.

It is a *basic* commitment because I suspect that, if we tried to locate some grounding for it, we would come up short. It does not seem that there is any natural feature of human beings that we all share in equal measure in virtue of which we can think that we ought to interact and relate as equals.[7] Indeed, it might even be, as Rousseau seemed at times to suggest, that it is precisely because of the pervasive inequalities in our particular natural features that we need to organize ourselves into a political society premised on a commitment to treating each other as equals.[8] Rather, we are often comfortable simply to begin with the idea that none is superior or inferior to any other as a starting point in our thinking in social philosophy. Importantly, this second idea can come apart from the first: whatever the fact of the matter is about the grounding of the basic commitment, it nevertheless can claim a sufficiently wide base of support to allow appeal to it just on its own terms. As Samuel Scheffler puts it, the ideal present in the basic commitment "represents a point of normative convergence:" some accept it as a part of a broader understanding of society as a "fair system of cooperation among free and equal people" that is "implicit in the public political culture of a modern democratic society," others think that "living in a society of equals is good both intrinsically and instrumentally."[9] There might be many different and perhaps conflicting arguments for that ideal, but we could disagree about those arguments and nevertheless agree that persons ought to interact with and relate to each other as equals. One feature of this shared agreement seems to me to be the pervasive sense in social and political philosophy that the sorts of arrangements that demand justification are just those that are not egalitarian in this sense, those in which one person appears to be in some way superior to another. As Isaiah Berlin put it, "equality needs no reasons, only inequality does so."[10]

All these considerations suggest to me that it makes sense to talk about a basic *commitment*. Such talk might be worrying insofar as it seems like a commitment is some kind of contingent feature of ourselves or our societies that we could abandon by free choice. But the notion of a commitment here is meant to be different than that. It is the idea that we cannot help but to endorse this idea,

[7] Waldron, One Another's Equals. I've also been helped immensely by the discussion in Sophia Moreau, Faces of Inequality: A Theory of Wrongful Discrimination (2020).

[8] We saw this point in discussing the *Social Contract* in the Introduction.

[9] Samuel Scheffler, Equality and Tradition 227 (2010).

[10] Isaiah Berlin, "Equality" 56 Proceedings of the Aristotelian Society 301, 305 (1956). And see Niko Kolodny, The Pecking Order (2023), for a systematic development of this idea.

because it seems to be presupposed by and to structure so much of our thought and talk about political morality. This idea of equality "conditions our whole way of thinking and talking, [so] we feel it to be non-contingent."[11] We can imagine societies that are structured by an idea of hierarchy and that do not meet the basic commitment, but it is generally thought that such societies are defective, that they are not, morally, an option for us. It is in this robust sense that we are committed to equality and to creating and fostering a society of equals.[12]

All that said about its status, we can now examine, in slightly more detail, the substance of the basic commitment and its notion of equal relations. In my experience, lawyers and legal theorists, when they hear words like "equality" or "egalitarianism," tend to think about the distribution of stuff, resources, money, welfare, what have you. In our present property-centric context, that assumption is even stronger: if there is more stuff that is mine than there is stuff that is yours, it looks like there is a kind of inequality in the picture. But as we saw in the Introduction and will elaborate at length later, the most pressing egalitarian critique of property does not rest on a distributive conception of equality. Rather, the critique is more pressing if it is presented as being about the way that, in being able to have something as mine, I seem to gain a kind of control over what you may or may not do that I could not have were it not possible for us to have things as mine or yours. The worry is not about distribution but about subordination and equal relations. And that is the substance of the basic commitment.

For you and me to relate as equals is for us to relate on terms such that neither of us is, nor can reasonably understand ourselves to be, the superior or inferior of the other, and for us each to understand ourselves and one another as capable of and required to govern ourselves according to those terms. This means that the parties to an egalitarian relation will not understand themselves to be superior and thus able to determine the relation's terms or inferior and subject to the relation's terms' being determined by the other party. In this way, the idea of an equal relation can be, to some extent, simply read off the wording of the basic

[11] P F Strawson, Individuals 29 (1964). As the Strawson reference might indicate, I take this as a kind of Kantian way of looking at things. The notion that plays the equivalent role in Kant's own political philosophy is the Universal Principle of Right, which he calls "a postulate incapable of further proof": Kant, Metaphysics of Morals 6:231. For a discussion of what *that* means (one that, fair warning, is not exactly light reading), see Arthur Ripstein, Force and Freedom: Kant's Legal and Political Philosophy 356–88 (2009). For those who are allergic to Kant, the formulation of the basic commitment may also be heard in a more pragmatic tone, along the lines of CS Peirce's pragmatism, on which, as Cheryl Misak puts it, some of our central practices are regulated by assumptions "that we have to assume are true if we are to carry on in the way it seems that we must carry on." See Cheryl Misak, The American Pragmatists 28 (2013). See the Appendix for more on these points.

[12] If you reject that line of thinking and believe that it might be just fine to live in a society structured by hierarchy as a matter of right, I feel like... maybe ... the arguments of this book as a whole are just not going to resonate with you. In any event, you're here, so you might just assume the basic commitment for argument's sake and see what comes of it. Also, though, maybe you want to think a bit more about why you'd think what you think you think.

commitment itself, by reference to the contrast with inegalitarian relations: to relate as equals is not to relate as superior and inferior. Elizabeth Anderson, in her important treatment of the subject, characterizes equal relations partly by reference to this same contrast:

> [Egalitarian] claims also have a negative and a positive aspect. Negatively, egalitarians seek to abolish oppression—that is, forms of social relationship by which some people dominate, exploit, marginalize, demean, and inflict violence upon others. . . . Positively, egalitarians seek a social order in which persons stand in relations of equality. . . . To stand as an equal before others in discussion means that one is entitled to participate, that others recognize an obligation to listen respectfully and respond to one's arguments, that no one need bow and scrape before others or represent themselves as inferior to others as a condition of having their claim heard.[13]

Here I follow Anderson in using the contrast with inegalitarian relations to help characterize the sort of relation that the basic commitment aims to foster. In such a relation, neither person is in charge of the other in the way that a master is in charge of a slave, which is just to say that each person should see the other as standing as an equal, as providing a source of reasons and claims for one another, as being a rational being with a capacity to set and pursue purposes, projects, and a conception of the good.

Let me now make six remarks about the basic commitment that will be important later on, all of which we will have more to say about. *First,* notwithstanding the usefully illustrative contrast between egalitarian and inegalitarian relations, the idea of equal relations is not just the idea that we not relate as inferiors and superiors. Rather, there is a distinctive and intrinsic value in relating to one another on terms of equality: this is the way that, at least in the realm of political morality, we ought to relate. A whole raft of familiar and valuable parts of our social world can and should be understood as particular realizations or instantiations of the more abstract idea of relating as equals that underlies the basic commitment. You and I relate as equals when we recognize that each is entitled to determine the terms on which the other may touch their body or when we take due care for one another's safety in our actions—when we treat one another as "neighbors" in Lord Atkin's sense.[14] And we relate as equals when we make promises to each other and take ourselves to be obligated to perform or more broadly when we resolve our disputes through an impartial judicial process

[13] Anderson, "What Is the Point of Equality?" at 313.

[14] For a discussion of this, see my "The Value of the Neighbour Relation" in Haris Psarras and Sandy Steel eds, Private Law and Practical Reason (2022).

rather than on the basis of strength. It seems to me that we should think of these phenomena, and many others, as constitutively realizing a positive value—the value of relating as equals—and not merely as good because they avoid subordinating relations.[15]

Second, the idea of equality in the basic commitment is relational and not comparative. We might be said to be of unequal wealth insofar as you have a lot of money and I have less, but that inequality is comparative, rather than relational: we can understand how wealthy you are and how wealthy I am independently of each other, and the question of equality is a question of comparing these two independent things. By contrast, the notion of equality in the basic commitment is entirely and irreducibly relational. We saw that, in thinking about this idea of equality, it is helpful to highlight its central idea by contrasting it with the paradigms of an unequal relation, such as the one that obtains between master and slave. But a master is not a master except in relation to a slave, so it is the relationship itself that is the site of egalitarian concern.[16] So it is with the egalitarian relation: what it is for you and me to relate as equals is not for us to be equal with respect to some quality that we can each be independently assessed in respect of, but instead for our relation itself to be one in which you are neither my superior nor my inferior. Such superiority and inferiority are entirely a matter of our relation, and cannot be understood independently of it.[17] So to know if our relation meets the basic commitment we do not (at least not directly) need to ask questions about the stuff each of us has, but rather about whether or not we relate on terms of equality. An important upshot of this relationality, which will become important later, is the way it fits comfortably with, first, the relational normativity that is at the heart of private law,[18] and, second, the core idea of a kind of liberalism according to which the concerns of political philosophy are about how we live together, or what we owe to each other, so that none of us is entitled to coerce another on the basis of some impersonal value but only on the basis of the possibility of our living together as equals in this way.

Third, the basic commitment is abstract and thus in an important way indeterminate. That means that it does not tell us, on its face, just what is required in order to relate as equals in any particular context. It also does not provide, in

[15] To put all of this in different words, I guess I think that a world of persons relating as equals is, just as such, a better world than a world with no persons, a better world than a world of persons unable to relate to each other as equals, and a better world than a world of persons relating systematically as inferiors and superiors.

[16] There might be nonegalitarian reasons to be concerned with the slave's lot, if they were deprived of certain goods or suffered in certain ways. But even if none of that were true, even if master and slave had empirically the same lives, with access to the same goods, the same protection from harms, and so on, there would still be an egalitarian complaint about the master's control over the slave.

[17] On the irreducibility of relational normativity, see Arthur Ripstein, Private Wrongs 36–38 (2016).

[18] On relational normativity in private law, see Ernest J Weinrib, The Idea of Private Law (1995).

those contexts where relating as equals requires a system of rights, anything like a "detailed blueprint" for that system of rights.[19] The basic commitment could be realized by a variety of different institutions in different times and places, depending on the different historical and social conditions that apply.[20] So determining what counts as an egalitarian relation and what does not cannot be entirely done in the abstract, but will often require specific, concrete, and intricate analysis of actual social facts.

Fourth, the idea of equality is, as the quote from Anderson indicated, responsive to social facts. At first glance, this point might seem in tension with the second. But, as we will see at length later, while the most basic way that a social institution can be in conflict with the basic commitment is by creating inegalitarian relations between individuals, there is another, more complex way in which such conflict can arise. It is possible, in some contexts, for the cumulative effect of egalitarian relations to generate forms of subordination in which no particular person can said to subordinate but in which someone may nonetheless be subordinated. Later we will come to see homelessness as a prime example of this phenomenon, which we will call *structural subordination*. This form of subordination is distinct from interpersonal subordination, and so requires a distinct response. But it does require a response. The basic commitment calls, ultimately, for the creation of a *society of equals*, and so requires not only legal and social institutions that create interpersonally egalitarian relations but also protections against structural subordination to ensure that none is the inferior of any other in either of these two distinct ways.

Fifth, building on the last two points, we can see that the rights we have in our persons can be understood as a specific realization of the basic commitment in their particular context. Whatever else is true of us, humans are physically embodied beings vulnerable to certain kinds of injury, able to set and pursue projects, purposes, and a conception of the good. It is in that guise that we relate to one another, and thus our relating as equals must recognize and protect our embodied agency or, if you like, personhood. (To be a person in this sense just is to be the sort of thing that is fit to relate to other persons on terms of equality.) So for you and me to relate as equals, we must each have rights in our own person, in the sense that it is up to me, rather than you, how you will be permitted to act with respect to my own person, and it is up to you, rather than me, how I will be permitted to act with respect to yours. Neither is the superior or inferior of the other with respect to this relation. There are lots of details, and I will say more about many of them throughout this book, but the core idea is

[19] Jacob Weinrib, Dimensions of Dignity: The Theory and Practice of Modern Constitutional Law 140 (2016).

[20] For historical discussion of this point, see James Q Whitman, "Enforcing Civility and Respect: Three Societies" 109 Yale Law Journal 1279 (2000).

a simple and familiar one. We are equals because neither of us is entitled to set the terms of our interactions unilaterally, in the way that a master is entitled to set the terms of their interactions with the slave. Instead, each of us is free to move through our world as an equal, neither inferior nor superior to anyone else.[21]

Sixth, and finally, notwithstanding the past several pages, I take the basic commitment to be pretty uncontroversial. You might disagree with me about some element of my particular characterization. But I take it that hardly anyone interested in this book's subject matter will want to deny the attraction of a notion of a society of equals structured by something like the idea I set out in this section. Nobody wants much to deny that we should not have a society in which some people are higher and some lower. The paradigmatic forms of unequal relation that history presents to us—master-slave, brahmin-untouchable—are interesting and enlightening to us here and now precisely because they display so clearly how things are *not* supposed to be for us. The central task of this book is thus to understand how this very simple, attractive, and, as I say, uncontroversial idea fits in with the idea of yours and mine.

1.3 A World without Yours and Mine

We can now return to the main thread of the argument. Remember that we are aiming to understand the relation between property and equality by trying to imagine how things would be in a social world lacking the idea of yours and mine. We saw in §1.1 that, in such a world, we could still have rights over our persons, and in §1.2 that these rights are one specific form of realization of the basic commitment to equality, in that we relate to one another through them on terms of equality. The egalitarian critique of property rests on the thought that the idea of yours and mine seems to introduce a kind of disturbance of those egalitarian relations. When an avocado is mine, it looks in a way like I am your superior, at least with respect to the avocado. To develop this line of thought, we need to explore more carefully the proposition that we would relate as equals in a world without yours and mine. That proposition, notice, is broader than the proposition that we would relate as equals with respect to our persons: it includes an inchoate premise that, without the idea of yours and mine, we would relate

[21] I've here been helped by Arthur Ripstein, "Embodied Free Beings under Public Law: A Reply" in Sari Kisilevsky and Martin J Stone eds, Freedom and Force: Essays on Kant's Legal Philosophy 183, 193–96 (2017) and Arthur Ripstein, "Political Independence, Territorial Integrity and Private Law Analogies" 24 Kantian Review 573, 579 (2019), where Ripstein puts the point as follows: "only a being capable of setting and pursuing ends could either subordinate another to its ends or be subordinated by another," as well as by many years of discussion of these ideas with Ripstein.

as equals with respect to the subject matter of property. As I indicated in the Introduction, I plan to argue that this inchoate premise turns out to be false. But first we need more precision. In particular, we need a more articulated understanding of how things would be, morally, in a world without the idea of yours and mine.[22]

Imagine a person who tried to claim something—an avocado, say—for their own in a world that lacks the idea of yours and mine. In disabusing this person of the notion that the avocado was theirs, we could say, on the one hand, "we do not have things as yours or mine, because nothing is anyone's," or, on the other hand "we do not have things as yours or mine, because everything is everyone's."[23] Properly understood, these replies exhaust the logical space: the claim that an avocado is someone's can be rebutted by showing that it is no one's or that it is everyone's.[24] And, indeed, treatments of this problem in the history of political philosophy can basically be divided into two rival camps, each of which models the situation that would obtain in such a world along the lines of one of those two answers. The two models go by different names depending on who is doing the discussing. I will adopt Pufendorf's language, and call the world where nothing is anyone's the "negative community" and the world where everything is everyone's the "positive community."[25]

A negative community, where spaces and objects are *nobody's*, is a kind of free-for-all, in which everything is available for taking and using, so that nobody has any complaint when another person takes something for themselves. If you get the avocado before me, you can eat it. Once you put it down, I can take it for myself, since it is not now (nor ever was) yours. In a positive community, by contrast, all spaces and objects are *everyone's*. Here nobody can have anything for themselves, as their own. I cannot take an avocado because the avocado is (in a way) your avocado and her avocado and his avocado, so it is not okay for me, without some special justification or else permission from every single other

[22] Let me emphasize that adverb: my concern here is not how things would be empirically in such a world, how happy or sad or rich or poor or productive or idle we would be. It is how things would stand between us in terms of our rights, duties, and so on.

[23] Or we might say both. In the Second Discourse, as we saw in the Introduction, Rousseau imagines a scene not unlike the one just described. The first person to enclose ground he calls the "true founder of civil society," and goes on to tell us how many "miseries and horrors" would have been avoided had the enclosure been rejected on the grounds that "the fruits are everyone's and the Earth no one's." Rousseau, Second Discourse II.1 [OC III 164].

[24] That is, {all, some, none} or {everyone's, someone's, no one's} exhausts the logical space. I understand "someone" to include individuals as well as groups that are a proper subset of "everyone," that is, I understand private group ownership as just an instance of private ownership. So does the law, as I will explain in more detail in §4.5.

[25] Samuel von Pufendorf, The Law of Nature and Nations IV.4 (1672). A negative community is sometimes called a commons and a positive community is sometimes discussed in terms of things being held in common, but those terms seem apt for confusion, which is why I adopt Pufendorf's language. Nothing turns on the terminology.

person, to take the avocado for myself.[26] Remember that each of these two different models can be understood as a kind of development and application of the basic commitment. In both cases, since nothing can be yours or mine, it is impossible for me to have a right with respect to a space and object that you do not have over me, or vice versa. So we seem in a way to be equals. And the idea of yours and mine seems to disrupt that equality. When something is mine, I get to determine how you may act with respect to it, in a way that seems worryingly parallel to (if admittedly narrower than) the way that a master gets to determine how a slave may act. As I understand them, the classical developments of both of these ideas, in the writings of Grotius, Pufendorf, Locke, Rousseau, Kant, and others, rested on this basic equality and on the thought that the idea of yours and mine seems to depart from it and so demands justification.

I said three paragraphs ago that to develop my argument, we need a more articulated account of the world without yours and mine. And now we have two. Which is one too many. So we should pick one. But as between the negative and positive community models, how should we choose the better depiction of a world without the idea of yours and mine? Echoing a point I made at the start of §1.1 we should emphasize that this is not an historical question, but a theoretical one. And I think the right answer to that question is that the negative community is the better model. One way to see why is by noticing that, in the actual world, we treat unacquired objects as we would treat them in a negative community. We do not treat them as if they were in the common possession of everyone but as if nobody has any rights in them at all. An unowned fox can be treated by anyone in any way they please, with no requirement that they secure the sort of permission from others that would be required in the positive community. It is only once someone catches the fox and makes it their own that any claim rights in the fox come into existence.[27] The law's understanding of the actual rights in our current system presumes that each of them was acquired in that way, and that unacquired objects, such as wild foxes, are nobody's, rather than everybody's. And the basic moral claim makes sense: in a world without the idea of yours and mine, it seems to me that I can walk where I want to walk, touch what I want to touch, eat what I want to eat, and so on, without anyone's permission. But that setup is unavailable in the positive community, where I would need everyone else's permission to do those things.

What is the attraction of the idea of a positive community? I think Locke's discussion, which is probably the most famous treatment of the idea, sheds some light here. Locke begins with the idea that God gave the earth to all of us

[26] For a more precise elaboration of these models, see my "Remarks on the Form and Justification of Private Law Rights, Liberties, and Powers" in Samuel Bray et al eds, Interstitial Private Law (2024).
[27] *Pierson v Post*, 3 Cai R 175 (1805).

in common, that is as a positive community. But Locke sees that, were we all to own the earth in common and thus require each other person's consent to use any of it, there would be trouble: "If such a consent as that was necessary, Man had starved, notwithstanding the Plenty God had given him."[28] As Locke sees it, in a positive community, since we all own the earth together, we cannot unilaterally take any of it for ourselves. Taking things unilaterally is inconsistent with the basic commitment, so it is wrong. That is an attractive idea. But surely the question here is what it means to "take" something unilaterally for oneself. The pull of the Lockean thought that taking is inconsistent with the basic commitment has to be that, when I take something, I change its normative status, I make it mine when it was not or make it not yours when it was. In the negative community, merely holding something is not a taking in this sense: there, I can pick the avocado from the tree to make guacamole, but as soon as I put it down, you may run off with it, since after all it is not mine. (I can only hold it, not have it.) But in the positive community, mere holding is a kind of taking.[29] In the positive community, I would need permission from everyone else to pick up a rock off the ground to examine it, or, indeed, to walk across the surface of the earth. That strikes me as a very implausible account of our relations to one another, to a sufficient degree that we ought to reject it as even an idealized model of what the social world could be, and how the basic commitment would operate, in the absence of the idea of yours and mine. Moreover, the negative community retains the capacity to see what is problematic about unilateralism. But it locates the problem in attempts to unilaterally claim rights in things and space—to have them and not merely to hold them.[30] In fact, this is the kind of unilateralism that we should be concerned with.

I will have more to say about that last point in the remainder of this chapter. For now, we will proceed on the basis of thinking that the world without yours and mine would be a negative community. We should be clear that such a world would not be a "pure" state of nature. We have already seen how there would be personal rights in the negative community. And we can assume that there could

[28] John Locke, Two Treatises of Government II.5, §28 (1690).

[29] Locke's discussion centers around examples involving food, which we use by eating and thus destroy. There is a difficult question about the permissibility of using something one does not own in a way that leads to its destruction. This question was the basis of the so-called Franciscan controversy, a (genuinely fascinating) thirteenth- and fourteenth-century dispute between the Vatican and the Franciscan order (whose main advocate was William of Ockham). The question was whether, by eating food, the Franciscans were implicitly claiming property rights in the food and thereby violating their vow of poverty, or whether eating was merely factual use (holding) that did not imply a claim of a right in the food and thus was consistent with the vow. For discussion, see Brian Tierney, The Idea of Natural Rights (1997).

[30] Pufendorf takes unilateralism as problematic only for having, not holding: The Law of Nature and Nations IV.6. Many of the classic liberal accounts of property center on this problem of unilateralism. For discussion, see Nicholas Sage, "Is Original Acquisition Problematic?" in James Penner and Michael Otsuka eds, Property Theory: Legal and Political Perspectives 99 (2018).

be rights arising out of promises and other such transactions. Moreover, both of those kinds of rights could implicate spaces and objects: you could not wrest the avocado I am holding from my hand without wronging me with respect to my person; I could promise you not to eat any avocados this week. Depending on your metaethical views, there could be other rights and wrongs involving spaces and objects: you (or others) might have a right that I not wantonly destroy all of the avocados; it might be wrong for me to mistreat a wild fox; you might have a right that I not cut down a tree whose shade I know you enjoy.[31] We could multiply these examples, but the essential thought does not require it: what we would distinctively lack in this imagined world would be reasons grounded on any idea of a space or object being yours or mine.

With this model of the negative community in place, we can turn to the first step in the overarching argument of this book. That step requires me to show that, without the idea of yours and mine, we would be unable to relate to each other on terms of equality with respect to spaces and objects. While we could use objects and occupy spaces in the negative community, we could not do so in a way that is consistent with the basic commitment.[32] I will approach this idea first, in §1.4 in somewhat compressed and capsule form, using a specific example and then, in §1.5, in more comprehensive and abstract terms.

1.4 Using Things as Equals

Suppose you, an inhabitant of the negative community, want to make some guacamole. We can imagine that you find a stack of avocados nearby, and that you grab one or two avocados from it during those few seconds when they are ripe enough to eat but not yet rotten. And we can imagine that something similar happens for whatever else you need: limes, onion, cilantro, salt, and . . . maybe . . . peas?[33] As you proceed, you will probably need to set the avocado down while you juice the limes, chop the cilantro, mince the onion, what have you. But without the idea of yours and mine, remember, the only entitlements you can have over these things arise when you are holding them. They are not yours. I cannot even think to myself that I should forbear from them because they are yours—that thought is unavailable in this world—and thus when you put them down, I cannot understand their being yours as giving me reason not to take them for my own purposes;

[31] Stilz's "located life plans" fit here, too. See Anna Stilz, Territorial Sovereignty 85 (2019).

[32] For a parallel, but distinct, line of thinking see Ernest J Weinrib, Reciprocal Freedom: Private Law and Public Right ch 3 (2022); Ripstein, Force and Freedom, ch 4; Rafeeq Hasan and Martin J Stone, "What Is Provisional Right?" 131 The Philosophical Review 51 (2022).

[33] Hey, you do you. (Or see https://www.nytimes.com/2015/07/03/dining/defenders-of-peacamole-step-up.html.)

I do you no wrong by doing so. You might succeed in getting everything together when nobody else is around, or on a day when nobody else wants to make guacamole (or avocado toast, or anything else involving your ingredients). But what you cannot do is have any kind of rightful or normative assurance. You could only make guacamole if I (and everyone else) let you. There would be no basis for you to say to anyone else that the avocados (or the other stuff) were yours, and no basis for anyone to take the (non-)fact that they were yours as a reason to act accordingly, so nobody would do you any wrong by interfering with your plans.

I think this situation would be bad. But we need to be clear about *why* it would be bad. Some of what I said might suggest that it would be bad because there would be no guacamole, that, more abstractly, there is something good about objects being used, or about our being able to use objects and spaces, or do those activities, and that we need the idea of yours and mine to access that good. But that is not the claim. As I said, you might be able to make guacamole because nobody happened to be around to interfere with your doing so or because you are the only one around who likes avocados and so nobody ever tries to take the avocados you need. And even if others were around, you might be able to achieve your ends because of some advantage you had over them: perhaps you are faster so you can run away with the avocados, or perhaps you are strong enough to build a wall others cannot penetrate. So the problem with the negative community is not a problem about things not getting done.

Nevertheless, these cases point toward a better understanding of the problem. To start with, notice that the possibility of doing things in a world without yours and mine turns, as I just indicated, on questions of particular powers. If you were advantaged in physical strength or speed, you could make guacamole after outrunning me with the avocado. If you were advantaged in various mental capacities, you could outwit me to escape or stay awake longer than me and make the guacamole after I fell asleep. If you were advantaged socially, you might be able to gather a group of friends to assist you in keeping the avocado away from me long enough to make the guacamole.[34] If your advantage was environmental, you might be able to make the guacamole after finding the avocado on your side of an impassible river. Notice also that, in any of these situations, you might elect not to press your advantage; you might as "an indulgence or connivance derived . . . from an accidental mildness,"[35] let me have the avocado. It is important to see that this kind of case is no different, in that what happens to the avocado

[34] These last two sentences can be understood as a development of Hobbes' thought that "the weakest has strength enough" to take from the strongest, "either by secret machination or by confederacy with others that are in the same danger with himself." Hobbes, Leviathan I.13 (1651). In these cases, the point is that the relevant particular power isn't strength but perhaps wiliness or popularity.

[35] Richard Price, "Observations on the Nature of Civil Liberty" (1776) in D O Thomas ed, Price, Political Writings 20, 26 (2012).

would still be up to you, as your letting me have it would just be a variety of having your way.[36]

To generalize from these cases, we can say that whether or not you would get to make your guacamole would be a matter of "morally problematic inequalities,"[37] as it would turn on whether you or I were advantaged with respect to various contingent personal and environmental characteristics. But this situation would be quite at odds with the basic commitment: in any of these cases, we would relate in the matter of the avocado not as equals but as superior or inferior with respect to the morally arbitrary differences in the relevant particular powers, be it strength, intelligence, popularity, luck, or what have you. And these inequalities, we might say, are a fundamental and almost ineradicable feature of human beings. Part of the idea of the basic commitment, as we saw in §1.2, is that we ought to organize our social and political institutions to assure the possibility of each relating to the other as equals; I employed the idea of a basic *commitment* precisely because we seem to lack any grounds to believe that we are actually equal in any basic quality. Here we see that the basic commitment actually has a kind of moral pull on us that is grounded precisely on the reality of difference: it is because of these morally arbitrary differences in our particular powers that we need to organize our institutions on these egalitarian terms.[38] So our problem is not about doing things. It is about *doing things as equals*. In a world without yours and mine, we would have no grounds on which to determine the question of who gets to use the avocado that rest on the basic commitment, and so the determination would turn on these morally problematic inequalities in our particular powers.

On the characterization I have given so far, we can discern a problem that arises because of the range of morally arbitrary differences between the particular powers of each person. I have described this difference as an almost-ineradicable

[36] Although, as I argued, a positive community is not a good account of the world without yours and mine, it may be helpful to note that there is a parallel argument available for why a positive community raises its own version of the same problem. The thrust of it is as follows. In the positive community, since everyone has a right that no others use any object or space without consent, your making guacamole would be permissible only if everyone else agreed to let you make it. It is doubtful that such consensus would be reachable in any but the most limited set of cases: as Finnis notes, unanimity is "far beyond the bounds of practical possibility in the political community": Natural Law and Natural Rights 231–33 (2d ed 2011). But even in that small set of cases, the decisions reached would be, arguably unavoidably, biased in favor of those members of the community advantaged in terms of a particular power, namely, those who are more persuasive, eloquent, popular, or so on. (After all, as Churchill put it, "Of all the talents bestowed upon men, none is so precious as oratory.") This is the lesson of Jo Freeman, "The Tyranny of Structurelessness," 17 Berkeley Journal of Sociology 151 (1972–73), as well as probably the best justification of rigid rules governing participation in seminars and workshops. That is, even here, there would be some who would be favored in a way that would be inconsistent with the basic commitment.

[37] Seana Valentine Shiffrin, "Promising, Intimate Relationships, and Conventionalism" 117 Philosophical Review 481, 485 (2008).

[38] For a related defense of the claim that a commitment to equality is at odds with letting important questions of political morality turn on morally arbitrary characteristics, see John Rawls, A Theory of Justice, rev ed 63 (1999).

reality, as a feature of human beings and our social world that seems something close to inescapable in our experience and thought about ourselves. If you accept that characterization, then you should accept the claim that this problem is unavoidable in the negative community, the world without yours and mine; that is, you should accept the claim that, in that world, we would be unable to settle questions like those about the use of the avocado on terms that are consistent with our relating as equals, and you can feel free to skip the next three paragraphs and meet me at the start of §1.5.

But you might worry that this characterization of the problem rests too heavily on what seems, after all, to be a kind of empirical conjecture. Perhaps we might aim to reform our social world to ensure that these morally problematic inequalities between persons disappear, to ensure that we do not differ in our particular powers. Assuming such a reform was possible, would we still face a problem about doing things as equals in the negative community? I want to argue that we would. One way of getting at the argument is by noticing that, as I described the negative community in terms of the differences in our particular powers, I painted a picture of what looks like pervasive subordination, a picture in which each question about the use of a space or object will be answered in terms of the relative powers of the parties to the dispute and thus in terms that seem to be understandable in terms of a superior prevailing against an inferior. But we might think about this situation differently. We might think that because the question of which of us will get to use the avocado cannot, without the idea of yours and mine, be answered in a way that allows us to relate as equals, the negative community can be understood not necessarily as a world of pervasively unequal (i.e., subordinating) relations but rather as a world without equal relations, a world in which relating to one another as equals is impossible because we lack the moral materials to do so.[39] Let me explain.

Think again about the avocado. Suppose that, at the same time, we both want it: I want to make guacamole and you want to make avocado toast. And suppose that you end up with the avocado because, in the circumstances, you are advantaged as a matter of your particular powers. How are we to think about this result? As I said, we might think that you subordinated me with respect to the avocado, that the interaction had a kind of might-makes-right character. But perhaps that would be too fast. Notice, first of all, that you prevailed only in the sense that you now happen to hold the avocado; nothing at all about what happened gives me any reason at all not to try again (and again, and again) to get it for myself. The avocado is not yours, because by hypothesis there is no yours and mine here; you

[39] Here I am echoing Kant's claim that the state of nature "need not . . . be a state of *injustice*, of dealing with one another only in terms of the degree of force each has. But it would still be a state *devoid of justice*." Kant, Metaphysics of Morals 6:312.

can hold it but you cannot have it. So it is not so much that might makes right but rather that, without yours and mine, there is no right and only might. Not only would I be unable to recognize the avocado as being yours, you would not be able to do so either.[40] We would be unable to recognize each other as equals, but we would also be unable to recognize each other as superior and inferior. Our relation would be more akin to the relations that we have with nonhuman animals: when the raccoons eat the strawberries growing in my garden, neither they nor I can think that they took something that is mine, and their holding it gives me no reason at all not to try to take it back (aside from the possibility of injury). Similarly, if you prevailed initially and ended up holding the avocado, but then I returned later and took it back, there would be no sense in which you could complain, no sense in which you could say that my taking it had wronged you,[41] no sense in which you could say that I had treated you as my inferior by failing to respect your claim to the avocado, because you could not have any such claim.

This is what it means to think that a world without yours and mine would not necessarily be a world of subordination with respect to spaces and objects but rather a world devoid of equal relations. It would not be possible for us to relate as equals with respect to the avocado because we would not have the moral materials to understand that relation. (One way to say this is that, to relate as equals, we need to make it possible for us to understand certain kinds of interactions as one party wronging another, and we cannot do that without the idea of yours and mine.[42]) To relate as equals, as we saw, is to relate in such a way that neither of us is, nor can understand ourselves to be, the superior or inferior of the other, and for us each to understand ourselves and one another as capable of and required to govern ourselves according to the terms of that relation. But without the idea of yours and mine, this kind of relation is impossible: there are no grounds on which we could do so, no terms to which we could look to ensure that neither is superior nor inferior to the other. The idea of yours and mine, we

[40] As Rousseau eloquently puts it: in a world like the one we are currently contemplating, "regardless of how they painted their usurpations, [those who prevailed] realized well enough that they were only based on a precarious and abusive right, and that since they had been acquired solely by force, force could deprive them of them without their having any reason for complaint." See Rousseau, Second Discourse II.30 [OC III, 177].

[41] As I noted, in some cases we might be able to concoct a derivative explanation of how my taking it had wronged you, along the lines of the considerations I mentioned at the end of §1.3: perhaps we're friends and my interfering with your projects (with the avocado or otherwise) would be a wrong with respect to that relation. But such reasons would need to be derivative in the sense that they'd rely on some *other* fact about the situation. Such explanations are inadequate because the idea of yours and mine as we generally understand it says is that the fact that something is mine (or yours) is, in the core case, *on its own* a reason for others not to interfere with my use of it (and so with the activities and interactions I enter into on the basis of the fact that it is mine).

[42] I argue something like that—that the possibility of certain kinds of wrongs is constitutive of egalitarian relations—in "Property Wrongs and Egalitarian Relations" in Paul B Miller and John Oberdiek eds, Civil Wrongs and Justice in Private Law 395 (2020), which is a predecessor to some of the arguments in these sections.

might say, turns out to be constitutive of the possibility of relating as equals with respect to spaces and objects.

1.5 The Problem of Yours and Mine

Of course, this is all about more than just avocados. The argument in the previous section, that without the idea of yours and mine we would be unable to engage in certain activities and relations, is meant to be formal, in the following sense. In a world without the idea of yours and mine, we would be unable to engage, as equals, in *any* activity or relation that requires control over spaces or objects. And, as we will see, that covers an extremely broad and diverse part of our social world. The set of activities and relations in which we could not engage as equals without the idea of yours and mine is so broad and so diverse, in fact, that it is effectively impossible to imagine how beings constituted as we are—embodied, vulnerable, finite beings subject to the basic commitment—would be able to live lives anything like the ones we do without being able to participate in them. In other words, a social world for beings like us that is governed according to the basic commitment is impossible without the idea of yours and mine. This is an initial characterization of one of this book's structuring ideas, which I will call the *Problem of Yours and Mine*, or, for short, the *Problem*. The Problem is the problem to which, I will argue, property is the solution: we need to solve the Problem in order to relate as equals,[43] and property is the only way to do that.

The easiest way to get at the formality of the Problem of Yours and Mine is by broadening and diversifying the range of cases that we understand as depending on the idea of yours and mine beyond the simple case we considered in the last section. To remind you: there we saw that we need the idea of yours and mine to engage in simple acts of using the avocado in a way that is consistent with the basic commitment. We concentrated on making the avocado into guacamole, a relatively solitary activity. So now we should broaden our focus. I said already that this is not about avocados: the argument applies in just the same way to making an apple pie with apples, building a house out of bricks and mortar, and so on. The point also applies just as much to space as it does to objects. Suppose I needed a few feet to pace to think over some argument I was trying to construct. Without the space being mine, that need could have no direct normative implication for you; I could have no complaint if you constantly inserted yourself into

[43] As I suggested in §1.2, the basic commitment is broader than the Problem of Yours and Mine. To live together as equals, we need, not just property but also personal rights, a law of contract, and a wide range of other legal institutions. It is in part for that reason that the basic commitment can be thought of as the overarching value in political morality, which is then specified into different forms, each of which is constitutive and regulative of different elements of the legal system.

that space and disrupted me, forcing me to alter my path, as long as you did it without touching me. Moreover, many activities require space not in the sense that the actor is moving into it but instead in the sense that the activity requires just that nobody else be in the space. It would be very hard to sleep, for instance, if you were permitted to stand right beside me and do whatever you wanted there, no matter how loud or disruptive it was.[44]

Next, and perhaps even more importantly, we need to see that the point does not apply just to solitary activities, with one person using an object or space; the Problem is not at all about anyone's wanting to keep things for themselves, on any kind of possessive individualism understood in that way. It applies just as clearly to the wide range of activities and relations that involve various kinds of collaboration with others. We need the idea of yours and mine not only to have things for ourselves but also to give them to and share them with others. You can only give what is yours.[45] The same is true of sharing, which is just one person inviting another to participate in the use of something that is the one's. Sharing is not an alternative to having things as yours and mine; it requires it.[46] Now, bringing together some of the points in the last two paragraphs, note how this idea of inclusion applies quite directly to space: an invitation to dinner or to stay the weekend are simply instances of sharing space, and so depend on the sharer's having the space as theirs to share. We cannot have hosts and guests without the idea of yours and mine. Notably, we can see in many of these cases the simultaneity of inclusion and exclusion: your dinner party invitation is what it is precisely because I invited you and not the others; children learn that they need to share with everyone present precisely because of the exclusionary message sent when they

[44] See Ellen Barry, "Desperate for Slumber in Delhi, Homeless Encounter a 'Sleep Mafia'" New York Times, January 19, 2016, p A6, <https://www.nytimes.com/2016/01/19/world/asia/delhi-sleep-economy.html>.

[45] Basically this argument was made by Aristotle in saying that property is necessary for what he called "liberality": Politics II.5 (1263b3-14). A similar point is made by Barbara Herman, "Being Helped and Being Grateful: Imperfect Duties, The Ethics of Possession, and the Unity of Morality" 109 Journal of Philosophy 391, 405 (2012). Herman's concern is more centrally those circumstances in which your need may require me to give you something by imposing on me a duty of beneficence; her thought is that, here too, the nature of the duty can only be articulated once I have something that is mine to give you.

[46] As the Canadian children's performer Raffi tells us: "It's mine but you can have some/with you I'd like to share it." Sharing as I understand it here includes the contemporarily popular and misnamed phenomenon of the "sharing economy." While this seems overwhelmingly obvious to me, people still seem to miss it, when for instance they argue that the "sharing economy" represents an alternative to ownership (or, as a blurb on the back of a book on the subject rather outlandishly says, "forces us to rethink what property means . . . shakes the very foundations of the idea of property"). Whatever we want to say about this phenomenon, it should not be *that*. Driving others around in *one's car*, letting strangers stay in *one's house*, lending others *one's tools* or *one's toys* indisputably rests on the idea of yours and mine. The sharing economy rests on, presupposes, and requires the idea of property. Someone owns those assets; they're just using them in a new(ish) way. In slightly different terms—terms used by James Penner—inclusion depends on exclusion. So there is no such thing, on my view, as a "post-exclusion understanding" of property, as suggested in Lee Anne Fennell, "Property Beyond Exclusion" 61 William & Mary Law Review 521, 564*ff* (2019).

share with some but not others; the value of the gift I make to you is in part that I chose you as the recipient, that I gave it to you rather than to someone else. This is a helpful way to see the importance of the fact that when something is mine or yours, it is mine or yours vis-à-vis everyone else. This is important because even if you and I could, in the absence of yours and mine, somehow agree that I would pass you a thing I was holding so that you could hold it, that agreement would not give third parties a reason to respect it, since it would not make the thing mine or yours.[47]

Now notice the possibilities opened up by the combinations of these relatively simple cases of exclusion and inclusion into broader syndromes and forms of life. The entire edifice of the market depends on the idea of yours and mine: a contractual exchange is (often) (roughly) what happens when I give something that is mine to you and you give something that is yours to me in return. Without the idea of yours and mine, I would be able to simply grab the thing you were holding once you put it down, since it could not be yours. So the market as we understand it would be impossible without the idea of yours and mine. In a different vein, a plausible way to start thinking about the phenomenon of the bourgeois home is in terms of the way that it allows one at the same time to exclude some and include others and thereby have a space and set of activities both alone and with others under one's control.[48] These broader cases illustrate an important abstract thought: the idea of yours and mine gives us opportunities to exercise what I will call *moral creativity*, by variously combining elements of the control I have in what is mine—inclusion and exclusion—to create new ways to act along with others with respect to spaces and objects. As we shall see throughout this book, by exercising this kind of moral creativity, we can and do get the idea of yours and mine to do quite a lot of important things for us.[49] Both the home and the market can be thought of in this way: as institutions that we invented through an exercise of moral creativity using the idea of yours and mine.

[47] To see this more clearly, imagine an attempt at exchange in a context without the idea of yours and mine. Think about Cicero's suggestion, while I'm in the audience in a theater, my seat is mine while I sit in it. Imagine an exchange in such a scenario. From my seat in the back of the theater, your preferred location, I spot you near the front, where I like to sit, and through an exchange of text messages we agree to swap. If I get up to come down to your seat and you get up to walk to mine, neither of us, in fact, has any complaint if some third party sits down in my seat before you get there, or vice versa. (The example apparently originates with the Stoic Chrysippus, but it was Cicero who made it famous: On Ends 3.67 (45 BCE). See Peter Garnsey, Thinking about Property 113–17 (2007).)

[48] Lisa Austin, "Person, Place, or Thing? Property and the Structuring of Social Relations" 60 University of Toronto Law Journal 445, 453 (2012). I'll have much more to say about homes.

[49] This is the source of my rejection of a view of property like Hanoch Dagan's, according to which property is first and foremost about the various inclusionary activities and relations it makes possible. I mean: I agree that property makes those things possible—I think it is partly constitutive of them—and I agree that they are valuable. I disagree with the "first and foremost," though, because it is the fact that it is mine and so that I have a choice about what to do with what is mine (or whether to do anything) that grounds any and all these inclusionary things.

Finally, notice the way that the activities and relations that depend on the idea of yours and mine vary along any manner of empirical dimensions. We need the idea of yours and mine both for quite intimate (hosting one's out-of-town parents or children for a weekend) and arm's-length dealings (a market transaction with a shopkeeper); we need it for short or one-off activities (a single instance of gift-giving or guacamole-making) and for those that take longer or involve repeated interactions (the sowing and then reaping of crops or the daily visit to the newsstand); again, we need it for interaction with small objects (the presentation of a diamond ring) and enormous spaces (the hosting of a polo match or baseball game). In all these cases, we are engaging in activities that depend on the idea of yours and mine which, without the idea of yours and mine, we could not do on terms of equality.

Given all of these differences, we can notice a couple of abstract features of the form that tie the members of this diverse set together. The idea of yours and mine arises in all these cases because in each of them we can think about some object or space being yours or mine (or someone else's). Built into that thought is the idea, first, that there is something that could be the subject matter of the idea, some "this" or "that" about which we can say or think "this is mine" or "that is yours." This subject matter, second, is distinct from the person whose it is: what is mine might just as well be yours and, indeed as we saw, some of the most central activities and relations that involve the idea of yours and mine are those in which something that is mine becomes yours. From the other side, third, the normative constraints that the idea of yours and mine imposes on others are in an important sense depersonalized: when an avocado is mine, you are obligated not to take it not because of any special feature of yourself or our relationship (unlike in a case of a promissory obligation) but simply because it is mine rather than yours. Finally, we can revisit the sense in which the idea of yours and mine is formal: when something is mine, there is in principle no limit to the use that I can make of it, and in the first instance there is no reason to think that any use I do choose to make of it (as long as that use does not infringe your personal rights) would be inconsistent with our standing as equals. This formality explains why, when something is mine, I have an "open-ended set of use privileges"[50] with respect to it; the various activities and relations considered so far are merely a few of the members of that set. I will have more to say about all of this as we continue.

Now it will be helpful to introduce a bit of terminology. I will use the expression *relating through the idea of yours and mine* to describe the category of the various activities and interactions that depend on the idea of yours and mine in the sense that that idea is part of what makes them the activities and interactions that they are. All the kinds of cases I have canvassed in this section fit into this

[50] James Harris, Property and Justice 72 (1996).

category: we relate through the idea of yours and mine when we share your spaces and my objects, when you keep others out of your home or I let them in to mine, and when we participate in larger and more elaborate structures and syndromes of such simpler interactions, as I do when we walk down the street and try to teach my children to keep off others' lawns or when we visit the supermarket to buy the ingredients to make guacamole.

In the light of all this, the breadth and depth of the Problem of Yours and Mine should become clear. A world without the idea of yours and mine would not, as the Everyday Marxist (or Burton Cummings) seems to imagine, be a world basically like ours but with less possessive individualism, a world in which we would share the land (and everything else), a world in which we would all live together. Rather, without the idea of yours and mine, we would be unable to participate as equals in any activity or relation that involved the kind of control I have described. (So any participation in these activities that we could get away with would not be consistent with the basic commitment.) And this is a huge category of activities and relations that extends across all walks of life, ranging from pacing and sleeping, through making and sharing guacamole, through entertaining guests and giving gifts, to the very idea of the home and the institution of the market. In short, we interact with one another through the idea of yours and mine countless times every day; imagining the social world without any of them seems almost impossible. Without the idea of yours and mine, we could not do any of these things on terms of equality. I should emphasize here that, although it will be convenient to talk in the next couple of chapters in rather abstract terms, these abstract terms encompass this wide variety of quite concrete parts of our actual social world. So the discussion here of these specific kinds of activities and relations that depend on the idea of yours and mine should be kept in mind throughout the abstract discussion to come.[51]

Putting all this together, we arrive at the claim that a social world without the idea of yours and mine is, as I will say, morally inconceivable: it is impossible to think that we could have a society of equals—one in which we could participate in this broad and important set of human activities and relations—without the idea of yours and mine.

[51] For a similar point about abstract and concrete notions in this kind of theorizing, see my "The Value of the Neighbour Relation" in Psarras and Steel, Private Law and Practical Reason 297 as well as the discussion at the end of my "What Makes a Home—A Reply" 41 Law & Philosophy 469 (2022).

2

The Law of Yours and Mine

2.1 Relating through the Idea of Yours and Mine

The basic commitment to equality requires that we create and arrange our social and political institutions to ensure that we interact with and relate to each other on terms of equality. The Problem of Yours and Mine is that it is impossible to do so without the idea of yours and mine. The obvious solution to the Problem presents itself. To relate as equals, we need to create an institution that lets us relate through the idea of yours and mine. The name of that institution is "property." So we need property to relate as equals. In this chapter, I elaborate that line of thought. In this section, I expand on the idea of relating through the idea of yours and mine and then show how, once we create a legal institution that realizes that idea, we can relate to each other as equals in respect to property's subject matter (i.e., spaces, objects, and, as we will see later, other stuff, too). After that, I will argue that familiar institutions of property are this sort of institution, that is, that "property" is the name of the law of yours and mine. And then I will show how no other kind of institution can solve the Problem: that anything that seems to solve the Problem either turns out to be an institution of property or else turns out not to allow us to relate to one another as equals.

Let me begin by characterizing in more detail what it is to relate through the idea of yours and mine. This characterization should not come as a surprise given the discussion so far.[1] The basic thought is that when it comes to an interaction over the use of some space or object, we can settle the (normative) question of what may happen simply when you (or I or they) say, "that is mine." What others may do with respect to your thing—your home, your avocado—is *up to you*, such that you have rightful normative control over the scope of their actions.[2]

[1] Moreover, it should not come as a surprise because you already understand it: after all, it is one of the first ideas that children come to grasp. See, for instance, Hildy Ross, Ori Friedman, and Aimee Field, "Toddlers Assert and Acknowledge Ownership Rights" 24 Social Development 341 (2015).

[2] There are other idiomatic expressions that get at the same idea. Avihay Dorfman, "Private Ownership and the Standing to Say So" 64 University of Toronto Law Journal 402 (2014), says the owner's "say-so" is determinative of the permissibility of others actions. Arthur Ripstein, Private Wrongs (2016), says that the owner is "in charge of" others with respect to what they own. It is also worth noting that the word "control" here may mislead, since we often have physical control over what is ours. But such control is not essential to the idea: what matters is the normative.

Property Law in the Society of Equals. Christopher Essert, Oxford University Press. © Oxford University Press 2024.
DOI: 10.1093/oso/9780197768952.003.0003

Relating through the idea of yours and mine has two important features that it is worth pausing on. First, the control over others associated with something's being yours is formal in the sense that we discussed in §1.5. At least in principle—more on those words later—you get to decide about the permissibility of *anything* that others may want to do with what is yours. This formality explains the way in which, when something is yours or mine, we have a control over what happens with it that is importantly *open*, that allows us not only to choose from the obvious activities and relations with others but also to exercise our moral creativity to concoct novel ways to relate with respect to what is ours. The second feature to notice requires a bit more explanation. The fact that something is yours settles the matter of what others may permissibly do with respect to it, such that the matter need not (and cannot) be resolved on the basis of our particular powers. Crucially, though, the idea of yours and mine brings with it a kind of independence from the particular person who invokes it in their thought and talk. That is, when you tell me to let go of the avocado because it is yours, you are not relying on anything distinctive about you or about me. Instead, your claim might be understood more explicitly as having two somewhat distinct parts: when you say, "put it down because it is mine," you are in effect saying first, "there is someone who gets to determine what others may do with respect to this avocado and their determination is that you must put it down" and, second "that someone is me."

This point is a bit easier to state within the context of a system of property, because in that context we have a word for the person who gets to determine what others may do with respect to an object or a space: we call them the owner. One crucial idea here is that the status of owner can and, in fact, must, be understood as detached from or independent of any particular person who happens to be the owner. When you tell me to put down your avocado you are not relying on anything special about you that would grant you control over me; instead you are relying on the status of owner, and it is constitutive of that status that the owner has the relevant control over what they own. Notice, also, how this point works in both directions: the fact that the owner gets to determine the permissibility of others' interactions with the avocado is also independent of any facts about those particular others. That is, there is nothing special about me in virtue of which you can tell me to put down your avocado except for the simple fact that the avocado is not mine, the fact that I am not its owner and you are.[3] Your control over

[3] From one point of view, we can understand feudalism as a development of the idea of control over spaces where the control is not independent from its holder in this way, where there is something "special" about those who control resources. That is, the inalienability of certain feudal incidents is surely not disconnected from feudalism's lords-and-serfs caste dynamic. For this point, see Joseph William Singer, No Freedom without Regulation: The Hidden Lesson of the Subprime Crisis (2015). A related way of making this point is in reverse. We might think that what is inconsistent with your equal standing to others is for you to be "set beneath [another] in a social hierarchy": Niko Kolodny, The Pecking Order 88 (2023). Your claim to be able to determine the permissibility of my actions with respect to the avocado is not a claim of that sort but merely a claim to your occupying the position

what is yours applies to me in precisely the same way that it applies to anyone else who is not its owner. There is nothing special about you as owner or me as nonowner; in fact, an entailment of the independence of the idea of yours and mine from our personalities is that the avocado that is now yours might just as easily be mine, or someone else's. So relating through the idea of yours and mine presupposes this structure of one person's contingently occupying the position—which we call *owner*—whose occupant gets to decide what others may do with respect to the relevant subject matter. This presupposition means that our relation is irreducibly mediated through the idea of yours and mine and is not a relation that is directly about you or me or anyone else.[4]

As I noted, most of us have a solid, intuitive grasp on the idea of yours and mine, such that what I have said in the past couple of paragraphs should not be surprising. But we need to notice that we actually need to do a fair amount of work to get from the Problem of Yours and Mine to the solution, property as the law of yours and mine. For one thing, notice that the idea of yours and mine, just as an idea, is in an important sense inert. Merely thinking it is insufficient to allow us actually to relate through it, which is what we need to be able to do. To do that, we need to *realize* it—that is, to make it real in our social world. One aspect of that realization is given by the way that the idea is abstract and indeterminate. Accepting that we must be able to have things as yours and mine tells us very little about how doing so could structure any particular interaction we might have. It does not tell us what could be yours or mine—avocados, land, ideas, debts, hair? The idea does not tell us what I need to do to make something mine or what you need to do to make something yours—when does that avocado I am planning to use become mine, rather than yours? The idea does not tell us, in any level of detail, what rights I get when I make this or that thing mine—you cannot eat my avocado, but can you draw it or use it to hold down some papers? You cannot enter my house, but can you fly over it or take photos of me when I am at home or send soundwaves through it? The idea does not tell us how to resolve disputes that arise regarding my rights over what is mine and your rights over what is yours—if you carelessly let your dog eat my avocado or if my barbecue's smoke kills your avocado tree, what should happen? In all these ways, the idea is indeterminate, which is to say that it does not provide precise answers to questions about how it applies in particular cases.[5]

whose occupant is entitled to the determination in question. So feudalism—or any system in which control over objects and spaces is attached to individual persons as part of a robust social hierarchy—is not a system of property on my view.

[4] Some find it useful here to talk about the "office of ownership." See *infra* note 16 for some thoughts on this.

[5] The idea that morality, or perhaps more generally what we have reason to do, is indeterminate and requires some legal institutional determination is a common one endorsed by many different

But the possibility of relating as equals precisely requires that each interaction have, at least in principle, a determinate resolution understandable as an actual judgment that the idea of yours and mine applies to the particulars of the case in this or that way.[6] And for it really to be the case that such a judgment allows you and me (the people to whom it applies) to relate as equals, it must be the case that the judgment itself treats us as equals. So it cannot be your unilateral judgment and it cannot be mine. For either one of us to assume the authority to make the judgment, to decide how to bring the abstract to bear on the particulars, would be to assume the authority to determine how the other could act in a way that is inconsistent with the basic commitment. To say that I could be the one to decide that, since it is my avocado, you must not bring your dog within x meters of it would be simply for me to assume that my right in my avocado entitles me to control over your dog. Such an assumption amounts to a kind of claim of superiority of me over you that is inconsistent with the basic commitment.

We should also remember the relational aspect of the basic commitment. Suppose that you were to declare that this avocado is yours and I were to declare that that avocado is mine. One might think that we could then relate as equals, on the grounds that since what happens to a single avocado is up to each of us, things would "come out even,"[7] in a kind of *détente*. But that would be a misunderstanding of the relevant ideas: for you and me to relate as equals is for us to relate such that neither of us is nor can understand ourselves to be the superior or inferior of the other, and for us each to regard ourselves and one another as capable of and required to govern ourselves according to those terms. When things merely come out even, this sort of relation is lacking: we need not regard ourselves as capable of and required to govern ourselves according to the terms of our relation any more than I regard the raccoons in my backyard as equals when I admit that while I can keep them out of the garbage, I cannot keep them from eating the occasional strawberry, but I can live with this state of affairs.[8]

theoretical approaches to law and legal institutions. (A prominent treatment is Tony Honoré, "The Dependence of Morality on Law" 13 Oxford Journal of Legal Studies 1 (1993).) However, most discussions seem to concentrate on some very limited set of cases where the phenomenon arises, notably traffic law and tax law. This concentration might be taken to suggest—on grounds of *expressio unius est exclusio alterius*—that other parts of the normative landscape, in particular those involving our present subject matter, *are* determinate in the absence of legal institutions. Not so. A central theme here will be that so, so much of what the idea of yours and mine might call for is indeterminate without institutional support. I am grateful to Barbara Herman for a conversation that crystalized my sense of how radical and pervasive this indeterminacy is.

[6] Again, the indeterminacy is metaphysical, not merely epistemic. In the abstract, the questions raised in the paragraph in the text have no answer. Someone needs to make an answer by exercising judgment in the bringing to bear of the abstract notion on the particulars of the case.

[7] This expression is from Russell Hoban, Bread and Jam for Frances (1964), which is, I should probably note, a children's book about badgers.

[8] Another nonhuman animal analogy might make things even clearer, with its echoes of the taking-turns structure of the relation of neighbors that I just described. Consider the expression,

To resolve this conflict in a way that allows us to relate as equals, we need a way to resolve the conflict that can be said to be ours, instead of just yours or just mine.[9] But whose does "ours" mean? Suppose we reimagined the case by having you and me mutually and bilaterally declare that this avocado is yours and that avocado is mine, and suppose moreover that we added further content to the declarations along the lines of the relevant form of mutual regard as capable of and required to govern ourselves according to the terms of the declaration. Would this solve things? Not quite, but we would be on our way. The central plank of our relation here is the fact of our mutual and bilateral endorsement of one another's status. Your avocado would be yours in part because I agreed that it would be and vice versa, and this mutual and bilateral endorsement of the realization of the idea of yours and mine with respect to our interactions with these avocados ensures that each of us has a claim to their status that is not unilateral. What does this tell us about the Problem of Yours and Mine?

If we zoom out a bit from this stylized example, we can see a kind of defect to be addressed.[10] Our bilateral agreement with respect to our avocados is, because it is bilateral, necessarily only our business, and cannot have any impact at all on the rights of anyone else. But a fundamentally important feature of the idea of yours and mine is that when something is yours or mine it is not anyone else's: it is yours or mine, as we say, *against the world*. This suggests that a more complete realization of the idea of yours and mine needs to be able to bind everyone at the same time in the same way that our bilateral declaration bound the two of us. In other words, we need to realize the idea of yours and mine *omnilaterally*, through an institution to which everyone is a party. Think about it this way. When something is mine, it is not anyone else's. So for each other person, it is true of them and me that we relate to one another through the idea of yours and mine with respect to the subject matter in question. And this is true at the same time for you with respect to whatever is yours and for everyone else with respect to whatever

given wide exposure in the movie *The Big Lebowski*, "Sometimes you eat the bear and sometimes the bear eats you." This seems to describe a kind of coming out even (with the bear or with fate more generally), but clearly does not describe anything like a relation (egalitarian or otherwise) between the bear and you, since persons and bears cannot stand in (normative) relations to each other.

[9] Many classical discussions of property center on the specific version of this problem that applies to the act of acquisition: in asking how someone could make something their own, they ask how what appears to be a unilateral act could be consistent with something like the basic commitment. As the discussion in the text will make clear, I think the solution to this problem of unilateralism is the omnilaterality of an institution of property. Applied to the question of acquisition, then, my view will be that things can only be acquired within such an institution. See §§ 1.3 and 4.3 for more.

[10] You might also suggest that we cannot relate as equals in the mutual declaration case because we lack the capacity to resolve any disputes over the avocados (if I am juggling my avocado and it falls and damages yours, have I wronged you?) in a way that treats us as equals. That's right, which is another reason why a genuine solution to the Problem of Yours and Mine requires an authoritative institution that can resolve disputes on terms of equality.

is theirs. Moreover, there are new people showing up all the time. So nothing like a series of actual (datable) bilateral agreements could be possible.[11] The idea of omnilaterality thus enters the picture not as an account of some kind of large-scale mutual declaration but rather as an idea of reason, as a tool for thinking through the way that relating through the idea of yours and mine can count as relating as equals. Since only such an omnilateral authority could realize the idea of yours and mine in a way that treats each of us as an equal, the creation of such an authority is itself required by the basic commitment.[12] In other words, the Problem of Yours and Mine requires us to create an omnilateral institution that can realize the idea of yours and mine and allow us to relate to one another through it.[13] We call such an institution "property law."

When we realize the idea of yours and mine in an authoritative omnilateral institution—through property law—we solve the Problem of Yours and Mine together. The institution realizes the idea by creating the possibility of ownership, the possibility of individual persons occupying the status of owner with respect to this or that subject matter. The subjects of the institution are thus able to relate to one another through the idea of yours and mine, because the idea has been realized—made real—using the mechanism of the actual determinate property rights through the institution's omnilateral capacity. So when I say "put down my avocado," I am not to be understood to be claiming any kind of superiority over you. Rather I am invoking the omnilateral authority of the institution: I am saying that everyone together made it possible to be the owner of the avocado and that I am the one who is the owner and thus has the capacity to exercise that institutional authority with respect to this avocado.[14] In order for this realization of the idea to be consistent with the basic commitment, of course, the position of owner must be "open to all under conditions of fair equality of opportunity."[15]

[11] See Ernest J Weinrib, Reciprocal Freedom: Private Law, and Public Right 52 n 22 (2022).

[12] One simple but not unhelpful way of thinking about this is by noting, with Kant, that we can think of "innate equality" as "independence from being bound by others to more than one can in turn bind them." Immanuel Kant, The Metaphysics of Morals 6:237–38 (1797).

[13] This is of course a version of a common Kantian argument, set out at length in the Metaphysics of Morals, as well as Arthur Ripstein, Force and Freedom: Kant's Legal and Political Philosophy (2009) and Weinrib, Reciprocal Freedom. For similar, but not quite as explicitly Kantian versions, see also Ronald Dworkin, Justice for Hedgehogs (2011); Seana Valentine Shiffrin, Democratic Law (2021). All of these views share the more general claim that law, in some form, is morally required. (Dworkin writes, at 320, that "collective coercive government is essential to our dignity," and Shiffrin, at 34, that "some of our mandatory moral ends require democratic law.") I leave coercion to the side here. But, in short, we need to be able to ensure that the judgments about what the idea requires are actually carried out, and ensuring that requires that the institution have the capacity to enforce its judgments if need be. See also *infra* note 58.

[14] As Ripstein puts it, "if the public authority is entitled to confer a power on me in the name of everyone, then the specific exercise of the power is also in everyone's name." Force and Freedom at 154. The way that institutional positions relate to a concern about subordination is also thematic in Kolodny, The Pecking Order.

[15] John Rawls, A Theory of Justice, rev ed 266 (1999). In saying this, I am ruling out of consideration here putative institutions of property that make it legally impossible for certain classes of people

But when this is true, our relation is mediated through the idea of yours and mine as realized in the institution of property and is thereby egalitarian.[16] We should also here remind ourselves of the breadth and open form of the idea of yours and mine that we saw earlier in this section and in §1.5: we relate through the idea not only when I exclude you from the avocado but also when I share it with you or give it to you or exchange it for your apple, and in so many other ways. In all these cases, the possibility of participating as equals in these activities and relations is conditioned on the omnilateral realization of the constituent idea.

This part of the account echoes many other well-known views in political philosophy. The term "omnilaterality" these days reads as Kantian, but I take the same idea to be invoked by certain elements in Rousseau's notion of the general will.[17] In particular it is present in Rousseau's brief discussion of property in the *Social Contract,* the discussion we noted in the Introduction. Rousseau characterizes property in terms of a kind of exchange, where each of us gives to the community everything we hold as a matter of fact and in exchange we get to have it back as a matter of right:

> What is remarkable about this alienation is that the community, far from despoiling individuals of their goods by accepting them, only secures to them their legitimate possession, changes usurpation into genuine right, and use into property.[18]

to own things, as, for instance, the English legal system did for married women until the late nineteenth century. See also note 3, *supra*, and chapter 3, note 3.

[16] There is some movement in property theory these days to talk about ownership as an "office." For the clearest development of the idea, see Larissa Katz, "Ownership and Offices: The Building Blocks of the Legal Order" 70 University of Toronto Law Journal, (Supplement 2) 267 (2020), and Katz's other works cited therein. I have in past used this terminology myself— see "The Office of Ownership" 63 University of Toronto Law Journal 418 (2013)—but I am no longer so sure it is helpful, because of the way that the notion of an office seems to involve a substantive purpose which limits the exercise of the powers of its holder, in a way that seems to me not quite consistent with ownership's open formal character—see "The Office of Ownership Revisited" 70 University of Toronto Law Journal (Supplement 2) 287 (2020). That said, a more basic notion of an office as an institutionally constituted site of rights, powers, duties, and so on, does seem apt here. As the argument in the text indicates, immanent in the idea of yours and mine is a kind of detachment between the status of owner and the person who has that status. This detachment, realized in the institutional context, is essential to the egalitarian character of property.

[17] To a somewhat similar effect is Shiffrin's account of democracy, by which, she says, she means "a political system that treats all its members with equal concern, regards their lives as of equal importance, and treats all competent members of the community . . . as, by right and by conception, the equal and exclusive co-authors of and co-contributors to the system, its rules, its actions, its directives, its communications, and its other outputs." See Shiffrin, Democratic Law at 20. I should note that some of what Shiffrin says is more comparative than relational. But the central thought that matters at the present moment in the argument is the thought that the state is made up of its subjects in an important way.

[18] Rousseau, Of the Social Contract I.9.6 [OC III, 367] (1762).

Rousseau's thought here is that, without a legal institution of property authorized by the general will—omnilaterally—we would each only be able to possess things as a matter of "usurpation," which is to say, not as a matter of right. That is, we could only hold them. By entering into a social contract, we transform that morally unacceptable situation—the negative community—into a rightful one. That said, this solution requires the existence of the general will, and thus "the right every individual has over his own land is always subordinate to the right the community has over everyone."[19] What precisely that "subordinate" means will concern us later, but for now the point is that each person's rights to their property are rights that come into existence only as the depersonalized rights of property created by an institution, so that none holds property on the basis of anything special about their own person but rather through the institution as the occupant of the position of owner of some bit of property.[20] In a slogan, we might say that something can be yours or mine only if it is, in this way, yours and mine.

2.2 Property Is the Realization of the Idea

When we relate through the idea of yours and mine as realized in an omnilateral institution, we relate as equals. I said that property is our name for such an institution. In this section and the next, I defend that claim, by arguing first (in this section) that familiar property institutions can be understood as realizations of the idea of yours and mine and then (in the next section) that nothing else can. It is worth my saying here that the structure of my account is non-instrumental in a specific way: my claim is that the idea of yours and mine is constitutive of the possibility of relating as equals with respect to spaces and objects. So it is not as if the idea is merely one among many potential tools for relating in this way; the Problem of Yours and Mine is that such relations are impossible without the idea of yours and mine. I will argue now that property and only property can realize the idea of yours and mine, which is to say, in other words, that property is not

[19] Rousseau, Social Contract I.9.7 [OC III, 367].

[20] A similar thought plays an important role in another well-known discussion of property from quite a different perspective. In "Dialogue on Private Property," Felix Cohen endorses the thought that property is that "to which the following label can be attached:

> To the world:
> Keep off X unless you have my permission, which I may grant or withhold.
> Signed: Private citizen
> Endorsed: The state."

With the final line, Cohen here echoes the point in the text. The state, as the embodiment of the general will, must be understood to "endorse" all exercises of legal rights; in the Rousseauian democratic tradition, the state, in a construction like that one, is just us, so that means that each of us must, in a sense, endorse all exercises of property rights, even those that keep us out. See Felix S Cohen, "Dialogue on Private Property" 9 Rutgers Law Review 357, 374 (1954).

merely one among many tools for allowing us to relate as equals with respect to spaces and objects but rather that it is constitutive of the very possibility of doing so.[21] Property is not one among a set of optional choices, it is an institution that we cannot morally do without.

My account of what an institution of property is may seem rather revisionist about what makes something an institution of property: not many people think that what does or does not count as property is a matter of answering a question about equal relations. But at the same time, as we will see, the account is, importantly, not very revisionist at all about what cases count as cases of property. That is, in saying what property is, I say something that is roughly consistent with our considered pre-theoretic intuitions about the question.[22] (I am not, in other words, giving a theory of "schmoperty.") I think my account, being revisionist about property's intension but not its extension, is therefore a very good one, in that it provides a new and attractive understanding of a part of the social world that we have a relatively solid grasp on, at least on the surface.[23]

Now on to the argument. Famously (or, perhaps, infamously):

> There is nothing which so generally strikes the imagination, and engages the affections of mankind, as the right of property; or that sole and despotic dominion which one man claims and exercises over the external things of the world, in total exclusion of the right of any other individual in the universe.

The picture of property rights painted by William Blackstone in this passage in his magisterial eighteenth-century treatment of English law is an evocative one that has, to this day, adherents.[24] It is the idea that, when I own something, *everything* that happens to that thing is up to me. A moment's reflection will show how that idea, just as stated, is on its face implausibly overbroad: I cannot choose,

[21] For more on this feature of the account see the opening section in my"Property and Homelessness" 44 Philosophy & Public Affairs 266 (2016). Also remember the point, briefly made in §1.2, that property is one constituent of a society of equals, and other formally different but parallel institutions (of personal rights, contract rights, etc.) will also be constituents in their own distinct ways.

[22] In other words: I'm making here an argument parallel to one made in general jurisprudence by Martin Stone. Stone's argument is that law as such solves a moral problem, and that "only law can solve [that problem]. Or better put, anything that solves it would perforce be law." Martin Jay Stone, "Planning Positivism and Planning Natural Law" 25 Canadian Journal of Law & Jurisprudence 219, 226 (2012). As I have said, I think that's the right way of thinking about property: only property can solve the Problem of Yours and Mine, and anything that solves the Problem of Yours and Mine is therefore property. In this section, I want to show that this understanding of property is also not radically revisionary in its extension, that the cuts it makes in terms of what is and is not an institution of property are cuts that we can endorse on the basis of our reflective intuitions about that question.

[23] Another version of the same structure applies to the question of what kinds of recognized legal rights within common law systems count as property, the subject matter of chapter 5.

[24] William Blackstone, Commentaries on the Laws of England II.2 (1766). Arguably Blackstone himself was not among the adherents of this view, but that is not a point I can consider here.

for instance, to hit you in the face with my avocado. A more general and important illustration of the same point is given by the law of nuisance—about which more in §4.2—which constrains my capacity to use my property to protect your capacity to use yours, and vice versa, through what the law calls an idea of "give and take, live and let live."[25] With that qualification, this Blackstonian idea comes into clearer focus. It is, I think, the same idea that interests A M Honoré in one of the most famous articles in property theory ever written. Honoré's project, as it is normally understood, is to show what ownership is by setting out the "greatest interest in a thing admitted by a mature legal system." Honoré calls this idea of the greatest interest "full" or "liberal" ownership; I call it "full liberal ownership."[26]

In that article, Honoré attempts to explain this idea in terms of a series of "incidents,"[27] which together add up to a kind of account of what it is to have something as yours or mine. To own something is to have, as he says, the right to possess it and keep others off, to determine how it will be used, both physically and economically, to be able to transmit it to others via gift or sale, permanently or temporarily, and generally to have all of this be the case in a very open-ended and indefinite way. Honoré is providing an analysis of what it is to have complete control over something. And the kind of control that Honoré is analyzing is what might intuitively come to mind when we think about something being yours or mine, the kind of control that gives its holder almost complete say over the actions of others with respect to the thing. I will call it the *most expansive* realization of the idea. It is also conceptually the most basic realization: when something is mine, the starting assumption is that everything that happens to it is up to me, since (cases involving violations of your rights aside) there is no reason that any particular choice I make with respect to how to use it would be inconsistent with our standing as equals. That is, in the abstract, the idea of yours and mine gives me the formal capacity to determine if I want to keep my avocado for myself, share the guacamole with you, trade the avocado for your apple, or anything else I might think of that does not involve violating your own rights over yourself or what is yours. That is not to say that reasons might not be offered to constrain what I can do with what is mine, but the point is that such constraints are constraints. Indeed, as I will now explain, the indeterminacy of the idea of yours and mine means that the most expansive realization of it is not required.

The easiest place to see this is by reference to the actual common law of property, which does not provide this most expansive notion of full liberal ownership.

[25] *Bamford v Turnley*, (1860) 3 B & S 62, 83–84.

[26] A M Honoré, "Ownership" in Anthony G Guest ed, Oxford Essays in Jurisprudence 107 (1961).

[27] They are: the right to possess; the right to use; the right to manage; the right to the income; the right to the capital; the right to security; the incident of transmissibility; the incident of absence of term; the prohibition of harmful use; liability to execution; residuary character. See Honoré, "Ownership" *passim*.

Blackstone himself knew this. The right of property, he said, "consists in the free use, enjoyment, and disposal . . . without any control or diminution, *save only by the laws of the land*."[28] In the common law, owners are burdened by any number of restrictions on the use of their property. Nuisance requires that owners not use their land in ways that unreasonably interfere with the use and enjoyment of others' land; zoning does something similar. The *numerus clausus* limits the kinds of interests that owners can create in their land.[29] The "accommodation" and "touch and concern" requirements in the law of servitudes constrain the power of neighbors to rearrange their rights with respect to each other's land,[30] and landlord-tenant law has a similar effect in its context. Necessity sometimes constrains the application of trespass remedies.[31] Some kinds of property cannot be easily abandoned.[32] That is not a short list, and these examples could be multiplied. For my purposes here I will define *constraint* as those rules and standards of various kinds which operate so that an institution provides owners' rights that are in some sense "less" than full liberal ownership. (As we will see in chapter 6, there are importantly different varieties of constraint that need to be teased apart; for now we can set those differences aside.)

Constraint brings with it a kind of tension that needs noticing here. On the one hand, we will want to say that the mere presence of constraint is not inconsistent with thinking that a system has realized the idea of yours and mine. As we saw already, the common law—arguably the paradigmatic institution of property—involves a wide variety of constraints. And as we will see later, a full understanding of the idea of yours and mine will turn out to *require* certain kinds of constraints. But on the other hand, it seems that too much constraint would be a problem: if I am not able to eat the avocado, or make guacamole with it, or share it or sell it, in what sense is it still mine?[33] I want to suggest that the idea of yours and mine itself provides a way out of this impasse. As I noted in §2.1, the indeterminacy of the idea of yours and mine explains how we need an institution

[28] Blackstone, Commentaries I.134 (my emphasis).

[29] Thomas W Merrill and Henry E Smith, "Optimal Standardization in the Law of Property: The *Numerus Clausus* Principle" 110 Yale Law Journal 1 (2000).

[30] See *In re Ellenborough Park*, [1955] 3 All ER 667 (accommodation); *Spencer's Case*, 77 Eng Rep 72 (KB 1583) (touch and concern).

[31] *Ploof v Putnam*, 76 A 145 (Vt 1910).

[32] Eduardo M Peñalver, "The Illusory Right to Abandon" 109 Michigan Law Review 191 (2010).

[33] Oliver Wendell Holmes' famous claim in *Pennsylvania Coal Co v Mahon*, 260 US 393, 415 (1922), that "the general rule, at least, is that, while property may be regulated to a certain extent, if regulation goes too far, it will be recognized as a taking" is based on this same idea. And to the same effect is Richard A Epstein, Takings: Private Property and the Power of Eminent Domain 97 (1985): "It would be a clear affront to the conception of ownership if a plaintiff were told that he was *never* entitled to redress if the defendant deliberately destroyed his property." Epstein takes this attractive idea to its most absurd implications, claiming that, since it would be an affront to completely constrain an owner's exercise of their rights, it is also an affront to constrain them at all. But Holmes' point is just the opposite.

of property in order to render it sufficiently determinate to realize it and actually allow subjects to relate through the idea. This means that an institution of property must provide rights that are sufficiently broad in a sufficiently wide degree of situations to allow its subjects to relate through the idea of yours and mine. The question about constraint then becomes just a form of the same abstract question: are the constrained rights of owners under a given institution sufficient to allow those owners to relate through the idea of yours and mine and solve the Problem? If the answer is yes, the constraints are consistent with thinking that a system of property exists. If the answer is no, they are not.

Two sets of familiar ideas can provide a helpful perspective on this inquiry. First, as we saw in §1.5, the idea of yours and mine constitutively enables a wide variety of ways for us to relate to one another through it. In investigating alternative institutions of property that are close to our own, our focus will be on the extent to which such alternatives would allow us to enter into these various relations, or ones somewhat like them. That is to say that an institution that did not allow us to keep others out, let them in, share things with them, transfer them to others, and so on—in short, an institution that did not allow us to relate to one another through the idea of yours and mine—would not be an institution of property. Second, Honoré's analysis indicated a set of familiar legal incidents of ownership. Rather than seeing the set as a cobbling-together—or, I guess I should say, "bundling"—of items that have no conceptual tie to one another, as some of those inspired by Honoré seem to do, we should see it instead as a way that the law provides determinate content to the idea of yours and mine.[34] I said that the most expansive realization of the idea of yours and mine provides for all of Honoré's incidents. But as Honoré says, we can still talk about property

[34] For my property-theory readers, I should probably say a bit more about this contrast. Honoré writes: "In stressing the importance of such common features, I do not wish to go beyond the claim that these resemblances exist *de facto* and can be explained by the common needs of mankind and the common conditions of human life. It would be rash to assert that the features discussed are necessarily common to different mature systems, or that their range and ubiquity proves that what is called 'general jurisprudence' is a reputable pursuit. These assertions may indeed be true, but for my purposes it is enough to show that the standard incidents of ownership do not vary from system to system in the erratic, unpredictable way implied by some writers but, on the contrary, have a tendency to remain constant from place to place and age to age." Honoré, "Ownership" at 109. Well, call me rash, but I very much want to go beyond *de facto* claims to provide a general account of ownership. Honoré suggests that he would not be opposed to my project—"these assertions may be true," he says—but many of those who follow in Honoré's footsteps would be: they deny the possibility that there is any unifying principle tying together the various "sticks" in the "bundle" of property rights that makes up ownership. (See, for still-cogent criticism, James Penner, "The 'Bundle of Rights' Picture of Property" 43 UCLA Law Review 711 (1996).) Others want to claim that ownership exists in some resource just when we have "enough" of Honoré's incidents to say so. (Muireann Quigley, "Property and the Body: Applying Honoré" 33 Journal of Medical Ethics 631 (2007).). The problem with this second approach is easy to see: if we have no unifying principle of the incidents, then there are no grounds on which we can say that we have "enough" incidents in a case to talk about ownership. By contrast, if we understand Honoré's analysis through the lens of the idea of yours and mine, we can use his determinate categories to answer the abstract question.

and ownership when only some proper subset of these incidents is granted to property right holders. This is not a matter of some determinate proportion of the Honoré incidents—it is not as though if I have eight I am an owner but if I have only seven I am not—but of the way that these incidents can guide us in answering the abstract question of whether or not I have sufficient control over others' interactions with something for me to be able to say that it is mine in the relevant sense. Importantly, too, we need to remember to approach this question from the point of view of diminution, in that the conceptually basic idea is full liberal ownership, such that constraints are to be viewed as takings-away from that basic idea.[35] Because the abstract idea suggests that when something is mine I get to determine what happens to it in any way I like, and that this breadth of control is consistent with our equal standing, the takings-away that are represented by constraints must themselves have a justification in terms of the idea of yours and mine or the basic commitment.

Generally, the question is one about whether or not a particular regime can be understood as a realization of the idea of yours and mine. We can turn to some particular instances of the question. One set of those concerns limitations on what we think of as the core capacities of ownership, cases where an owner's liberty to use or right to determine others' use or power to alienate is constrained. Much will depend on details here, but the basic picture is clear: we need to ask if individuals can relate to each other through the idea of yours and mine in such cases, viewing the constraints as constraints on the formal idea of full liberal ownership. Constraints on the liberty to use are familiar: there are lots of ways I may not use my car, but it is clearly my car, because what happens to it within those constraints is entirely up to me. Constraints on the right to exclude can sometimes bring us closer to the line. While a rule that allows strangers to roam across my rural land, keeping a distance from my home, seems consistent with thinking about it as my land,[36] a rule that allowed them into my home to sit on the couch and watch tv between the hours of 9 am and 5 pm would make it much harder to do so. So an institution that claimed to grant its subjects property in homes while denying them the right to exclude to this degree would arguably not be an institution of property in homes, because it would not be giving its subjects the homes as their own.

Restraints on alienation are a more familiar version of the same dynamic. The right starting point for thinking about them is the one seen already: alienability

[35] So I disagree with Anderson's claim that each of the incidents of full liberal ownership requires "a separate argument," but I agree (for what it's worth) with her conclusions about what kinds of results we want, so I need (as I will suggest, later) arguments about which constraints are justified. For Anderson's view, see Elizabeth Anderson, "Freedom and Equality" in David Schmidtz and Carmen Pavel eds, The Oxford Handbook of Freedom (2016).

[36] For a discussion of the details of the Swedish case, probably the best known, of a right to roam, see R Campion and J Stephenson, "The 'Right to Roam': Lessons for New Zealand from Sweden's *allemansrätt*" 17 Australasian Journal of Environmental Management 18 (2010).

is built into the very idea of yours and mine in terms of its role in understanding the idea as consistent with our standing as equals. Equally importantly, we can see that alienation of property can easily be understood as just one end of a spectrum whose other end is a simple licence or temporary sharing. That is, we saw that for my home to be mine means that I can keep you out of it but also that I can invite you in. Inviting you in, though, means inviting you for dinner or inviting you for the weekend or asking you to house sit for the day or for the year, and so it seems to extend to giving the home to you outright.[37] This means that restraints on alienation should be understood as constraints on a power that is built into the idea of yours and mine. This is another clear illustration of the operation of the formality of the idea: we ought to think about inalienable property as constrained property, rather than thinking that we might choose to "add" alienability to some notion of something's being mine that could be conceivable in the absence of alienability.[38] This is, of course, not to say that we cannot or even that we should not restrain alienation. There may be very good reasons to do so. As to the question of how significant a restraint on alienation is consistent with thinking about something as mine, we need to consider particular cases in detail. Some simple restraints are obviously not problematic: a rule that says you cannot sell alcohol to a minor does not mean that the alcohol is not really yours. Other cases are closer to the line: tenancies with social housing providers often limit alienation. A core part of the common law's idea of a tenancy is that it is freely alienable—more on this in §4.6—but some statutory rules restrain such alienation and yet continue to conceptualize tenants as property holders. I tend to be of the view that such constraints are consistent with thinking about the spaces in question as instances of property, because their residents are still able to participate in a very wide array of relations through the idea of yours and mine: they can keep others out and invite them over for stays of whatever length, and thus do any of the things that require those elements of control. But, again, this is all rather indeterminate in the abstract, and my own read on the specifics of such cases matters less than the structure of our thinking about it.

A distinct, but similar, set of questions arises in another context. Here the questions are about the scope of the institution of ownership, about what kinds of spaces and objects can be owned. Probably the most familiar version of this question is about the ownership of the means of production, the question of whether what is sometimes called "socialism" is a form of property in my sense. Rawls' treatment of this question fits well with my account. He assumes that "among the

[37] Adolf Reinach, The A Priori Foundations of the Civil Law 70 (1913/2012), trans John Crosby. And see Ben McFarlane, The Structure of Property Law 692 (2008): "Across the property law system, there is a clear rule that if B1 has a right to exclusive control of a thing . . . then B1 *does* have the power to transfer that property right to B2."

[38] For a different view, see Anna Stilz, Territorial Sovereignty 71–72 (2019).

basic rights is the right to hold and to have the exclusive use of personal property, [which] would seem to include at least certain forms of real property, such as dwellings and private grounds."[39] Then Rawls contrasts two different models, which differ in whether or not they allow for private control over the means of production: the common law does allow for such private control, and it is a realization of the idea of yours and mine; so the question is about the alternative, which Rawls calls "liberal socialism,"[40] where "the means of production and of natural resources, [are] socially, not privately, owned." Rawls' view is that either of these systems may "be justified. This depends on existing historical and social conditions."[41] But is liberal socialism a system of property in my sense?

It is. The important point is that under liberal socialism, there is a relatively narrow set of cases in which private ownership is prohibited,[42] so subjects are still able to relate to one another through the idea of yours and mine in a sufficiently wide variety of different ways, as they still own their homes and personal property in a quite robust sense. We can see this by noting the contrast, as Rawls does, between liberal socialism, on the one hand, and, on the other, "state socialism with a command economy," which involves a "one-party regime" and a "general economic plan adopted from the center,"[43] for the use of resources. Under this latter system, subjects cannot relate to one another through the idea of yours and mine at all and thus cannot relate as equals with respect to resources like spaces and objects. Rawls' treatment is instructive also in regard to the claim that the idea of yours and mine is abstract and allows for a wide range of institutional realizations. That is, the idea does not provide a "detailed blueprint" for a society,[44] but instead structures our thinking about how to relate to one another. It would be odd if such an abstract idea ruled out, as a matter of definitional fiat, actual institutions in the world that many of us think of as institutions of property. That said, it is not as though the theory provides no grounds on which to choose between these systems. The present point is just that the permissibility of such institutional variation will mean that our choice is properly understood not

[39] John Rawls, Justice as Fairness: A Restatement 114 (2001).

[40] Rawls, Justice as Fairness at 135.

[41] Rawls, Justice as Fairness at 114; and see also at 138–39 to the same effect.

[42] It may be worth noting that the expression "means of production" does not make it self-evident where the line of permissible private ownership is to be drawn in liberal socialism. That is, it's not clear what the means of production are. One proposal, which is congenial to my account, is that the means of production are determined in part by reference to questions about what scope of ownership is required by the abstract notion of justice. See William A Edmundson, "What Are 'the Means of Production?'" 28 The Journal of Political Philosophy 421 (2020). This way of thinking allows us to generalize beyond the means of production context, and say that we have an institution of property whenever the institution applies the idea to a sufficiently wide range of cases, defining "sufficiently wide" in terms of the basic commitment and the idea of yours and mine.

[43] Rawls, Justice as Fairness at 138.

[44] Jacob Weinrib, Dimensions of Dignity: The Theory and Practice of Modern Constitutional Law 140 (2016).

as a choice between property and some alternative but as a choice *among* systems of property. I return to that question in §3.3.

2.3 Only Property Is the Realization of the Idea

We have seen that we can understand a variety of familiar property institutions as solutions to the Problem of Yours and Mine. Now it is time to turn to the claim that *only* a system of property can solve the Problem. What I will do here is consider some counterexamples—familiar proposed alternatives to property—and show that either they do not represent a solution to the Problem or else turn out not to be an alternative to property but to be a system of property after all. Obviously we should not proceed by arguing cases—that black swan might be out there somewhere. But my argument is going to aim to demonstrate a kind of strategy for dealing with putative counterexamples and so by the end of this section it should be relatively clear what I might say about other cases that I do not discuss here. I return to this point later in this section.

We can start with a rather broad set of cases exemplified by the command economy that, with Rawls, I rejected as a system of property in the last section. A command economy can be understood as an instance of what I will call *substantive resource allocation schemes*. Any such scheme approaches the question of how an object or space should be used by beginning with a principle—a "noble or beautiful purpose,"[45] comprehensible entirely independently of the idea of yours and mine—and then asking, at any given moment or in the context of any given dispute, what or whose use of the space or object would best or most efficiently serve or respect or promote the principle. Experience provides a variety of such schemes, which for our purposes differ only in their constituent principle: think of systems that make the use of an object or space depend on welfare maximization, or on welfare equalization, or some combination of those (which probably describes real-life command economies), or on desire or preference satisfaction, or on the glory of God (as in various religious orders' organizations, including in particular various monastic orders whose members take themselves to lack any property in anything[46]), or even on the basis of some kind of random turn-taking (as in the "job wheels" used by roommates). Of course one important set of questions about such schemes is practical: how could it be determined whether one or another candidate use actually promoted the value, who would make such determinations, and so on. We will set those question aside and assume it could

[45] Stone, "Planning Positivism and Planning Natural Law" at 228.

[46] On whether or not they could be right in that self-understanding, see the discussion of the Franciscan controversy in Brian Tierney, The Idea of Natural Rights (1997).

be done. By hypothesis, such a scheme is not a system of property: permissible use turns on the abstract value and nobody gets to decide what happens to something on the basis of the idea of yours and mine.[47]

The question to answer is this: does a substantive resource allocation scheme solve the Problem of Yours and Mine even though it is not a system of property? And the answer is no: such a system fails to respect the basic commitment, because it does not allow its subjects to relate as equals. This might come as a surprise, since the substantive principles I suggested could be said to have in common precisely that they apply to their subjects in the same way, that they treat them all equally. But there is an important difference between treating people equally and treating them as equals, which is to say giving them the means to relate as equals.[48] Recall, again, that for you and me to relate as equals is for us to relate on terms such that neither of us is, nor can understand ourselves to be, the superior or inferior of the other, and—of particular note here—for us each to understand ourselves and one another as capable of and required to govern ourselves according to those terms. No scheme based on any of the principles I set out, or any other similar principle, could satisfy this requirement, since they do not allow their subjects to relate to each other in this way; instead, subjects of such a scheme are treated merely as the means for the production of whatever value the system aims to promote or respect. Interestingly, the point here applies even if the substance of the principle that determines the permissibility of uses is itself substantively egalitarian. The Marxian principle "to each according to his

[47] An exchange in the movie *Guardians of the Galaxy* illustrates:

> Corpsman Dey: I have to warn you against breaking any laws in the future.
> Rocket: Question. What if I see something that I want to take, and it belongs to someone else?
> Corpsman Dey: Well you will be arrested.
> Rocket: But what if I want it more than the person who has it?
> Corpsman Dey: Still illegal.
> Rocket: That doesn't follow. No, I want it more, sir. Do you understand?

The bit lands because everyone—except Rocket, who, perhaps, it should be noted, is a talking raccoon—understands that, in an institution of property, how much you want something that is another's is immaterial to the permissibility of taking it. A system in which the strength of our desires or preferences for the use of spaces and objects was determinative of the permissibility of using them would not be a system of property. Rocket's mistake here, of course, parallels the one Rawls noted in his account of promising: "what would one say of someone who, when asked why he broke his promise, replied simply that breaking it was best on the whole? Assuming that his reply is sincere, and that his belief was reasonable . . . I think that one would question whether or not he knows what it means to say 'I promise' (in the appropriate circumstances). It would be said of someone who used this excuse without further explanation that he didn't understand what defenses the practice, which defines a promise, allows to him." See John Rawls, "Two Concepts of Rules" 64 The Philosophical Review 3, 17 (1955). The present thought is the same: someone—whether a talking raccoon or an economist—who thinks that the permissibility of using another's object depends on the account of some impersonal value *does not understand what property is.*

[48] The treating as equals versus treating equally distinction is from Ronald Dworkin, Taking Rights Seriously 227 (1977).

need," for instance, fails to relate its subjects as equal persons but instead merely treats them as vessels for the primary site of moral concern, namely, needs.[49] For the system to tell me that my intended use of the avocado is not permitted because yours better achieves the relevant value, whatever that value may be, does not allow you and me to relate as equals. The fact that your use is *your* use is immaterial. And none of the activities and relations that, as we saw in §1.5, depend on the idea of yours and mine could happen here: the permissibility not just of your using the avocado for yourself but also of your sharing it or handing it to me would depend on whether that would respect the scheme's principle.

Notice also that a denial to me of permission to use the avocado because your use better serves the principle would be no different than a denial on the grounds that avocado use tends to increase greenhouse gas emissions or that a raccoon could use the avocado more efficiently. In none of these cases is anything like an idea of relating as equals present: I could only see you in the way I could see the raccoon or the environment, as parts of the universe to which the value could be applied rather than as party to a relation of equals. And the same thing would be true in reverse. We might characterize this situation by saying that you and I (and everyone else) are experiencing the system in parallel, wherein the normativity of the system is applied to each of us individually, severally but not jointly. The decision would be based not on any relation between us but rather (at most) on a comparison between how each of our proposed uses, understood monadically, met the relevant principle.[50] So the question of whether or not we related as equals would not be answered negatively (i.e., it would not be that we related as superior and inferior): it would misfire, since there would be no relation between us at all. In this way, we might think about the world of a substantive resource allocation scheme as a kind of parallel to the world without property, in that here we would be unable to relate to one another on terms of equality and so to meet the basic commitment. In the pure negative community, there would be no terms on which to determine how objects and spaces could be used; here there would be rules, but those rules would fail to allow us to relate to one another as equals (or indeed, at all) and thus fail to meet the basic commitment.

A different familiar sort of proposed counterexample to a claim that property is necessary is a regime of use rights or "usufruct." The basic idea of such a system is that a person who is using an object or space has a right to that use, so that others cannot interfere with it during the use, but that, once the use is completed, the object becomes available for others' use.[51] The difficulty with such a proposal

[49] So, as Rawls thought utilitarianism did, it fails to "preserve the distinction of persons, to recognize the separateness of life and experience": Rawls, Theory of Justice at 167.

[50] On relations versus comparisons, see Ripstein, Private Wrongs at 36–38.

[51] Something like this is, for instance, what Grotius took to be the moral situation in the state of nature; for a defense of a similar idea see Stilz, Territorial Sovereignty.

is that the idea of use is too unstable to allow for us to relate through it on terms of equality. The worry, in a nutshell, is that there is an irresolvable ambiguity in what it means to "use" something. Recall that, in the negative community, I was permitted to take the avocado you had picked and put down because it was not (and could not be) yours and so, once you were not holding it, you could have no right to it. Here the proposal is that you would have a right to it because (and while) you were using it. In our world, it does seem natural to say that you are using the avocado that is beside your cutting board about to be chopped. But what about the avocado in the bowl, or the one in the fridge, or the one still hanging on the tree in the backyard? Arguably you are using at least some of those, or you might claim to be using them. To know if you are, we need a way to determine what use is. And here is where the instability of this proposal arises. As anyone who has been near kids (or at least my kids) knows, it is very easy to dispute the fact that a person is using something: "I was using that toy (that I have not touched in a month)," says the older one to the younger. More generally, a maximalist interpretation of use would amount to letting you decide what counts as using the avocado: but this would be simply to treat the avocado as yours, and so to introduce property through the back door.[52] (Conversely, allowing me to determine what counts as using the avocado would be to make it mine.) In other words, simply giving an individual person the capacity to determine whether or not they are in fact using the avocado (and so whether or not another's use is interfering with theirs and is thus permissible) just amounts to making it theirs, where that is understood through the idea of yours and mine, and so cannot be an alternative to a system of property. A system of usufruct, in order to count as a genuine alternative to a system of property, would require a way to set a limit on the permissible uses of the avocado: a way to say that using in *this* way counts (to preempt others' uses) but using in *that* way does not. But such an alternative seems to turn out to be a substantive resource allocation scheme, by making the determination of permissibility turn not on our relation but on something independent of us.

Let me say something slightly more schematic in terms of counterexamples. You may notice that I argued here using the method of cases, and that is not a particularly good way to prove a point: although I think substantive schemes (sufficiently broadly understood) and usufruct are the most obvious candidates for alternatives to property, there might be some other case out there that I missed. You might be thinking about one now! But let me just suggest that (at least in my experience) many other such counterexamples are actually pretty underdescribed or undertheorized or unstable and then to turn out, upon closer

[52] See Weinrib, Reciprocal Freedom; Arthur Ripstein, "Possession and Use" in James Penner and Henry E Smith eds, Philosophical Foundations of Property Law (2013) 156.

examination, to reduce to one of the two I discussed or to actually presuppose an institution of property (or all three, depending on how the example is developed).[53] Here is one example: the library. Some people think (or tell me that they think) that the rights I have in a book I borrow from the library are sufficiently wide to solve the Problem of Yours and Mine while narrow enough that we would not say that the book is mine, and since the library's rules apply to everyone in the same way the library is an institution that is consistent with the basic commitment. But the devil is in the details. First of all, an actual library comes nowhere near being a counterexample to my claim: the library owns the books. And in §1.5, we saw that lending and borrowing depend on the idea of yours and mine.[54] The books are the library's books and I can use them because the library has let me; the library and I relate through the idea of yours and mine. Next you might try to modify the example so that the library cannot think of the books through the idea of yours and mine, perhaps by suggesting that the permissibility of my borrowing or the time I can borrow would be determined not by the library but instead by some independent value. But now you have described a substantive resource allocation scheme. Similarly, if you modify the permissible use of the book so that I could only keep it out as long as I was using it, you have created a scheme of usufruct, and then would need to develop its details in the way that, as I suggested, would reduce to either of the alternatives. You might go the other way instead and propose to significantly broaden the scope of what I can do with the book once I have it: maybe I can keep it as long as I want to, give it to others or trade with them, mark it up to my heart's content, and treat it as mine, perhaps even against the library itself. Well, now you have described an institution of property in books, with the library playing something like the role of the state.

Notably, this would be true even if the library chose to broaden the scope of its borrowers' rights on the basis of some substantive principle. Suppose, for instance, that more reading would get done this way. This would be a kind of rule-consequentialism,[55] because the idea would be that we would better promote the value in question by assigning broad control rights to individuals. This might be how to think about some other real-life cases, like the assignment of offices to faculty members or of cells to monks, if such assignments are not made on the basis of the faculty or order's property rights but on the basis of some substantive principle—that is, if the order (/Dean) does not take itself to

[53] I set aside alternatives—like feudalism: see *supra* note 3—that fail to solve the Problem because they are inegalitarian.

[54] See chapter 1, note 46.

[55] I set aside here the familiar difficulties that rule-consequentialist-type schemes face. I wrote about those difficulties earlier, but I now take no position on the soundness of my arguments. See my "Legal Obligation and Reasons" 19 Legal Theory 63 (2013) and "A Theory of Legal Obligation" in Sciaraffa and Waluchow eds, The Legacy of Ronald Dworkin (2016) 245.

have the right to decide who gets what cell, but only to carry out God's will (/ make efficient use of Faculty resources).[56] My point now is that how we should think about these cases will be a matter of some rather fine details. The question will be about the form of thought that is appropriate to the specific regime. My sense is that in most real-life cases, the idea of yours and mine is inapplicable: if I come back from class to find you in my office, privacy concerns aside, my complaint is not that you wronged me but that you broke the rules.[57] But in other cases subjects might be allocated sufficient control to allow themselves to relate to each other through the idea of yours and mine. We need to be careful here, because the real-life cases do not have this structure.[58] But in an imagined world where all the spaces and objects within a jurisdiction were allocated by a state authority to its subjects with a degree of control sufficient to realize the idea, we would have a system of property. The central point here is that the history of the institution or the motivations of those who created it are immaterial if it actually allows its subjects to relate to each other through the idea of yours and mine. This book is not about how states actually create institutions of property; it is about the form of thought or idea of reason that is appropriate

[56] For discussion of this set of points, see David Owens, Bound by Convention 177 (2022).

[57] This is also Harris' view as developed in the case of "Red Land": see J W Harris, Property & Justice 17–19 (1996).

[58] Some readers have suggested that the real-world cases are closer to the theoretical case. For instance, one might think that in the university offices setting, individual faculty members have property rights as against one another, and the Dean (or the university) plays a role like the state plays in the actual legal system, enforcing private rights held by individuals. The suggestion is not that these are *legal* rights, but that they are of the character of social norms, sufficiently determinately realized to allow for a genuine (although nonlegal) institution of property, such that faculty members can really be said to have property rights in their offices *inter se*, so that there are in effect two institutions of property at play, one legal (in which the university is the only holder of property rights) and one social. Similar things could be said about property within families, and, extrapolating even further, to other well-known instances of social norms, including Ellickson's famous discussion of cattle ranchers in Shasta County. (See Robert C Ellickson, Order without Law: How Neighbours Settle Disputes (1991).) Getting clear on this set of cases requires us to understand in detail the nature of the rights and their enforceability as between the parties to them. Social norms in general fail to count as law because the rights they generate are insufficient to ensure that their holders actually relate on terms of equality as required by the basic commitment: there is nothing internal to the idea of social norms among cattle ranchers that can explain what would be wrong if one rancher were systematically subordinated by the others in the application of the relevant norms. More generally, in the world of social norms, the strong (i.e., popular, skilled at debating, etc.) can always have the possibility of manipulating the social norms in their favor, allowing them to subordinate the weak, and, at least from the point of view of the social norms themselves, there will be nothing wrong with this. In other words, social norms are insufficient to solve the Problem because they are insufficient to ensure equal relations. At the same time, if such norms develop in a sufficient way to ensure equal relations, they would cease to be social norms and would become a kind of legal system of their own. Where exactly that line is drawn is impossible to say in the abstract and requires an application of judgment to particular cases. It seems obvious to me that the cattle rancher case does not meet the bar, nor do relations with respect to spaces and objects among members of a family (regardless of what he thinks, my older son does not have property in his room or toys against his younger brother). I can imagine a version of the university case that did meet the bar, given the prevalence of quasi-legal procedures in university dispute resolution, but I have never experienced it.

to understanding the possibility of the justification of such institutions as elements of a society of equals.

Now there remains one other possible counterexample to my argument, close to those we have just been considering, that merits our attention. Roughly, this is the proposal that we could relate as equals if we owned everything in common, in a positive community, along the lines of the way that we seem to own public property like streets and parks, schools and museums, courthouses and legislatures. Indeed, I agree that, with respect to these public spaces, we can be said to relate to one another as equals, since our interactions in the street or the park, say, are governed according to a set of norms that seems constituted by the idea that none is the superior or inferior of any other and at the same time that the space is not yours or mine (or anyone else's) but (in some sense to be developed) *ours*.

This is a genuine form of egalitarian relation, and one that has an essential role in a society of equals. But it cannot replace the essential role played by an institution of property understood as the realization of the idea of yours and mine. Both public property understood as ours and private property understood as yours or mine are necessary for us to relate as equals in a democratic society. Arguing for that conclusion now, though, would derail us from the presentation of the argument, because it requires a detailed examination of the nature of public property. That examination and the defense of the thought that we need both of public and private property are the substance of chapter 7.[59] If you are anxious to see that argument, you can skip to it now. If you want to wait, that would be fine. The elevator pitch goes like this: just as we need private property to relate as equals in certain essential ways, we need public property to relate as equals in other essential ways. But these two forms of property are constituents of different parts of a society of equals and neither can be allowed to overtake the other.

[59] In §7.4, I also discuss schemes of resource allocation associated with some Indigenous groups, which in some cases may have a similar structure to public property.

3
The Community of Yours and Mine

3.1 Illusory Equality and Structural Subordination

In chapters 1 and 2, I argued that the basic commitment to equality requires the realization of the idea of yours and mine in an institution of property. As I mentioned in the Introduction, Rousseau's brief discussion of property in the *Social Contract* has a similar structure. There Rousseau can be understood to claim that we need property to relate as equals, as it "substitutes a moral and legitimate equality for whatever physical inequality nature may have placed between men, [so] that while they may be unequal in force or in genius, they all become equal by convention and by right." But Rousseau also says, in the same breath, "under bad governments, this equality is only apparent and illusory; it serves only to maintain the poor in his misery and the rich in his usurpation."[1] Whereas the point of property, in a deep sense, is to allow us to relate as equals, a look around at the actual world and its pervasive inequality in property might suggest that our actual institutions of property are systematically failing to achieve their purpose, that as Proudhon, one of the most famous and trenchant of property's critics, puts it, property, "resting necessarily on equality, contradicts its own rationale."[2] It is time to confront this reality.

We can begin by clarifying our focus. The history of property is a history of domination, of those empowered by property using their power to disadvantage others, systematically or randomly, of slavery, racism, class conflict, and so on. As troubling as this history is, it is important to notice that in almost all these cases, property is used merely as one among other potential tools to effect some non-property-based idea of domination or subordination. If I am right that property is fundamentally an egalitarian institution, we might think that these are cases of property being more or less willfully distorted in service of domination of various kinds.[3] There are also forms of subordination or inequality that

[1] Rousseau, Of the Social Contract I.9.8 [OC III, 367] (1762).

[2] Pierre-Joseph Proudhon, What Is Property? 63 (Donald R Kelley and Bonnie G Smith eds, 1840/1994).

[3] Recent years have seen a flourishing of scholarship making this point, especially in the United States, where the connections between systematic racism and property run deep. For one comprehensive account, whose central claim is broadly consistent with the point in the text, see Bethany R Berger, "Race to Property: Racial Distortions of Property Law, 1634 to Today" 64 Arizona Law Review 619. As Berger argues, if we have a clear conception of the point of property, we can see reformist projects aimed at eliminating various distortions of it not as external limitations on property

Property Law in the Society of Equals. Christopher Essert, Oxford University Press. © Oxford University Press 2024.
DOI: 10.1093/oso/9780197768952.003.0004

seem more internally related to or dependent upon property, that seem not to require any kind of bad acting or bad actors, but instead to flow from the very idea of yours and mine, perhaps even necessarily or inevitably. As we saw in the Introduction, many egalitarian critics of property base their critique on the way that, as Rousseau said, property seems through a "slow succession of events" to lead to inequality. Proudhon's view was similar:

> the perpetual and absolute right of retaining one's patrimony . . . involves the right to alienate, to sell, to give, to acquire, and to lose it; and [it] tends, consequently, to nothing less than the destruction of that equality for which it had been established.[4]

I think both Rousseau and Proudhon are pointing out the same thing: property seems (uniquely?) to allow for accumulation of spaces and objects and, in the face of any kind of scarcity, unchecked accumulation by some can—and almost always does—lead to deprivation for others. In many contemporary societies, this process is most clearly realized as the phenomenon of homelessness. Homelessness looks like about as clear of a case of subordination as we can find; and at the same time, it seems plausible to say that homelessness is "partly produced by property," or that it is "a property problem."[5] How can an account of property as an egalitarian institution allow us to think about this?

Here is a way into the problem. I said previously (in §2.2 in particular) that familiar institutions of property like the common law can be understood as

but as attempts to more fully bring property into line with its justificatory basis. A more difficult problem arises when a putative property institution legally disables some of its subjects from owning property, as the English did under the system of coverture. Such a system, of course, does not make it possible for those subjects to relate to others on terms of equality and so cannot be said to realize the idea of yours and mine. Just what, precisely, to say about it, though, is something I set aside here. For discussion of a parallel case, see Jacob Weinrib, Dimensions of Dignity: The Theory and Practice of Modern Constitutional Law 92*ff* (2016).

[4] Proudhon, What Is Property? at 65. Part of Proudhon's pessimism seems to me to come from his assumption of the thought (associated commonly with Lockeans and libertarians) that property is a "natural right," fully determinate and enforceable absent any institution, and thus that internal to the very idea of property is the illegitimacy of constraint: "If property is a natural right . . . all that belongs to me by virtue of this right is as sacred as my person; it is my blood, my life, it is myself: whoever touches it offends the apple of my eye." (*Id.* at 39.) Here Proudhon is echoed in strikingly similar terms by Nozick: "Seizing the results of someone's labor"—that is, his property—"is equivalent to seizing hours from him and directing him to carry on various activities." Robert Nozick, Anarchy, State, and Utopia 172 (1974). What both of these views share, opposed though they seem to be, is the mistaken commitment to the thought that constraint is necessarily external to property. (For another recent view that shares Proudhon's mistake, see Liam Murphy and Thomas Nagel, The Myth of Ownership (1995).) Once we free ourselves of this mistake, we can see that constraining property solves the problem Proudhon is concerned with and, indeed, is required by property itself.

[5] Nicholas Blomley, "Homelessness, Rights, and the Delusions of Property" 30 Urban Geography 577, 581 (2009); Jane B Baron, "Homelessness as a Property Problem" 36 Urban Lawyer 273 (2004).

realizations of the idea of yours and mine. Because the idea of yours and mine is an egalitarian idea, whenever we relate through our property—when you exclude me from your home or you invite me in; when I am your tenant and you are my landlord; when we interact as neighbors in a nuisance dispute—we relate as equals. Recall that our relation is, as I put it, mediated through the idea of yours and mine, so that your capacity to determine the conditions of my entry into your home rests not on anything special about you or me but instead on the fact that the owner of the home has that capacity and that you happen to be the owner. Recall also that this mediation rests on the independence of the subject of my ownership from me and you, so that your right as owner applies in just the same way to everyone else as to me.

Now ask: does this set of ideas apply to our relation with respect to your home if I have no home of my own? In the first instance, the answer is surely "yes." Your right to exclude me does not depend on anything particular about me, and so whether I have a home or not is utterly irrelevant: the right applies to everyone just in their capacity as not-the-owner-of-your-home. Indeed, were my homelessness relevant—so that, as homeless, I was entitled to enter your property—we would very quickly lose the sense in which the home was yours.[6] Since your right to exclude me rests on your status as owner of your property—a status which I might hold, although I presently do not—its exercise does not subordinate me. However, what is true of you is true of every other owner in just the same way. No other owner subordinates me when they refuse to allow me entry to their property. But without a home of my own, I am now in a position where I lack any private space onto which I am entitled to go.[7] Let me emphasize that point by writing it again: the homeless are not entitled to go anywhere unless an owner lets them. This does not just look like a case of subordination. It *is* a case of subordination, a case so bad that it is hard in most contemporary societies to find a worse one. The homeless are dependent on the will of others to be in any private space at all, and thus to participate in any of that wide variety of activities and relations that, I am arguing, we need property to be able to enter into.

We seem, then, to be faced with a kind of contradiction or paradox. On the one hand, because the idea of yours and mine, as realized in an institution of property, is egalitarian, you do not subordinate me when you exclude me from your property, even when I am homeless. On the other hand, because every owner is entitled to exclude me, and I have no home of my own to go to, I am

[6] "If homelessness were once admitted as a defence to trespass, no one's house could be safe. Necessity would open a door which no man could shut. It would not only be those in extreme need who would enter. There would be others who would imagine that they were in need, or would invent a need, so as to gain entry. Each man would say his need was greater than the next man's." *Southwark London Borough Council v Williams*, [1971] 2 All ER 175.

[7] There are public spaces, but they do not present a solution to this problem; I say why in chapter 7.

left entirely under the control of others with respect to everything that happens in a home, and so I am (we might say) subordinated with respect to homes.[8] So it seems that the homeless are subordinated even though nobody subordinates them. The solution here is to embrace the paradox: homelessness is an instance of what, in this book, I will refer to as *structural subordination*.[9] Structural subordination obtains when the accumulation of nonsubordinating actions results in someone's being subordinated. This idea of structural subordination can be understood as a theoretical development of Rousseau's and Proudhon's notion that property leads to inequality through a slow succession of events. As Proudhon saw, a very basic part of the idea of yours and mine is that I can give you things, that I can make what is mine yours. When this is left unchecked (typically paired with a market-price mechanism), everyone can exchange property freely and eventually prices can rise in a way that leaves some homeless.[10] No propertied person seems to be acting in a way that is inconsistent with the basic commitment by accepting the highest bidder's price for their home, nor are they doing so by excluding strangers, homeless or not. But as we have seen the homeless are left in a position where they are unable to obtain any property of their own and are thus subordinated.

Thus we arrive at Proudhon's point that an institution designed to solve a problem about subordination "contradicts its own rationale" by allowing subordination to arise structurally as an effect of the institution's rules. The possibility of structural subordination as I understand it here emerges only once we have an institution of property. The structural subordination of the homeless is generated by the very idea of yours and mine: it is only when we can have things as yours and mine that we can exclude others and thus, through a slow

[8] The formality of this argument means that it could apply to any kind of property. But we worry about homelessness in a way that we do not worry about "boatlessness" or "avocadolessness" because of the wide and important set of activities and relations that are constituted by property in the home. One's life as a member of a society of equals can proceed apace without one ever owning a boat or an avocado, which is to say that boatlessness or avocadolessness do not tend to involve subordination as homelessness does. See my "What Makes a Home: A Reply" 41 Law & Philosophy 469 (2022).

[9] I think, but am not sure and do not feel obligated to decide (or argue), that what I am calling "structural subordination" is related to or the same as what some people mean when they think and talk about "structural domination," or "structural injustice" and what Kant calls "general injustice." But I think unpacking that would take us too far afield here. On structural domination, see Jennifer Einspahr, "Structural Domination and Structural Freedom: A Feminist Perspective" 94 Feminist Review 1 (2010); on structural injustice, see Iris Marion Young, Responsibility for Justice (2011); and on general injustice, see Kant, Lectures on Ethics at 27:416 or Kate A Moran, "Neither Justice nor Charity? Kant on 'General Injustice'" 47 Canadian Journal of Philosophy 477 (2017). I should probably note that the relation to Young's notion of structural injustice may be a bit more complex. Young uses homelessness as an instance of her own category, but defines the abstract category in a way that excludes cases of "specific actions and policies" (Responsibility for Justice at 47) of the state. Depending on how precisely those words are to be interpreted, we could find a way to include the unintended cumulative effects of the property system or not.

[10] For detailed discussion of the facts, see Gregg Colburn and Clayton Page Aldern, Homelessness Is a Housing Problem: How Structural Factors Explain US Patterns (2022).

succession of events, arrive at a situation of structural subordination. But the connection here is not merely causal: the subordination that the homeless face is only understandable as subordination with respect to the idea of yours and mine. The point of property is to allow us to relate as equals with respect to spaces and objects, but structural subordination interferes with this, which is why Rousseau wanted to say that the equality property provides is illusory. Here is the thing to notice, though: because the subordination of the homeless is best seen as subordination with respect to the subject matter of yours and mine, it seems like this illusory equality is comprehensible internally, in the sense that the very same considerations that lead us to see the need for an institution of property can also explain the sense in which the actual institutions of property that we have are defective. That is, an institution of property that, like those we are familiar with, fails to eliminate structural subordination should be understood as defective from the point of view of an internal standard of adequacy. Property has built into itself the conceptual material to see what is wrong with homelessness. A system of property that fails to meet this ideal is not just bad; it is a bad instance of its kind. I think this thought is immanent in the prevalent critique of property as an inegalitarian institution. Correctly understood, we should not think of property as subject to some external egalitarian constraint, so that a claim that our systems of property are inegalitarian amounts to a claim from the outside whose resolution requires balancing distinct or conflicting values. Instead, we should see such claims as internal to property, as claims that these institutions need to do a better job of the thing that makes them what they are, which is to say of allowing us to meet the demands of the basic commitment with respect to spaces and objects. Allowing us to see that property is internally defective is among the central theoretical virtues of thinking of it as an egalitarian institution.

To talk about property in this way, we can use a new idea, *the community of yours and mine.*[11] The community of yours and mine is the regulative ideal of property, which is to say it is a way of thinking about what an institution of property should look like. In a community of yours and mine, there is no structural subordination with respect to the idea of yours and mine, so that not only do the community's subjects relate to one another on a pairwise basis on terms of equality (through the idea of yours and mine), but the institution is structured in such a way as to guarantee that no subject is or can be subordinated with respect to the idea. As a regulative ideal, the community of yours and mine has a few notable features. First, it is regulative of property institutions: any institution of property should strive for the closest possible adherence to the ideal of the community of yours and mine, and an institution of property is defective insofar

[11] I took the phrase from Kant, The Metaphysics of Morals 6:258 (1797), but Kant means something rather different.

as and because it fails to meet this ideal. Relatedly, though, we need to see how a defective institution of property is still a valid (and morally required) institution, one which can still obligate its subjects. So the fact that our institutions are defective does not mean that they do not bind; I cannot point to the prevalence of homelessness in our society (mine or others') as a defense to my trespassing on your land.[12] Finally, the ideal is internal in that it is a standard of adequacy that is generated conceptually by the same ideas that explain the need for an institution of property in the first place.[13]

[12] The language of the regulative ideal calling for the closest possible adherence is drawn from Weinrib, Dimensions of Dignity, to whose careful articulation of the role of a regulative ideal I am deeply indebted.

[13] Many theorists of property of quite widely different orientations will concede that there is reason to impose some kind of egalitarian regulations or limitations on a system of property. Perhaps this is justified on efficiency grounds or as a matter of political expediency, or perhaps it is justified because equality is a value that is important and needs to be balanced against whatever other values, such as freedom, ground property. According to these views, equality comes from the outside, as it were, and so needs to be balanced (but: how?) against whatever values are internal to property. In my view, the egalitarian demand is not imposed from without but rather is part of the self-same set of considerations that call for the creation of an institution of property in the first place. We need not, that is, import any further principles or ideals in order to justify the regulation or limitation of property on egalitarian grounds. Rather, all we need to do is to take seriously the nature of the institution itself. In my view, then, if you're attracted or even committed to the idea that property is a good thing, then you're automatically also committed to the idea that property must be constrained to aim for conformity with the ideal. In slightly different terms, we might say that the egalitarian project of property begins with solving the Problem of Yours and Mine but remains *incomplete* in the presence of structural subordination; completing the project thus requires not only realizing the idea of yours and mine in the sense we have already seen but also pursuit of the regulative ideal. Here I'm aiming for the same kind of "judo" that Niko Kolodny describes in *The Pecking Order*, by showing how an institution whose backers tend to see equality as their enemy is, properly understood, egalitarian, which means that these backers are actually committed, rather than opposed, to egalitarianism. Perhaps I should indicate that I know that many people (including many of my friends who have read this) do not sign on to the requirement that property be justified and evaluated according to a single view with anything like the monomaniacal devotion that I do (if they do at all). These people want to say that there are *lots* of values that property promotes or respects and that there is nothing gained by insisting on monism here. (They might concede that equality is property's "first virtue," to use Rawls' phrase—see John Rawls, A Theory of Justice, rev ed 3 (1999)—but argue that that does not prevent others from applying.) The worry in this approach is that a pluralistic account of the value of a social institution as central to our lives as property seems utterly inadequate to its subject matter, as it will always make the final determination a matter of "yeah, maybe, there are some good things and some bad things here, but I guess on balance property is acceptable." That kind of answer is fine when it comes to choosing something to cook for dinner or to watch on TV one evening, but it strikes me that the stakes here are too high for that kind of answer, that we should ask for more in the context of the central social, legal, and political institutions that literally make up the social world that we inhabit. Another point worth noting in this connection is that the force of external critique can only be contingent in yet another way (beyond the contingent applicability of the evaluator's purpose or perspective). It is always an open question whether or not some external value will be better served by a system of property or not: we don't know, actually, whether there would be more guacamole made in the negative community or under a system of property. What we do know is that guacamole could not be made on terms of equality in the negative community. At this stage of the argument, the parallel point is this: if one were to critique property on the grounds that it did not promote welfare as well as some alternative might, one would need to marshal a significant amount of counterfactual evidence about the ways that the proposed alternative would do better. And the counterfactual nature of that evidence makes it seem like the best answer we could give to the comparison on which the external critique would be based would be, "yeah, maybe?" By contrast, the ideal of the community of

It is important to keep track of the sequence of ideas presented here. The possibility of structural subordination and the regulative ideal of the community of yours and mine come into view only once we have an institution of property. So we cannot "skip" straight to them; nor can we achieve the possibility of a community of yours and mine without an institution of property. To look at an existing institution of property beset by homelessness and to argue for property's abolition is to misunderstand this structure. Morally, the elimination of property is not an option. So the correct response to homelessness is not a call for abolition but a call for reform to move the institution closer to its ideal.[14]

3.2 Different Worries about Inequality

Structural subordination and the need for the idea of the community of yours and mine can be brought out clearly with the phenomenon of homelessness, but there is more to say. I want to consider some broader questions about property and inequality, questions about whether or in what way the distribution of property in a society might be problematic from the point of view of this ideal.[15] A helpful way to begin to think through these questions is, once again, provided to us by Rousseau. He wrote:

> by equality, we should understand, not that the degrees of power and riches are to be absolutely identical for everybody; but that power shall never be great enough for violence, and shall always be exercised by virtue of rank and law; and that, in respect of riches, no citizen shall ever be wealthy enough to buy another, and none poor enough to be forced to sell himself.[16]

Here Rousseau begins with a reminder that the notion of equality that underlies the basic commitment is not one that demands a certain distribution of goods, but rather one that requires relations between persons to be structured in certain ways. In our particular context, he then, in the well-known final sentence of the quoted passage, gestures toward the way that equality seems to have implications

yours and mine presents us with all the conceptual resources we need to know the degree to which it is being met.

[14] As I noted in the Introduction, Rousseau makes the same point, if more evocatively than I do. "What, then! Must we destroy our societies, annihilate yours and mine, and return to live in the forests with the bears? A conclusion in the style of my adversaries, which I would like to prevent rather than to leave them the shame of drawing." See Rousseau, Discourse on the Origin and the Foundations of Inequality among Men Note IX, [14] [OC III, 207] (1754).

[15] What I will not discuss here is the question of discrimination and property. It requires additional resources so I will return to it with those resources in hand in §6.5.

[16] Rousseau, Social Contract II.11.2 [OC III, 391–92].

both with respect to some having too little and with respect to some having too much. Others have shared Rousseau's core intuition here: Martin Luther King, Jr, for instance, put the point in a speech by saying: "No one should be forced to live in poverty while others live in luxury."[17]

Rousseau's idea that none should be so poor as to be forced to sell themselves can easily be tied to the ideas in this chapter, by seeing that phenomena like homelessness (or lack of other important forms of property) lead to subordination, in the way that, without property of one's own, one's capacity to participate in important and valuable activities and relations falls under the control of others. Ensuring that everyone has sufficient property to avoid such subordination would be a way to ensure that none of us falls into this position. The idea of a floor or minimum might seem overly austere or conservative. But I do not think it is. It is actually quite demanding in that it requires (among other things) each to have a home that is adequate to protect against subordination with respect to the activities and relations that property realizes. Getting near that state of affairs would require quite radical social reorganization in most contemporary societies, and certainly all those societies that have an institution of property along the lines of the common law's. What the ideal calls for is not that each has merely enough to live or to survive, but instead that each has enough to protect against structural subordination.[18] And that turns out, as we shall see in detail later, to be quite a lot.[19] Moreover, the idea here is not one merely of what is sometimes called "formal" equality. I am not—definitely, definitely not—arguing that what the basic commitment requires is no more than that everyone have a chance to get some property or that everyone be eligible to own property.[20] The argument here is much more robust, or if you like "substantive" than that: it demands that each have enough property to ensure that they are not subordinated with respect to property. Meeting that demand would require quite a radical reorganization of our existing institutions. And it is worth noticing, once again, how we got to this conclusion: the same normative considerations that require an institution of property also demand that such an institution be regulated in such a way as to ensure that each of its subjects has sufficient property of their

[17] For discussion, see Tommie Shelby, "Prisons of the Forgotten: Ghettos and Economic Injustice" in Tommie Shelby and Brandon Terry eds, To Shape a New World: Essays on the Political Philosophy of Martin Luther King, Jr. 187, 194–96 (2018).

[18] In Rainer Forst's terms, this is a point about justice, not a humanitarian concern. See Rainer Forst, "Law, Morality, and Power in the Global Context" in The Right to Justification 241 (Jeffrey Flynn trans, 2007/2012 in English).

[19] Still, as Rousseau reminds us, "The bounds of the possible in moral matters are less narrow than we think." Social Contract III.12.2 [OC III, 425].

[20] As Kant might have when he wrote that the "thoroughgoing equality of individuals within a state, as its subjects, is quite consistent with the greatest inequality in terms of the quantity and degree of their possessions." Immanuel Kant, "On the Common Saying: That May Be Correct in Theory but It Is of No Use in Practice" 8:291 (1793). I say "might," because Kant's views are more complicated.

own. A view that property is a good thing necessitates, on its own terms, a significant redistributive program.

Still, you might demand more. Rousseau, in the quoted passage, seems to call not merely for a lower bound on property but for an upper bound, too. I think there is something to this idea, but to see it, we need to proceed cautiously. First, notice that the idea of yours and mine, as realized in an institution of property, is not affected by the amount of property that you and I have. We saw this already in the context of the discussion of homelessness, where I argued that, when you exclude me from your home, you and I relate as equals through the idea of yours and mine even if I have no home of my own. So *a fortiori* the same point applies if you are rich and I am not. Suppose that we are neighbors, and that you are the CEO of a large technology company and I am a professor: I am financially comfortable and I own a home, but you are magnificently wealthy and own homes around the world. How does this matter? With respect to our bilateral relation as neighbors, it matters not at all: the fact that you are much richer than me plays no role in thinking about whether or not you may enter my land or I enter yours, about what activities each of us could do that would unreasonably interfere with the others' use of their own land, or anything else. The private law of property is utterly insensitive to considerations of relative wealth.[21] As between you and me, I think, Rousseau's worry about your being too rich does not apply, since, given that I have enough of my own, you cannot "buy" me.

However, things are more complicated. We need to think also about the systematic interplays of property rights, and about the ways in which the exercise of those rights might accumulate to generate problems of subordination. More simply put: property is the basis for accumulation of wealth and wealth confers its own kind of power. As Morris Cohen notes in a famous essay, "dominion over things is also imperium over our fellow human beings."[22] Cohen is thinking that the very rich gain, via their wealth, the capacity to shape, more or less directly, important elements of their society to an extent that might be seen to subordinate others. Now we need to contrast two different versions of this phenomenon, both of which Cohen gestures toward. One is the role of wealth in democratic politics: the wealthy have, thanks to their wealth, an undue influence over the priorities of politicians (through lobbying), elections (through private campaign financing), and so on. The other is the role of wealth in the broad category that we can call the financialization or commodification of property in land: here I am thinking about the concentration of wealth in financial institutions and the process of financialization of mortgages which, really roughly, all together result in a huge proportion of the privately owned land in

[21] See Ernest J Weinrib, The Idea of Private Law 76–80 (1995).
[22] Morris R Cohen, "Property and Sovereignty" 13 Cornell Law Review 8, 13 (1927).

many contemporary societies being ultimately owned by a very small number of very rich individuals.[23]

What I want to suggest is that the first of these two things is, in an important sense, external to property, whereas the second might be understood to be at least closer to internal. Think about it like this: the control that the wealthy have over democratic politics and the reasons that such control is wrongful can be understood, at least in principle, absent any concept of yours and mine. The problem is that democracy is fundamentally inconsistent with an inequality of power among citizens with respect to their capacity to control and influence the democratic process. The whole point of democracy is that it is the egalitarian form of government.[24] So allowing for this inequality of power is inconsistent with the idea of a democracy precisely because it seems like it can create a kind of subordination of the powerless by the powerful. But wealth is merely a contingent source of power: we would have just the same problem, from democracy's point of view, if influence on elections or on politicians' decision-making were distributed according to beauty or height or popularity. The solution to these problems is laws that regulate the democratic process to exclude the influence of power, whatever its source. When the source of the power is wealth, we might have reasons given to us by the normative ideals of democratic government to do something about it, to (say) limit the amount of property that any one person can have; but we might also solve the problem in different ways, by making it impossible to use that form of power to exert influence on the democratic process (by making all elections publicly funded, say). The point is just that all such rules are external to property, since they are not about the idea of yours and mine. (One more way to see this: although they would take different forms, we would need rules ensuring the integrity of our democratic politics in the negative community, without property, and the community of yours and mine, where the ideal is fully reached, just as much as we would need them in our actual world.)

Cohen's other kind of case is more complicated, because it has to do with housing. As we noted, the problem of homelessness is comprehensible as wrongful because of its connection to property; that is, we can only understand homelessness as such by seeing it as a kind of structural subordination generated by the operation of the system of property. Housing plays a similar role in thinking about Cohen's other example, about financialization of the real estate sector. A common thought is that something has gone systematically wrong in the way that housing has come to be treated primarily as a commodity rather than as a space in which to live a life.[25] Of course, the idea of a home as

[23] Cohen, "Property and Sovereignty" at 14.

[24] See Ronald Dworkin, Freedom's Law: The Moral Reading of the American Constitution 15*ff* (1996); Seana Valentine Shiffrin, Democratic Law 20 (2021); Niko Kolodny, "Rule over None II: Social Equality and the Justification of Democracy" 42 Philosophy & Public Affairs 287 (2014).

[25] See David Madden and Peter Marcuse, In Defense of Housing (2016).

mine or yours is expansive enough to encompass both of these different kinds of use. The difference between them from the point of view of this book is material: use of a home as a commodity (on its own or through some more complex financialization process) is a narrower and more limited form of use than use of it as, well, a home, as a place in which to live a life, as the grounds for the wide variety of activities and relations that require a home. Homelessness is a pressing social concern because to lack a home is to be unable to access the latter set of uses, a set of uses broad enough that a person unable to access them would have difficulty participating as a member of a society of equals. That does not seem to be true of an inability to use a home as a commodity. And the obvious problem here—a matter, again, of the accumulation of the effects of permissible options through a slow succession of events—is the way that financialization can lead to increasing prices and other changes that make the housing market inaccessible to many. There are good reasons to think that a housing market ought to be regulated to protect against such changes. Notably, though, in regards to our current concern, this is not itself a matter of anyone's having too much but instead a matter of the regulation of the rules around mortgages, tenancies, and so on, regulations aimed at protecting the capacity of individuals to have homes of their own. So some of the reasons to worry about concentration of ownership of homes or real property through financialization seem internal to the law of property, but others not. These issues will also intersect with the extent to which a state approaches compliance with the ideal of the community of yours and mine by ensuring that each of its subjects has a home of their own.

Finally, I should say that I am sympathetic to the idea that "there is more to a society of equals than a just scheme of distribution of material goods,"[26] and in particular that the members of a society of equals ought to share a certain generalized set of egalitarian attitudes toward one another. And I am open to the thought that an extremely unequal distribution of property, even if each person has enough property to satisfy the minimum I set out earlier, is inimical to such a set of egalitarian attitudes.[27] I do not know if there is much that an account of property's justification as a legal and political institution can say about this. I should note that the egalitarian account here might be exploited to demonstrate that property need not be tied to anything like an unchecked accumulation, that it would be better for all of us and for each of us if we recognized the egalitarian basis of our property institution and acted in a way that is consistent with it. But I leave the details of that for others.

[26] Jonathan Wolff, "Fairness, Respect, and the Egalitarian Ethos" 27 Philosophy & Public Affairs 97, 104 (1988).

[27] Shelby argues that this might have been King's view. See Shelby, "Prisons of the Forgotten."

3.3 Toward the Ideal: Institutional Choice and Public Law

The ideal of the community of yours and mine sets an internal standard for property institutions. We can turn to the practical upshots of this idea. The first, about which I say just a bit, is that we can use the ideal as a rubric against which to measure different institutions. We saw in §2.2 that the idea of yours and mine is itself sufficiently abstract and indeterminate to permit quite a wide range of institutional variation in its realization, and that what a particular form an institution should or will take will often be a matter of "existing historical and social conditions."[28] As the ideal of the community of yours and mine applies to all these institutional variations, we should notice that they might fare better or worse with respect to the ideal. This strikes me as the way to understand both familiar calls for things like an increase in the provision of social housing or the socialization of the means of production and familiar claims that one system of property is better than another because it has less homelessness or less of a gap between rich and poor or some similar thing. As to how to respond to such claims, I can make only one very schematic remark. The question of whether or not one or another institution of property conforms better to the ideal of the community of yours and mine involves significant empirical elements. So to answer it we must examine such institutions and judge, on the basis of a review of all the relevant considerations, which one does a better job from the point of view of the internal standard applicable to property institutions as such. Such examination is outside my scope here.

The second site at which the ideal of the community of yours and mine has some practical upshot is something I can say more about. I will do so, in abstract terms, in the remainder of this chapter, and then, more concretely and at greater length, in chapter 6. For now, let us return to the discussion of homelessness and structural subordination. Remember that the basic thought was that the introduction of property—the realization of the idea of yours and mine—seems to have within it the seeds of this structural subordination. The idea of yours and mine brings with it right from the start the thought that what others may do with respect to what is mine is up to me, and it is the accumulated exercise of that feature of it that, as I argued, generates the structural subordination of the homeless. The subordination of the homeless, being structural, is not the result of any individual act. But it depends on the institution: without the institution of property there could be no such thing as homelessness. It is only because that institution gives us the rights that it does, with the features that they have, that the subordination of the homeless

[28] John Rawls, Justice as Fairness: A Restatement 139 (2001).

is possible. We might then say, not at all inaccurately, that it is *the system itself* that subordinates the homeless.[29]

This feature of structural subordination presents us, quite clearly, with the outlines of the right approach to it. Since those subordinated structurally are not subordinated by other private persons, their complaint is not one that sounds in private law; instead, they are subordinated by the legal structures operating at a higher level of generality, so their complaint is with the state itself. In other words, structural subordination is a problem that requires a public law solution. As I understand it, public law is the solution to a problem about the relationship between the state and its subjects.[30] The basic commitment requires a variety of legal institutions that have what we can think of as the familiar private law form: the idea of yours and mine, for instance, must be realized through private law mechanisms like trespass and nuisance law (about which more later). But the creation of legal mechanisms like courts and legislatures—the creation of a state—creates a new problem: it creates the problem of the vulnerability of individuals not to one another but to the state itself.[31] Public law is the solution to this problem. The idea that homelessness is the result of structural subordination fits here by allowing us to see that homelessness arises because of and through the operation of the legal institution of property, which means that the solution to the problem of structural subordination is a matter of public law. Doctrinally, the basic thought here will be that each member of a state has a right against the state that the state legislate to eliminate homelessness: this is a public law right since it is a right of individuals against the state.[32] It is not a right to a specific thing but rather to "state action and institutional structures" aimed at eliminating the relevant form of subordination.[33]

[29] Here's another kind of case that is messy as an example but whose messiness might bring out the point. Think about a seminar room, and imagine you show up right before the seminar starts to find that there's no seat left for you. It seems that nobody in the room is on the hook for the fact that you're left without a seat, as each of them is entitled (in just the same way as you are) to come in and sit at any available seat. So you're left without a seat even though nobody has kept you from having a seat. You might think, actually, that this means that nobody is ever permitted to sit down (for a parallel argument, see Dylan Dodd, "The Cookie Paradox" 92 Philosophy and Phenomenological Research 355 (2016)), but that solution to the problem here parallels returning to the negative community as a "solution" to the Problem of Yours and Mine. You might also think that the university, or whoever set up the seminar room with too few seats, is the one who is on the hook for your being left seatless. Actually, that's pretty close to the view I defend in the text: the state, in setting up the system of property, plays the parallel role in the homelessness case.

[30] For one elaboration of this view of the role of public law, see Ernest J Weinrib, Reciprocal Freedom: Private Law, and Public Right (2022).

[31] "Legal systems are both a solution and a problem," says Fred Wilmot-Smith, Equal Justice: Fair Legal Systems in an Unfair World 12 (2019).

[32] Cf. Ernest J Weinrib, "Poverty and Property in Kant's System of Rights" 78 Notre Dame Law Review 795, 817 (2003): "the duty is incumbent on the people (and derivatively on the sovereign) rather than on any particular person. . . . The systemic difficulty that property poses . . . is resolved by the collective duty imposed on the people."

[33] Jacob Weinrib, "Maitland's Challenge for Administrative Law Theory" 84 Modern Law Review 207, 210 (2021).

This idea then allows me to draw a more comprehensive notion of the law of property as I understand it here, and thus to preview where we are headed. As I said, property is the law of yours and mine. We can see now that such an institution has two distinct parts. First there is what we will call the *private law of property*, which is the part of the law of property that allows individual private persons to relate to one another on terms of equality through the idea of yours and mine. I will turn to an elaboration of the private law of property as it has been developed in the common law tradition next: there we will see how the various familiar doctrines of the private law of property—trespass, nuisance, licences, acquisition, transfer, servitudes, and so on—allow the parties to interactions with respect to private property to relate as equals. As the last three sections have shown, the private law of property, left unchecked, can result in the structural subordination of some of the members of a society, and this structural subordination requires a public law response, in the form of, in particular, provision of property to the homeless. Laws providing such housing, among other parts of the legal system, form what we will call the *public law of property*. Later, with a picture of the private law of property in hand, we will return, in Part III, to an elaboration of these ideas and discussion of some familiar parts of the public law of property.

And the law of property as a whole is made up of both of its parts, and neither can exist without the other. The private law of property left unchecked by public law would result in a system of property that utterly failed to adhere to the ideal of the community of yours and mine. Such a society would be a laissez-faire dystopia that not only would be a moral disaster but would also be defective from the point of view of property's own internal standards, as it would, by allowing structural subordination, fail to ensure adherence to the basic commitment, leaving the egalitarian project of property incomplete. At the same time, though, the public law of property cannot exist without the private law of property. This is true not only conceptually—as I argued, the idea of structural subordination, and thus public law as a solution to it, only comes into view once we already have a private law of property—but also substantively and normatively. The role of the public law right to housing is to ensure that each subject of the institution has sufficient property (understood as private rights realizing the idea of yours and mine) to avoid subordination.[34] It is this set of ideas that I think develops Rousseau's remark, quoted earlier, that "the right every individual has over his own land is always subordinate to the right the community has over everyone." The notion of subordination Rousseau invokes cannot be that none

[34] I want to maintain the possibility that the private relations constituted by property are "coherently preserved as a semi-autonomous order within a totality that actualizes" the basic commitment, modifying a thought set out in Alan Brudner and Jennifer Nadler, The Unity of the Common Law 152 (2d ed 2013).

of us can really have anything as our own, since that would efface the private law realization of the idea of yours and mine. Rather, it is the idea that the public law constraints on the private law realization are internal to the sequence of ideas here and thus should not be seen as somehow an external limitation on them but rather as a proper part of the complete development of those ideas. Public law completes the egalitarian project of property as the law of yours and mine.

PART II
THE PRIVATE LAW OF PROPERTY

4
The Common Law of Property

4.1 Trespass and Licences

In this Part of the book—that is, in this chapter and the next—I will expand upon the claims of §2.2 at much greater length. That is, I will show how the common law of property can be understood as (an instance of) the law of yours and mine, an institutional realization of the idea of yours and mine that allows us to relate to one another as equals. In this chapter, I will show how the stuff of what is sometimes called "land law" can be illuminated by my account. We can think of trespass, licences, nuisance, acquisition, and transfer as elaborations of the idea of yours and mine, which is to say as workings-out of what it can look like for parties to relate to one another as equals in paradigmatic forms of interaction with respect to some space or object. In chapter 5, I will expand the account in a different direction, by showing how it helps us to think about the boundaries of property law as a department of private law. I will show how the account differentiates property from contract and the law of the person, and also show how to think about other interesting liminal cases of property, in particular those involving intangible resources. But here we will concentrate on land and objects.[1]

We begin with trespass. At its core, the idea of yours and mine says that when something is mine, it is up to me to determine what you may do with it or to it. When it comes to spaces and objects, that means that I get to determine whether and under what circumstances you may enter or physically interact with them. And, basically, realizing this core is the job of the law of trespass, since trespass just says that when something is mine I have both a right that you not enter it or physically interact with it and a power to license such entries or interactions. In other words, trespass makes it the case that, legally, it is up to me to determine how others can treat what is mine. Hence trespass can be seen as the most basic element of the law of property. Saying that might strike some (pedantic?) private lawyers as imprecise or inaccurate, so I should clarify it in two ways. (If you do not identify as such a person, feel free to skip the remainder of this paragraph.)

[1] I cannot cover *all* the doctrines in this area, and I apologize if I do not cover your own favorite. It may be worth mentioning one omission explicitly: I say nothing much in this book about remedies. I take the topic of remedies to be an important one, but one that is, strictly speaking, outside the scope of the book, in that it is a more general topic in private law theory. The essential work on the topic is Stephen A Smith, Rights, Wrongs, and Injustices: The Structure of Remedial Law (2020).

Property Law in the Society of Equals. Christopher Essert, Oxford University Press. © Oxford University Press 2024.
DOI: 10.1093/oso/9780197768952.003.0005

First, I will write rather loosely about "trespass" as if the word encompassed a single tort. But that is not quite right. There is a tort of trespass to land, there is trespass to chattels, and, depending on the jurisdiction, a whack of other torts—conversion, ejectment, detinue, trover—that cover specific fact scenarios. Here I ignore these complexities and focus at the conceptual level on the notion that the basic wrong in property involves interfering physically with a physical space or object that is owned by another.[2] That is basically what I will mean by "trespass." (I say more about the details in a moment.) Second, I know that some private lawyers want to say that trespass is part of the law of torts and not the law of property. I find that an odd thing to think. Tort law is not a rival body of law to property law: it is (roughly) the law of infringements of noncontractual private rights, so it rests upon the bodies of law that constitute those rights.[3] Some torts, like battery, are infringements of personal rights and others, like trespass, are infringements of property rights.[4] Our target, trespass, is a property tort. So it is a part of tort law (since it is a noncontractual private wrong) *and* a part of property law (since it protects property rights).

Once again, trespass is the most basic legal realization of the idea of yours and mine, precisely in the sense that, when something is mine, I get to decide how you may interact with it. To realize the idea, the law says that I have a right that you not interact with what is mine, coupled with a power to license such interactions and render them nonwrongful. Importantly, there are two distinct steps in that thought. The right to exclude comes conceptually first: in law, for it to be up to me how you act in some respect, I need a right that you not act in that respect. But I also need more: the idea of yours and mine requires not just that I can exclude you but also that I can include you, through the power to license. Conceptually, the power presupposes the right: I can only include you if I could exclude you, because unless your permission to enter is premised on my right to exclude, you would not properly be thought to be entering something that is mine in any familiar sense.[5] This complete realization of the idea of yours and

[2] See Simon Douglas, Liability for Wrongful Interferences with Chattels (2011). Perhaps there are principled reasons to insist on a division among these different torts, but I do not see them. In my view, a trespass to chattels and a conversion are both basically the same wrong, and any legal distinctions between the two torts are explained by a combination of history and legal procedural grounds. It is worth saying that Ben McFarlane, whose work is notable for its focus on the intricacies of legal doctrine, also references the centrality of an abstract notion: "the principal means by which B can vindicate a property right is by showing that the defendant, by breaching a duty not to interfere with B's protected use of a thing, has committed a wrong." See Ben McFarlane, "Equity, Obligations, and Third Parties" [2008] Singapore Journal of Legal Studies 308, 311

[3] For a helpful development of this thought, see Jacob Weinrib, "What Can Kant Teach Us about Legal Classification?" 23 Canadian Journal of Law and Jurisprudence 203, 224–25 (2010).

[4] I say more about the line between persons and property in chapter 5.

[5] Smushing the right and power together would give an owner something like a right that <others not enter unless the owner desired them to>, where desire would be understood as a psychological state not fully under the control of the owner, and thus would play an empirical rather than

mine can be associated with a familiar notion of trespass according to which a trespass is an unauthorized entry onto another's property. This notion is fine in most cases—and certainly in everyday thought and talk—but we will separate the right and power at this stage to clarify the presentation.[6] Importantly, the conceptual priority of the right over the power should not be taken to amount to any normative priority of exclusion over inclusion. We saw already that including others is at least as important as excluding them in understanding the idea of yours and mine. The priority is a matter of the logic of rights and powers, not a claim that exclusion is in a normative sense more important than inclusion.[7]

What does "exclusion" mean here? We saw in §2.1 that when we relate through the idea of yours and mine we relate as equals. The same is true of trespass. While a trespass is in its basic form a physical intrusion on the space or object owned by another, it is about neither what a defendant does nor what happens to a plaintiff. Instead it is about an interaction between them, about the way that the intrusion can be understood as an act by defendant that is inconsistent with plaintiff's rights as owner. That is, when I trespass, I act as though it is up to me rather than you to determine what I may do with something that is yours, and thereby deny the force of the egalitarian relation that your ownership constitutes between us. This abstract thought generates a set of familiar doctrinal points.

First, trespass is said to be an "intentional" tort. To trespass, I need to intentionally act in a way that is inconsistent with your right over what is yours, by entering your land or placing some foreign object there.[8] There is no such thing as an attempted trespass: if I aim to take your avocado but forget that you had already traded the avocado to me for an apple, I commit no wrong. Nor do I commit a wrong if I do not act intentionally at all but merely end up on your land, perhaps because others carried me there.[9] Trespass is about legal relations between persons and does not concern itself with the locations of bodies when those locations are not a matter of the actions of persons. The relational nature of trespass also explains how the tort requires that I intend to be in the physical location that I was but not that I knew or intended to be <on your land>

normative role, so that it would not actually be *up to* the owner in the relevant sense what others would be able to do on their land.

[6] The forthcoming provisions on trespass in the Restatement (4th) Property helpfully work through this same structure, in setting out the "gist" of trespass to be an unlicensed entry to the land of another and at the same time setting out a complete definition of trespass that separates the right and the power to license entry.

[7] For a different view about the relation between the right and power, see Avihay Dorfman, "Private Ownership and the Standing to Say So" 64 University of Toronto Law Journal 402 (2014). I think Dorfman's view confuses conceptual priority with normative priority. It's possible to track down a handful of footnotes in papers written by Dorfman and by me arguing this point, but I'll leave that tracking down to the reader.

[8] *Athwal v Pania Estates* (1981), 11 CELR 17, [16].

[9] *Smith v Stone* (1647), 82 ER 533 (KB).

under that description.[10] This makes sense because it ensures that trespass turns on considerations that are, we can say, public as between us. My ignorance of the fact that I am trespassing does not matter, because if it did matter it would make the legal relationship between us a matter of what I knew, which would subordinate you to me (since I could make my liability a matter of my own subjective psychology). This is consistent with trespass' role as a part of private law where, as a general matter, questions of liability do not turn on the subjective mental states of the parties.[11]

Famously, a central part of the basic law of trespass is that there is no requirement that the plaintiff be harmed by the defendant's entry:

> By the laws of England every invasion of private property, be it ever so minute, is a trespass. No man can set his foot upon my ground without any licence but he is liable to an action, though the damage be nothing.[12]

This element of the law of trespass is difficult for any kind of instrumentalist account of property law to explain, since it is clear that it will result in inefficient results in individual cases. In my view, it is not only easy to explain, it is absolutely central to the entire edifice of the law. I do not invoke the law of trespass to keep you off of what is mine in order to promote some other value, I invoke it to keep you off of what is mine *because it is mine*. Trespass allows me to keep you out of my land regardless of how good or bad that would be in property-independent terms. That is a good thing, because that allows us to relate through the idea of yours and mine and such a relation is necessary for and constitutive of our ability to relate rightfully in terms of space.[13] When you trespass on my land we can understand your action as wrongful because, in a way, it is subordinating. You treat me as your inferior by acting as though you, rather than I, had the right to determine the permissibility of your action on my land, denying the application of the idea of yours and mine.[14]

[10] *Basely v Clarkson* (1681), 3 Lev 37; *Costello v Calgary*, 1997 ABCA 281, [33].

[11] See my "Legal Powers in Private Law" 21 Legal Theory 136 (2015). And more generally, see Ernest J Weinrib, The Idea of Private Law 177–183 (1996) for the clearest exploration of the way in which making private law interactions depend on the subjective mental states of one of the parties is inconsistent with their relating as equals.

[12] *Entick v Carrington* (1765), 95 ER 807 (KB). To similar, if more contemporary effect, see *Athwal*, and *Jacque v Steenberg Homes*, 209 Wis 2d 605, 563 NW2d 154 (1997). *Entick* itself is a case about the relation between private owners and the state. We'll come back to that sort of question later.

[13] The point of trespass is to partly constitute an egalitarian relation, not to be a means to some non-property value. On that contrast, see my "How Law Matters in *Why Law Matters*" 12 Jerusalem Review of Legal Studies 1 (2015).

[14] Here I embrace a relatively common view on which private wrongs can be understood as a form of subordination, which suggests why the default remedy for trespasses and other property wrongs has, historically at least, been an injunction. I offer a brief treatment that is along these lines in my "Nuisance and the Normative Boundaries of Ownership" 52 Tulsa Law Review 85, 118–19 (2016).

Now turn to inclusion. To completely have something as mine, I need not only to be able to keep you out of it but also to be able to invite you into it.[15] In fact, keeping-out and letting-in are two sides of the same coin: whether I enforce my right to exclude you or exercise my power to include you, the permissibility of your interaction with what I own is up to me. Property law gives us the means to let others in, in the first instance, through the licence. When I grant you a licence to enter my space (or use my object), I make it the case that your entry (or use), which otherwise would constitute a trespass, is rightful. People grant licences for all sorts of reasons and thus the granting of a licence might be of interest from various psychological, sociological, or economic points of view. But in law, the grant of a licence is a legal act, in that it changes the legal situation between us and changes our relative rights, liberties, duties, and so on. In other words, it is the exercise of a legal power.[16]

When we put the right against trespass and the power to license together, we see a more complete picture of the legal realization of the idea of yours and mine, in the sense that my right and power make it up to me whether and under what circumstances you may enter or use what is mine. It is important to be explicit about the strength of this point: just as a trespass does not depend on any showing of harm, there are no circumstances in which I am obligated to exercise my power to license, nor am I, in the normal course of things, required to give, or even to have, reasons for choosing or not choosing to exercise it. As far as the private law of property is concerned, I may choose to keep you out of it or share it with you for any reason or no reason at all. That is just what it is, in the common law, for something to be mine.

The grant of the licence, like the basic act of exclusion, is a relational event that involves both parties, so the law insists that it be constituted by an event that is public as between them. Whether or not I licensed your entry onto my land cannot be a matter of what I intended to do or a matter of what you took me to do. Rather it is a matter of what I *communicated* to you, where I understand, and hereby define in this book, "communicated" to mean made public such that a reasonable person in your position would understand a reasonable person in my position to have been manifesting the intention to grant the licence. So if you thought you had a licence but did not in fact, you are still trespassing;[17]

[15] Just what "need" means here is a matter of some (pretty inside baseball) dispute, as to whether we can arrive at the necessity for the power to license through a transcendental argument about the nature of rights in property or whether we need a normative argument that the power to license is itself valuable. I tend toward the former view, but I don't think anything turns on that at the doctrinal level. For a defense of the claim that a parallel argument has a transcendental character, see Seana Valentine Shiffrin, "Promising, Intimate Relationships, and Conventionalism" 117 Philosophical Review 481 (2008); for a defense of the alternative view, see James Penner, Property Rights: A Re-Examination 28–31 (2020).

[16] Again, see my "Legal Powers in Private Law."

[17] *Athwal.*

conversely, if I communicated a licence to you but thought I had not, you are not trespassing.[18] This communication's being an objective matter of what is public as between the parties means that many acts of licensing can be implicit: I need not utter the words "come in," but instead can merely open the door and step aside. And in crowded circumstances such as those many live in these days, various forms of physical setup can be taken as communicating some limited set of general licences, so that the presence of a paved path from the public way to a house's front door can be taken to communicate a licence to walk to the door to knock on it. (Explicit communication trumps implicit communication, so that a "Do Not Enter" sign beside the walk means that there is no licence to enter.)

The importance of the communication element also arises because the licence sets the terms or scope of the licencee's permission to be on the licensor's property, such that exceeding the licence's scope counts as trespassing.[19] This is again part of the idea that owning property is a matter of being able to determine if and how others may act in it,[20] which is to say that included in the idea that I can decide whether or not you can enter is the idea that I can decide, having allowed you to enter, what you may and may not do once you have. With trespass as the starting point, we see that I can grant you a licence to enter the kitchen, but that grant does not affect the impermissibility of your entering the bedroom. Related to this is the common-law rule that a licence is generally revocable at will by the licensor:[21] having communicated to you that you may enter, I can communicate to you that you must leave. The revocability of the licence is crucial to understanding the value of the relationships that are grounded in licensing: part of what makes our relation as host and guest worth having is the way that you are, while at my house, governed by me. But we must be sure not to take this too far. In order to ensure that your legal status, while a licencee, is not entirely subject to my whims, my revocation brings with it a permission to take a reasonable time to leave the property.[22] One kind of case that looks as it if involves an irrevocable licence is the public accommodation—inns, stores, and the like. To understand these cases, we need some more infrastructure—in particular, an account of public property—so I will leave them for discussion in §7.3.

[18] This is the licence-specific version of the argument in the text accompanying note 11.

[19] *Gross v Wright*, [1923] SCR 214. This point has been established at least as far back as the *Six Carpenters' Case* (1572), 8 Co Rep 146a, 77 ER 695. That case also stands for the proposition that, in some cases, exceeding the scope of a licence can lead to a holding that the entire entry, even that which was covered by the licence, was a trespass. I do not think the account here determines the validity of that doctrine (of trespass *ab initio*).

[20] The law is more developed for land than chattels, but *mutatis mutandis* the same points apply.

[21] *Wood v Leadbitter* (1845) 13 M & W 838; *Marrone v Washington Jockey Club*, 227 US 633. See also Charles E Clark, "Licenses in Real Property Law" 21 Columbia Law Review 757 (1921).

[22] *Mellor v Watkins* (1874), LR 9 QB 400, 405.

4.2 Boundaries and Nuisance

Trespass and licences, by allowing an owner to determine if and how others enter or use what they own, work together to realize the possibility of relating as equals through the idea of yours and mine with respect to objects and spaces. Notice how this characterization, to be made to work, needs an account of when one person is entering or using another's property, that is, of what its boundaries are. The point seems simple. But some think that if I send an object (an airplane, a drone) high over your land, I am not trespassing.[23] The common law's traditional rule says that "my land" extends indefinitely up into the air (and below it to the center of the earth). Courts apply the content of, and sometimes still invoke, the centuries-old maxim *cujus est solum, ejus est usque ad coelum et ad infernos*, roughly meaning "who owns the soil also owns from the depths to the heavens."[24] This suggests that the content of my right in my land is some three-dimensional object, sometimes called a "column of space,"[25] raising worrying objections about my owning infinitely far into space. An alternative would be to impose a "ceiling" on what I own, although such a ceiling would necessarily be worryingly arbitrary. (If I could build a building or fly a balloon x feet high, I could do the same thing $x + 1$ feet high, so allowing you to use the space above x feet seems like it would allow you to control what is mine even below that line.)

In fact, the law here is better understood as more robustly relational. The point of the maxim is not that I own some (possibly) infinite three-dimensional object. The point rather is best understood in terms of the law of trespass, because the question of the boundaries of my property is, in law, the question of what does and does not count as a wrongful with respect to what is mine. So the maxim just tells us that there is no height over my land at which you can be understood as being above or outside the scope of my rights. However high above the surface of the earth (or whatever depth below it) you can go or use, I can also go or use, so there is no way to say that at some height you are not trespassing because you would not be interfering with what is mine.[26] (Of course, legislation can

[23] *United States v Causby*, 328 US 256 (1946).

[24] *Edwards v Sims*, 232 Ky 791, 24 SW2d 619 (1929), *Didow v Alberta Power Ltd* (1986), 70 AR 199 (QB), *Anchor Brewhouse Developments Ltd and Ors v Berkley House (Docklands) Developments Ltd* [1987] 38 BLR 82. And see also Stuart S Ball, "The Vertical Extent of Ownership in Land" 76 University of Pennsylvania Law Review 631 (1928). Things are more complex—or perhaps more confused—in the United States. See Stuart Banner, Who Owns the Sky? The Struggle to Control Airspace from the Wright Brothers On (2008).

[25] I feel compelled to point out that, contrary to the somewhat common use in the text, the space would not be a column, but a polygonal pyramid with its apex at the center of the earth.

[26] This is how the maxim is understood in *Bocardo SA v Star Energy UK Onshore Ltd*, [2010] UKSC 35, [14–15]. Of course, the maxim is simply a default: property can be subdivided vertically such that a particular legal parcel of land can have vertical as well as horizontal bounds. See Stuart S Ball, "Division into Horizontal Strata of the Landspace above the Surface" 39 Yale Law Journal 616 (1930).

for public purposes limit the rights of owners in subadjacent or superadjacent space,[27] but this is no different than any exercise of public powers to limit private rights, on which more later.) When it comes to private persons, we set the boundaries of what we own not physically but relationally, by reference to the question of when others commit wrongs.

This idea that what we own is a relational legal construct is extremely helpful in understanding the law of nuisance. Nuisance can be seen as a further development of the basic idea of trespass, in that nuisance, like trespass, works to ensure that we can use land as equals, as I put it in §1.4. We saw that a trespass can be understood as a kind of disruption of an egalitarian relation, as it involves my presuming the authority to decide what I may do on your land in a way that is inconsistent with the application of the idea of yours and mine. I will argue now that the subject matter of nuisance can work this same sort of injustice, in a more complex way. To wit: I can disrupt your dinner party by coming into your dining room, but (as your neighbor) I can also disrupt it by turning my music up to 11 or starting a fire that emits smoke that interferes with your breathing; in each case we might think that I subordinate you, by failing to let you determine the uses of your own land. But notice that the latter two disruptions involve the use of land that is mine. This means that we cannot simply treat them in the way we treat trespasses. Were *any* noise or smoke generated on my land to count as a wrong against you, I would be unable to make use of what is mine, and we would have the converse problem of subordination, in that I would be unable to determine the use of my land. Nuisance aims to solve this problem, to allow each to use their land in a way that is consistent with others using theirs, thus allowing us to relate to each other on terms of equality.

This is, as Coase put it, "a problem of a reciprocal nature," and so one that is particularly well-fitted to be analyzed here.[28] The central doctrine of nuisance says that a nuisance is an unreasonable interference with the use and enjoyment of the plaintiff's property. As the UK Supreme Court recently noted in its important decision in *Fearn v Tate Gallery*, this rule can be understood as a principle of "equal justice" or "reciprocity."[29] This rule involves two closely related but importantly distinct applications of the idea of yours and mine. In the first, we focus on the fact that a nuisance is an unreasonable interference with the use and enjoyment *of the plaintiff's property*; in the second, we focus on the fact that a nuisance

[27] See, e.g., the American Federal Aviation Act, 48 USC 40103(a)(1). In *Kelsen v Imperial Tobacco Co*, [1957] 2 All ER 343 (QB), the Court saw this point clearly, in stating that the relevant English legislation providing rights for public air overflights was necessary to "negative" the action of trespass which would otherwise have been available, given the *ad coelum* rule.

[28] Ronald Coase, "The Problem of Social Cost" 3 Journal of Law and Economics 1, 2 (1960).

[29] [2023] UKSC 4 [34–35].

is an *unreasonable interference* with the use and enjoyment of the plaintiff's property. We can take them in turn.

Nuisance is a tort that protects property rights in land, a "tort against land."[30] That means that the defendant must interfere with the use of the plaintiff's land *as land*. It is not enough for your activity to make it difficult for me to do what I want on my land; the test requires that your interference be one that affects my use of the land as such.[31] This means that there is no liability for interferences that are personal to me or that are, even if more objective in nature, not sufficiently tied to my use of the land.[32] (Some of these cases might be private wrongs, but because they are not interferences with the property rights of the plaintiff, they cannot be nuisances.) But what is a tort against land? The discussion of the *ad coelum* rule can help to structure our approach, by reminding us that the question is a legal question, about the realization of the idea of yours and mine. This helps to rule out one potential account. The paradigmatic forms of nuisance—smells, smoke, noise—all involve, in a way, an emanation of something—volatile organic compounds, particulate matter, soundwaves—from the defendant's activity onto the plaintiff's land. One might suppose that all nuisances must have this character, that a nuisance is a kind of invisible or intangible trespass.[33] But this is not quite right, for at least two reasons.

First, it simply is not the case that all nuisances involve emanations: it is well-settled law that removal of lateral support, denial of access, and interference with the use of an easement are nuisances.[34] Second, and more fundamentally, this notion of nuisance as emanation depends on an unmotivated reduction of nuisance to the physical. But—and this is thematic in this book—property in land is not about land as physical space, it is about the possibility of relating as equals with respect to space. As the toy example three paragraphs ago indicated, the paradigmatic forms of nuisance are actionable not because of their physicality—there

[30] Donal Nolan, "'A Tort Against Land': Private Nuisance as a Property Tort" in Donal Nolan and Andrew Robertson eds, Rights and Private Law (2011) 459. I will just note very quickly that there is no direct analogue for property in chattels, but the same form of protection is provided in the law through a patchwork of other legal protections, mostly the law of negligence. In brief, the relevant rule there says (among other things) that you are not entitled to use your own objects in a way that imposes an unreasonable risk of harm to mine. Thus each of us is given a kind of sphere of control over our own things that is consistent with the other having a like sphere of control over theirs. But negligence also covers a lot more than that, so I cannot here go into detail about its workings.

[31] See, for example, *Fontainebleau Hotel Corp v Forty-Five Twenty-Five Inc*, 114 So 2d 357 (Fla Ct App 1959). There could have been no claim in this case because the defendant's building on its land did not affect the use of the land as land, it merely affected the profitability of that use.

[32] For the former, see *Rogers v Elliot*, 15 NE 768 (Mass 1888), for the latter, see *Hunter v Canary Wharf*, [1997] AC 655, 691, and in particular Lord Goff's discussion of harassing phone calls as not sufficiently about the use of land to be actionable in nuisance.

[33] See, e.g., Simon Douglas and Ben McFarlane, "Defining Property Rights" in James Penner and Henry E Smith eds, Philosophical Foundations of Property Law 219 (2013).

[34] For these and other examples see *Fearn* at [12–17] as well as my "Nuisance and the Normative Boundaries of Ownership" at 96–97.

is no plausible story on which volatile organic compounds entering my land should constitute a wrong in some brute or basic sense—but because they interfere with the possibility of using the land in a way that is consistent with thinking about it as mine. They are wrongs because, as the law says, they interfere with "the ordinary comfort physically of human existence."[35] My land, then, is not space considered physically (or spatially) but space considered legally, that is, space considered as *mine*, as mine to use on terms of equality with everyone else. Seen this way, nuisance does not require an emanation onto my land, because the use of land as such by creatures like us may be interfered with through other means than emanations.

The *Fearn* case illustrates this point very clearly. There the defendants' property had upon it a public viewing gallery from which hundreds of thousands of people each year had a very clear view into the apartments of the plaintiffs who lived directly across the street (about 30m away). The Court held unanimously that the fact that no emanation from the defendants' land ended up on the plaintiffs' land was no bar to recovery, since the viewing and photography that took place on the viewing platform could materially intrude into the privacy and use of the plaintiffs' homes as homes: the fact that the plaintiffs' homes were essentially open to the public for viewing was, the Court found, a way for the defendants to subordinate the plaintiffs with respect to their use of what was theirs, no different than the intrusion of smells, smoke, or noise. The plaintiffs reasonably could have understood their ability to make use of what was theirs to be subordinated to the use of the land being made by the defendants, since whether or not the plaintiffs could wander around in their pajamas (say) was, in a sense, up to the defendants (and their patrons).[36]

So understood, nuisance, considered as a body of law as a whole, plays an important part in constituting the scope of property rights in land. As I noted two paragraphs ago, this fits well with the point about subsurface and aerial trespass: in both cases, the "boundaries" of land are determined not purely physically but in reference to the fact that the boundaries are *legal* boundaries. Nuisance does this, first, by constructing categories of actionable interferences, that is, by determining what can count as the kind of interference which, if I were to impose it upon your land, we could worry that I had subordinated you with respect

[35] *Walter v Selfe*, 64 ER 849, 852 (1851).

[36] Importantly, in reaching the result it did, the majority insisted that the defendants' viewing platform actually made the use of the plaintiffs' land *as land* unreasonably difficult, distinguishing this case from the well-known decision in *Victoria Park Racing & Recreation Grounds v Taylor*, [1937] HCA 45, where the defendants overlooked the plaintiffs' racecourse to broadcast the results over the radio. The distinction is helpfully tied to our discussion here: in *Victoria Park*, the overlooking did not affect the use of the land as land—as the court said, nobody on the plaintiffs' land could have known what the defendants were doing—but merely affected its profitability. But that is not the right kind of interference to count as a nuisance. For more on *Victoria Park* see chapter 5 note 71.

to your use of your land as such. The established forms of nuisance all meet that test, and, as the Court said in the *Tate Gallery* case, there is no reason to think that these categories should be closed. Instead, in confronting new potential instances of nuisance, the common law can limn the boundaries of what it is to own land, that is, of what you or I have when some land is yours or mine.

So nuisance helps us to understand what property in land is, legally, by understanding what can count as an unreasonable interference with the use and enjoyment *of the plaintiff's land*. As I said, nuisance has another role, in determining the contents of our equal relations with respect to the idea of yours and mine by deciding what counts as an *unreasonable interference* with the use and enjoyment of land. We can turn to that now. The key here is to remember, again, that nuisance is a reciprocal phenomenon. We have noted that many uses of my property can generate effects on your property that could not be wrongful nuisances since, if they were, that would amount to giving you control over how I may use what is mine. It simply cannot be the case that your ownership of your land means that I cannot make any sound on my land at all. The law of nuisance has for a long time helpfully made this point by contrasting nuisances with permissible interferences that are characterized as a matter of "give and take, live and let live."[37] We relate as equals with respect to our property when we relate through this reciprocal principle: a nuisance is when my use of my property goes beyond that reciprocity—when it is unreasonable—and has the effect of subordinating your use of what is yours to my use of what is mine. The idea of reasonability here is an idea of equal relations in my sense; indeed, the reasonability standard in nuisance is perhaps the most explicitly egalitarian part of the law of property.

Saying that the standard is an application of the idea of equal relations is still very abstract. That might seem worrying, but it is actually consistent with the doctrine. The law of nuisance lacks any systematic account of what counts as an unreasonable interference, and courts often disclaim the capacity to say anything beyond that nuisance is "a matter of degree," where "difficult questions may sometimes arise."[38] In itself, this is not a problem: the role of a fact-finder in a nuisance dispute is to bring these abstract ideas to bear on the particulars of the dispute before it, as "the question in each case ultimately reduces itself to the fact of nuisance or no nuisance, having regard to all the surrounding circumstances."[39] This also explains a wide range of reasonable disagreement about the application of the rule to particular cases.[40] Various particular doctrines in nuisance law, in

[37] *Bamford v Turnley* (1860), 3 B&S 62, 83–84.

[38] *Miller v Jackson*, [1977] QB 966, 986 (CA).

[39] *Appleby v Erie Tobacco*, (1910) 22 OLR 533.

[40] Notably, in the *Fearn* case, while the entire Court agreed that a nuisance does not require an emanation, the Court actually split 3–2 on whether or not the interference caused by the overlooking was unreasonable. The way to gloss the dissent here is to say that it would have held that the overlooking was a matter of give and take, live and let live.

particular the so-called locality rule, can be understood as guides to that process of judgment in determining what counts as an unreasonable interference.[41]

However, one idea that can be seen to run through many of the prominent cases is a relational idea of generality and specificity.[42] According to this idea, an interference is unreasonable when the defendant's interfering use can be characterized as a more specific instance of a general category that aptly describes the use the plaintiff cannot make. Conversely, an interference can be reasonable if it prevents the plaintiff from using their land in a way that can be characterized as a specific instance of which the defendant's interfering use can be characterized as a general category. Or, as the Court in *Fearn* put it, in slightly different terms:

> A person who puts his land to a special use cannot justify substantial interference which this causes with the ordinary use of neighbouring land by saying that he is asking no more consideration or forbearance from his neighbour than they (or an average person in their position) can expect from him. Nor can such a person complain on that basis about substantial interference with his special use of his land caused by the ordinary use of neighbouring land. By contrast, a person who is using her land in a common and ordinary way is not seeking any unequal treatment or asking of her neighbours more than they ask of her.[43]

So on the one hand, the smells emitted by a defendant tobacco factory that interfere with any ordinary human use of the plaintiff's neighboring land constitute a nuisance,[44] and on the other, a demand that a defendant not erect any structure at all on their land to allow plaintiffs to sunbathe on theirs could not be a complaint that sounds in nuisance.[45] This understanding of nuisance is comprehensible as a development of the requirement that parties relate as equals because to claim that my specific use of what is mine should take priority over your more general use of what is yours amounts to a claim that I should be able to do precisely what I deny to you, and thus a claim to a kind of superiority inconsistent with the basic commitment; by contrast, the priority of the general over the particular is consistent with equal standing, since none claims a right denied to another.

[41] See Sandy Steel, "The Locality Principle in Private Nuisance" 76 Cambridge Law Journal 145 (2017).

[42] Here I aim to develop Ernest Weinrib's discussion of nuisance in The Idea of Private Law at 192–93, which in turn draws on *Hay v Cohoes Co*, 2 NY 159 (1849). Weinrib now takes a rather different view of nuisance: see Ernest J Weinrib, Reciprocal Freedom: Private Law and Public Right 89–92 (2022). Allan Beever defends a view somewhat similar to mine on this point in Beever, The Law of Private Nuisance (2013).

[43] *Fearn* at [35].

[44] *Appleby v Erie Tobacco*.

[45] This is a different reading of the facts of *Fontainebleau*.

Let me say finally that, on this view, the difference between trespass and nuisance is not sharp. It lies in the way that a trespass involves occupation of space, and so makes the use of (some part of) the plaintiff's land essentially impossible, whereas a nuisance merely makes such use unreasonably difficult. In the case of a trespass, I cannot stand where you are or put anything where you parked your car; but in the case of a nuisance, because it does not occupy space, the smoke you send onto my land may make it impossible for me to do some things (like eat or sleep) but not others (like storing scrap metal). The traditional test that requires trespasses to involve objects visible to the naked eye aligns with this. Notably, though, the line is not impenetrable or perfect. Your use of my land in familiar physical ways (like building an airstrip) is not actually inconsistent with my using it in any way at all: I might be holding it for investment and not care who enters or leaves.[46] Conversely, some nuisances—say the emission of gamma radiation—might come very close to making any use of the property impossible.[47] And doctrinally, nuisance and trespass often overlap.[48] Perhaps a different account of the division between them is possible. But for my purposes, the important point is that trespass and nuisance work together to more fully realize the idea of yours and mine than trespass could on its own.[49]

This returns us to the point that nuisance helps to limn the boundaries of rights in land and thus reminds us that we should in my view think of both trespass and nuisance as playing a role in constituting, as a matter of law, what it is that I own when I own something. Think of it this way. Property is relational: it is not about me and my stuff, but about me and you, and how we can relate as equals with respect to all the stuff. So when we realize the idea of yours and mine what we are doing, in part, is constituting the boundaries of ownership for the law's purposes, which is to say constituting the subject matter of relations of yours and mine. In other words, we are determining what I am referring to when I say "this is mine." Because that idea is an idea not about the relation between me and what is mine but an idea about the relation between me and you, we should understand the law here—the law of trespass and nuisance—to be constituting the subject matter of the relation, the object of property, which I will describe as the *res*.[50] In other words, *what I own* is a matter of our relation and thus a matter of the legal

[46] This phenomenon causes some problems for the law of adverse possession: see *Masidon Investments Ltd v Ham* (1984), 45 OR (2d) 563 (CA).

[47] Penner calls this "constructive ejectment." See James E Penner, "Nuisance and the Character of the Neighbourhood" 5 Journal of Environmental Law 1 (1993); Penner, Property Rights, 148–52.

[48] For discussion of this point, see *Martin v Reynolds Metals Co*, 342 P2d 790 (Or 1959).

[49] Implicit in this account is the thought that I can license you to commit what would otherwise be a nuisance. And that is the law: see *Pwllbach Colliery Co v Woodman*, [1915] AC 634, 638 (HL).

[50] Although "res" is a Latin word, it occurs enough in what follows that I've decided not to italicize it after introducing it here.

rights I have against you that you not act in certain ways that can be described (in the cases discussed so far, at least) simply and entirely by reference to an object or space. So my land, as a matter of law, is not simply a three-dimensional space. Rather, the boundaries of the space (for trespass law) are defined, by the *ad coelum* rule, in terms of the possibility of others' entrances. Moreover, I also have a right that you not emit unreasonable smoke from your land (or commit any other nuisance). The boundaries of my land—and the boundaries of any other res—are determined by the law on the basis of an application of the idea of yours and mine to the context in question. Thus the law of nuisance helps (with trespass) to constitute the res that is the land from the law's point of view and so renders its legal boundaries determinate.[51] This is not to deny the physicality of trespass as we normally understand it, but to emphasize that the idea of yours and mine is an abstract normative idea that has a kind of conceptual basicness in our legal thinking, and that it applies to the physicality of spaces and objects without reducing into brute (and worryingly nonrelational) physicality. Moreover, because nuisance itself is a development of the basic commitment, so that nuisance disputes are resolved in a way that ensures the equal standing of the parties, the very idea of a res—the idea of the subject matter of a property right—is itself an egalitarian idea, in that what I own when I own something is determined in part by reference to the way that my ownership must be consistent with the requirement that I relate to others on terms of equality.

4.3 Acquisition and Possession

With this idea of the res in hand, we can turn to our next set of doctrines. We saw in §1.5 that the idea of yours and mine has built into it an independence of its subject matter from particular persons. What is mine might be yours. This means that we will need an explanation of why what is mine is mine rather than yours. This is why one of the first questions about property encountered by law students is the question about, as it is called, first possession: where do particular property rights come from? I own the pencil on my desk because my mom bought it for me as a gift, and my mom bought it from a pencil seller, who bought it from a pencil manufacturer, who made it out of wood (along with paint, rubber, metal, graphite) that it bought from a logging company which had the right to cut the trees down because . . .

[51] A res, as I'll understand it, is the legal subject matter to which the idea of yours and mine applies in a given case, it is the "this" to which I refer when I say "this is mine." As we'll see, the lesson here from nuisance applies more generally and the res should not be mistaken for the physical object on which it is based, and indeed, we'll see cases in which there is a res without a physical object. We'll discuss these points more in §5.4.

At some point, all property rights need to bottom out in a story about one person taking some unowned object and, somehow, making it their own. It is well-known that Locke argued that the labor that goes into acquiring an unowned object grounds a natural right—a right not arising out of any particular legal or political order—in the object, and that the entire law of property exists in order to work that right up into an institutional form, to protect it against others, and so on. There are many criticisms of that view, which we do not need to explore in detail here.[52] Instead, we will consider how my account of property conceives of acquisition. The short answer is simple: acquisition is not some magical moment where property comes into being, as in Locke's (or perhaps Hegel's[53]) view, but instead a merely technical question that can be answered entirely within the confines of the institution. Put differently the answer to the question "How can I make something mine in a state of nature?" is "You cannot."[54] The question about acquisition arises because we need an institution of property and such an institution needs to have rules about how objects that have not been owned become owned, about how they enter into its purview, as it were. The common law's version of those rules is the law of first possession.[55]

One way to see this is by reflecting on the classic case of *Pierson v Post*.[56] Post, the plaintiff in the case, had been hunting foxes in what was then the "waste and uninhabited ground" of Long Island when the defendant Pierson, a "saucy intruder," killed and took the fox that Post had been in hot pursuit of. Post claimed that Pierson had stolen his fox, but Pierson's reply was that Post had not gained

[52] The most comprehensive discussion of Locke's view is A John Simmons, The Lockean Theory of Rights (1992). Cogent criticism from different points of view is found in Jeremy Waldron, The Right to Private Property (1988), Arthur Ripstein, Force and Freedom: Kant's Legal and Political Philosophy 96–105 (2009), and Liam Murphy, "The Artificial Morality of Private Law: The Persistence of an illusion" 70 University of Toronto Law Journal 453, 464–64 (2020). To my mind, the most persuasive reconstruction of Locke is Seana Valentine Shiffrin, "Lockean Arguments for Private Intellectual Property" in Stephen R Munzer ed, New Essays in the Legal and Political Theory of Property 138 (2001). In Shiffrin's reconstruction, Locke's view becomes not unlike mine, in that her Locke sees God's gift of the earth to man as requiring an institution of property in order to prevent starvation and then sees the role of acquisition as merely internal to the institution rather than generating a pre-political claim on what is acquired.

[53] For clear discussion, see Nicholas Sage, "Is Original Acquisition Problematic?" in James Penner and Michael Otsuka eds, Property Theory: Legal and Political Perspectives 99 (2018).

[54] To the same effect, see Katrin Flikschuh, "Innate Right and Acquired Right in Arthur Ripstein's Force and Freedom" 1 Jurisprudence 295, 297 (2010) and Florian Rödl, "The Legitimacy of Civil Freedom" 69 University of Toronto Law Journal 159, 174–75 (2018).

[55] Even according to the Lockean or Hegelian view, the act of picking up an object is of normative interest only because the end state—a property right—is of normative interest. The idea of original acquisition is a helpful heuristic for thinking about the justification of property, as it forces us to ask how *this* person became the owner of *this* thing. But that question is just a particular version of the more general question, how is *any* person the owner of *any* thing. And that question, as I argue in the text, needs an institutional answer.

[56] 3 Cai 175 (1805). For a deep dive into the case, see Angela Fernandez, The Hunt for the Fox: Law and Professionalization in American Legal Culture (2018).

a property right in the fox and that therefore Pierson had not wronged Post. The majority of the court agreed with Pierson: Post had not acquired a right in the fox because he had not caught the fox. But the court was clear that catching the fox, in this context, was a broader notion than actually physically getting one's hands on it:

> actual bodily seizure is not indispensable to acquire right to, or possession of, wild beasts; but that, on the contrary, the mortal wounding of such beasts, by one not abandoning his pursuit, may, with the utmost propriety, be deemed possession of him; since, thereby, the *pursuer manifests an unequivocal intention of appropriating the animal to his individual use*, has deprived him of his natural liberty, and brought him within his certain control.[57]

I have italicized the passage that I think is the key to the decision. What is required to acquire a property right in some unowned object is an act that "manifests an unequivocal intention" of doing so. Let us see why.

An act of acquisition is the exercise of a legal power. By acquiring some object, the first possessor makes the object theirs, and thereby gains a right that they did not previously have and—what is the same idea viewed from the other direction—puts everyone else under a legal obligation that they did not previously have not to touch or take the fox. To acquire an object is thus to bring it under the purview of the system of property, to make it the subject matter of an application of the idea of yours and mine (i.e., to make it a res). Because the right is good against the world, because it imposes duties of non-interference on everyone else, acquisition needs to be accomplished in a way that can be understood to be public, which is to say available for the world to see: since everyone else now has a duty not to interfere with the now-owned fox, they need to be able to know that fact in order to be able to govern their conduct accordingly. And because the right is only contingently connected to its holder, the acquisition needs to be accomplished in a way that can establish a sufficiently public connection between the acquirer and what is acquired.[58] Putting these formal features of the property right together, we might say that the generic way to acquire an object is to manifest the intention to do so in the language of property, to treat it in the way that an owner would treat it.

In *Pierson v Post*, the capture of the fox does this: by actually getting his hands on the fox, Pierson both establishes that the fox is owned and that it is he who

[57] *Pierson v Post* at 178.

[58] For a well-known similar view, see Carol M Rose, "Possession as the Origin of Property" 52 University of Chicago Law Review 73 (1985); and for a recent restatement, see Carol M Rose, "The Law Is Nine-Tenths of Possession: An Adage Turned on Its Head" in Yun-Chien Chang ed, Law and Economics of Possession 40, 51–52 (2015).

owns it. This rule allows all potential acquirers (and all potential bearers of the duties correlative to the right created by the acquisition) to relate on terms of equality, since it makes the relevant normative event—the bringing into being of a new property right—something that is public, equally available to all. The fact that Post *really wanted* the fox, or that he had *worked really hard to try to catch* the fox, or anything else that is only about Post is, from this point of view, just not relevant. Acquisition is an exercise of a legal power, so what matters must be what happened in the world, publicly, in a way that all parties can understand as having the relevant effect. At the same time, it is important to see that the role of actually physically getting the object is in one important sense derivative. First possession is not about getting your hands on the object to establish some kind of special connection between you and the object.[59] Rather it is about publicly establishing that the object is owned, and that you are its owner. For some objects, actual physical possession (manucaption) does this most effectively. But for others, manucaption is not required to establish the relevant legal control, because manucaption is not required to act like an owner would act.[60] Moreover, it is certainly conceptually possible to imagine a law of property that solved the problem of initial acquisition without any system of private actions of possession, perhaps through a lottery system.[61] It is essential, given the egalitarian

[59] First possession does require what in the phenomenological tradition is called a nonintentional (or real) relation to the acquired object, as opposed to an intentional relation, where the latter but not former type of relation is consistent with the object not actually existing, because it is a relation of thought rather than of real objects: see Franz Brentano, Psychology From an Empirical Standpoint (1874)). Thus wishing for it or dreaming about it or wanting it could never count as acquiring it, since one can wish for or dream about or want things that lack any existence outside one's wishing, dreaming, or wanting them. But that is a low bar, which, notably, *Pierson*'s dissenting judgment's "reasonable prospect" test meets: I cannot have a reasonable prospect of catching a nonexistent fox. So the reason to reject the reasonable prospect test is not that it's only happening in someone's head; it's that it does not sufficiently communicate that the acquisition has taken place.

[60] According to some views, the physical possession of the fox is necessary to ensure that the possessor has actually physically acquired the object and so brought it under their will. (See, e.g. Ripstein, Force and Freedom.) But this seems to me to be a misstep and to fail to see how thoroughly relational acquisition is. First possession should not be thought about in terms of the acquirer's relation with the acquired object, but instead in terms of their relation with others; so the sine qua non must be that the act of acquisition is *unequivocal*. It is true that physical possession will very often be the best candidate for an unequivocal act of acquisition. But not always: the law contains a variety of cases in which the relevant act is not a matter of physically getting one's hands on something. Consider the various norms for the acquisition of whales as discussed in Robert C Ellickson, "A Hypothesis of Wealth-Maximizing Norms: Evidence from the Whaling Industry" 5 Journal of Law, Economics, & Organization 83 (1989) or for shipwrecks, as in *The Tubantia*, [1924] P 78. A different way to see the point is to move outside the context of tangibles. In patent law, the acquisitive act is registration of the patent, an act that is purely communicative in my sense. The importance of physical acquisition in the contexts of tangibles is thus explained by reference to the idea that only such acquisition can properly be understood as unequivocal; in other contexts, things might be different.

[61] Cicero notes that, in ancient times, some colonial lands were assigned by lottery. See Cicero, De Officiis 1.7. On lotteries as basic commitment compliant see Alexander A Guerrero, "Against Elections: The Lottocratic Alternative" 42 Philosophy & Public Affairs 135 (2014). See also chapter 5 note 19, where I consider and to some extent endorse the possibility of a different norm of initial acquisition in the context of human biological materials.

character of the idea of yours and mine, that acquisition be consistent with the requirement that ownership be "open to all under conditions of fair equality of opportunity."[62] The law of first possession in the common law meets that test, but alternative arrangements might, too.

Once we see all these points about acquisition, it is an easy step to apply the same basic framework to our thinking about any situation involving possession in the law of property.[63] In short, possession just is not a fundamental idea in the law of property when the law is understood in terms of rights-based principles. Rather, possession is merely an epistemic or evidentiary device coupled with a generalized preference in the law for there to be someone to exercise the rights of ownership for each owned object.[64] The doctrine of adverse possession—according to which someone who trespasses in what we might call a particularly egregious way on the land of another for a long period of time can become the owner of that land—illustrates this most clearly. There are some sophisticated theoretical treatments of the law that attempt to make serious hay out of adverse possession.[65] They aim to show that an adverse possessor is somehow morally entitled to the land, that it is just or right for the original owner to be ousted. But we might notice that in a world of land registries, the doctrine has lost most of its power, suggesting that the traditional, naïve story is the right one: adverse possession is a way of making legal facts determinate in the face of nonlegal indeterminacy about what happened, a way of settling titles in a world without easy access to information and records.[66] We need to know who the owner of land is and we need this to be relatively settled, so that the various relations grounded in ownership can be securely possible and not dependent always on the possibility that someone might emerge from the mists of time with a better claim. So the law limits the scope of older claims, such that we need not look, as Blackstone put it, before "time out of mind,"[67] and says that claims relying on evidence older than the relevant period are not admissible. This is the legal structure of the law,[68]

[62] John Rawls, A Theory of Justice, rev ed 266 (1999). Recall the role this point played in §2.1.

[63] For some recent treatments of possession, see the essays collected in Eric Descheemaeker ed, The Consequences of Possession (2014).

[64] Larissa Katz, "Ownership and Offices: The Building Blocks of the Legal Order" 70 University of Toronto Law Journal, Supplement 2 267 (2020).

[65] Margaret Jane Radin, "Time, Possession, and Alienation" 64 Washington University Law Quarterly 739 (1986); Alan Brudner, "The Unity of Property Law"4 Canadian Journal of Law and Jurisprudence 3 (1991); Larissa Katz, "The Moral Paradox of Adverse Possession: Sovereignty and Revolution in Property Law" 55 McGill Law Journal 47 (2010); Sarah E Hamill, "Enduring Trespass: What Adverse Possession Reveals about Property" 96 Supreme Court Law Review 216 (2020).

[66] For a comprehensive discussion, see Charles C Callahan, Adverse Possession (1961). And see also the discussion in Thomas W Merrill, "Property Rules, Liability Rules, and Adverse Possession" 79 Northwestern University Law Review 1122, 1126–37 (1985).

[67] William Blackstone, Commentaries on the Laws of England III.13 at *217.

[68] See, perhaps while reflecting on its title, the *Real Property Limitations Act*, RSO 1990, c L-15.

and it makes good sense.[69] As with first possession, adverse possession is an empirical tool that we use to solve a problem that can itself be understood without reference to the idea of possession. In the first case, the problem is "how do we decide who will own previously unowned objects?" and in the second, it's "what do we do about disputed ownership of land grounded on historical uncertainty?" or something along those lines.[70]

The same basic point applies in other possession cases. Possession is merely a tool to help figure out who holds the relevant normative position that matters, but it has itself no independent moral or legal significance.[71] The same idea can be put in the reverse order to clarify it. To physically possess something is merely to hold it, which, as we saw in §1.1, is a situation that has no intrinsic legal import; a crucial idea in understanding the need for property is the distinction between holding and having. Property is about having, which is to say about rights over something that one is not presently holding. Once we grasp the concept of having, holding falls away and becomes normatively secondary. Its main role becomes epistemic, in that the question of who holds something can be a clue to the important question of who has it.[72]

Possession also plays a different kind of secondary role that arises in the nonideal case in which someone who is not the owner of something ends up holding it. In these kinds of cases, an idea of physical possession generates a kind of proxy or "surrogate" ownership.[73] The basic and easiest case of this is the law of finders,

[69] Arthur Ripstein, "The Rule of Law and Time's Arrow" in Lisa M. Austin and Dennis Klimchuk eds, Private Law and the Rule of Law 306(2014); John G Sprankling, "An Environmental Critique of Adverse Possession" 79 Cornell Law Review 816 (1994).

[70] I mean here to account only for the basic private law cases of adverse possession. More complicated versions of the problem involving wider historical injustice (as in colonial acquisition of land) or other moral considerations (as in, perhaps, objects with cultural heritage significance) require a different treatment.

[71] To the same effect see Rose, "Law Is Nine-Tenths of Possession" at 45.

[72] Further evidence for this lies in the decreasing importance of physical possession for kinds of property for which registration is possible, as in the unavailability of most adverse possession claims for registered lands. Rudden characterizes both possession and registration as instances of an idea of publicity. See Bernard Rudden, "Things as Things and Things as Wealth" 14 Oxford Journal of Legal Studies 81, 82 (1994). To be clear, then, I do not think physical possession plays a constitutive role in our thinking about property, and it is not impossible to imagine systems of property in tangibles that make little or no use of possession in the way that ours does. This somewhat instrumental story about possession is thus meant to show why possession is pervasive in our law and consistent with the idea of yours and mine even though it is not an essential element of the institution.

[73] For a careful development of this idea, see Larissa Katz, "The Relativity of Title and *Causa Possessionis*" in Penner and Smith eds, Philosophical Foundations of Property Law 202, 205–208. To the same effect, see Thomas W Merrill, "Ownership and Possession" in Chang ed, Law and Economics of Possession 9, 23. Merrill goes on, in my view confusing the relationship between possession and ownership in his discussion of finders law, which he characterizes as the law according rights to possession "independently of ownership." It is not clear to me why Merrill does not endorse the obvious thought that finders law as a whole is just a development of the idea of what he calls surrogate ownership. Rose makes the same basic claim: "Possession for the law means *acting like an owner*": "Law Is Nine-Tenths of Possession" at 49 (emphasis in original).

where a person who is holding a lost object is treated by the law as the owner of that object with respect to everyone in the world except the true owner.[74] The law does this because, again, the whole point of property is to realize the egalitarian structure of the idea of yours and mine. We treat the holder of an object as an owner (unless there is evidence that someone else is the owner) so that we can treat someone as the owner and allow individuals to relate with respect to the object as equals through the idea of yours and mine.

This brings us to the law of bailment, about which a couple of brief words are in order, primarily because they will be helpful in thinking about some different problems later on. Cutting through a whole lot of complexity, bailment is the legal relation that occurs when one person—the bailee—has possession of an object owned by another person—the bailor.[75] Some of the law of bailment is concerned with the relations between these two people, and the duties that the bailee owes to the bailor to take care of the bailor's goods. Another part is a working-up of the considerations that I mentioned in the last paragraph, to the effect that the law treats the bailee, when it comes to other people, as a stand-in or surrogate for the owner, such that a bailee can bring claims against those others if they interfere with the object without their consent. At the same time, the owner herself—the bailor—also generally has claims against third parties, so if someone steals the bailed goods from the bailee's possession, the bailor has a right to recover them herself, directly. (And of course there are rules about how the bailor and the bailee's claims against the third party need to be rendered consistent, so that the third party is not subject to double liability.) Interestingly, in this way, bailment is helpful as a very clear illustration of the distinction between having and

[74] *Armory v Delamirie* (1722) 1 Strange 505. In fact, a fuller explanation of the law of finders, one that fits well with the rest of this chapter, involves this account of possession's role in two different ways. First is the one already mentioned. Second is what is required to understand the most common scenario in which the law of finders is relevant, namely, where one person (the locator) finds a lost object on land occupied (which is to say possessed) by another person (the occupier) who was unaware that the object was there and did not themselves own the object as an object. The law here can be understood basically by asking if the locator was, in locating the object, trespassing against the occupier. There is a clear rule that says that when a locator is on the land of an occupier without permission, the occupier will have superior title to what the locator finds. But there is also a rule that says that if the locator finds something that is "attached to or under" the occupier's land, the occupier again has superior title. See *Hannah v Peel*, [1945] KB 509. This makes sense, since such an object is effectively part of the occupier's land, so the occupier is already in possession of it, which is to say that they already found it and thus have superior title to the finder. The locator can thus, absent specific consent, be understood to be trespassing by taking it: you don't normally have consent to take parts of people's land with you when you visit, and the physical unity of the land and the found object can be understood as communicating that the occupier also possesses the object. (The same basic analysis, modified to highlight the varying role of certain social norms, can apply to the law of fixtures. An object becomes a fixture if its owner attaches it to their real property in such a way as to communicate, in the sense articulated in the text, that the object is now a fixture, that is, a part of the realty. See, e.g., *Strain v Green*, 25 Wash. 2d 692 (1946).)

[75] A still-helpful comprehensive treatment of the common law can be found in Joseph Story, Commentaries on the Law of Bailments, with Illustrations from the Civil and Common Law (9th ed 1878).

holding that was so central to the argument in chapter 1. The law of bailment took a while to develop, but it became, properly understood, a part of the law of property when "[t]he use of the word *property* was . . . extended so as to include the mere right of one who had bailed goods so that he might at any time retake them, or from whom goods had been wrongfully taken. In other words, it was recognized that a man might have property in goods, although he had no *thing* in possession, if he had a good claim to take some particular *thing* for himself out of others' possession."[76] Property is precisely always about when you have a right to some thing and not about when you actually hold it, and the law of bailment recognizes and vindicates that understanding.

4.4 Alienation

The independence of me and what is mine means that, when something is mine, I need an explanation of how it became mine. It seems that such an explanation can take two forms.[77] I can acquire things originally, in the way we contemplated in §4.3. Or I can get them from someone else. The latter is our next topic.

How does one transfer property to another? The straightforward and basic legal answer, typically attributed to a case called *Cochrane v Moore*, is easy to state: there must be a donative intent and there must be delivery.[78] Indeed, as one court put it,

> there cannot be a gift unless there is a deed or an actual delivery of possession. The delivery is an essential part of the gift. *Cochrane v. Moore* shews that words of gift and an acceptance by the donee, communicated to the donor, are not enough where there is no delivery.[79]

There is a lot to say about this. We want an account of transfer that takes seriously the status of both the transferor ("donor") and transferee ("donee"), such that they can relate in this transaction as equals. Based on considerations parallel to others we have seen already, such an account will be one that does not make the transfer's metaphysics entirely dependent on one or the other party to it.[80] Of course, an owner has the upper hand in that an owner is the one who

[76] T Cyprian Williams, "Property, Things in Action, and Copyright" 43 Law Quarterly Review 223, 227 (1893) footnotes omitted.

[77] For discussion of this point, see Peter Benson, Justice in Transactions 326–27 (2019).

[78] *Cochrane v Moore* (1890), 25 QBD 77 (CA).

[79] *Kingsmill v Kingsmill* (1917), 41 OLR 238 (HCJ).

[80] To the same effect, see Samuel von Pufendorf, The Law of Nature and Nations IV.9 (1672). Pufendorf defends this view by noting that it is "inconsistent with Human Society, that bare Internal Acts should be allow'd a Power of producing Rights to hold Valid and Effectual with other men."

gets to determine, at the start of things, whether and under what circumstances any transfer at all will take place. Generally, though, gifts need to be accepted: I cannot force you to become the owner of something you do not wish to own.[81] Suppose, then, that such a decision is made and ultimately a successful transfer takes place so that the donee ends up as owner. When, precisely, should we say that the transfer happened? This is the crucial question about transfer, both theoretically—capturing the moment of transfer is, as we will see, crucial to capturing what transfer is—and practically since, as the cases show, questions about transfer often arise when some event—an object's being lost, a donor's death—seems to have interrupted a transfer, and a court needs to decide whose object it was at the relevant time, that is, whether or not a transfer was completed.

First, notice what happens when the gift is complete. The primary legal change that takes place is in the rights, duties, powers, and so on of the two parties to the transfer. Unlike in the case of original acquisition, when the act of first possession changes *everyone's* rights and duties, an act of transfer has very little effect on the rights and duties of third parties—they still owe the same duty to <the owner> not to enter the land or touch the object they owed before the transfer. The only difference is that the person to whom they owe that duty—the owner—changes.[82] That difference does matter, for instance, if a third party would like a licence to use the property. But in general third parties are not able to know definitively who owns most things, so a change in ownership does not have a particularly significant effect. The parties whose interests matter most in understanding transfer are the parties to the transfer.

In the light of that, we can see that the donor's merely having the intention to make a gift (or wanting to do it, or dreaming about it[83]) is insufficient to complete the gift. The donee cannot have access to the donor's subjective mental states, and

[81] In the common law, gifts are presumed to be accepted, but they can be disclaimed. In most civilian systems, affirmative acceptance is required: Richard Hyland, Gifts: A Study in Comparative Law 484–95 (2009).

[82] This was a point emphasized by James Penner, The Idea of Property in Law (1997), in criticizing what he plausibly took to be the upshot of a Hohfeldian understanding of property law. In brief, since Hohfeld understands property rights as a collection of rights against particular persons, he seems committed to the view that, as one Hohfeldian put it, "What happens, for example, upon a so-called transfer of title to real property from A. to B. is, that the rights and other jural relations of A. in relation to his fellowmen with respect to the object transferred are extinguished or divested and that B. becomes invested with similar though not necessarily identical rights and other jural relations." See Walter Wheeler Cook, "The Alienability of Choses in Action" 29 Harvard Law Review 816 (1916). If that is the right analysis on the Hohfeldian account, then Penner is correct in thinking that it is a bad account, as it would seem to imply that my rights and duties change billions of times each day upon each transfer of property between two strangers to me. I've argued that Hohfeldians need not accept that conclusion, since the better view is that the duties can be understood to be owed to "the owner," whoever that may be—see my, "The Office of Ownership" 63 University of Toronto Law Journal 418 (2013) and "The Office of Ownership Revisited" 70 University of Toronto Law Journal 287 (2020)—but the details of that claim and of the disagreements between Penner and me need not detain us here since we both agree about the point as it's put in the text.

[83] See *supra* note 59.

it would be inconsistent with the equality of the parties for the transfer (and concomitant changes to legal relations) to take place, as it were, entirely within the donor's head. After forming the intention to make the transfer, the donor's next act might be to say something about it: "I plan to give you my car." Does such an utterance count? The law says it does not, and it is not hard to see why: does such an utterance mean that the car is meant to be the donee's at the time of the utterance? Or the next day? Or at some unspecified time in the future? There seems to be no way to know, or, more strongly, no actual fact of the matter that is equally available between the parties. (Perhaps the donor knows what they mean, but what they mean is once again entirely in their head.) Suppose that the donor is specific: "I will give you my car next Tuesday at noon." And then suppose something unexpected happens, either under the control of the donor (they decide to take that long-awaited drive to the Grand Canyon) or not (the car is struck by lightning), and suppose it happens on Monday. What happens on Tuesday? Depending on how you think about the transfer, things can get pretty complicated. But the law avoids a lot of problems by saying that the transfer can only be said to be completed when the donee actually is in possession of the property. We saw in §4.3 that there is nothing magical about actual physical possession in the law of property, and that its apparent importance is derivative. The same point applies here: possession is the test only because it is the clearest and most salient point at which both the donor and donee can ordinarily understand the transfer to have been completed. Once you hand the car over, I know, and you know, that it is my car.[84]

One implication of that story is that parties should be able to identify the relevant moment of transfer in other ways than actual physical delivery: just as in the case of first possession, physical possession is merely a tool for understanding a more basic normative or legal idea centered on manifesting the intention to exercise the relevant legal power, in that case acquisition and in this case alienation. Now I am sure you will be quite as pleased as I was to learn that, indeed, that is the law. It has been settled for hundreds of years that certain symbolic acts—what Grotius called "mute signs"[85]—can count as delivery, as when the passing of a key to a piece of property counts as delivery of that property.[86] And this position is continually affirmed even by courts, such as the one quoted at the start of this

[84] For a similar analysis, see Philip Mechem, "The Requirement of Delivery in Gifts of Chattels and Choses in Action Evidenced by Commercial Incidents" 21 Illinois Law Review 341, 348–49 (1926), along with the accompanying second and third parts of the same article, at starting at pages 457 and 568 of the same volume of the journal.

[85] Hugo Grotius, On the Law of War and Peace III.24.v and *passim* (1625). To the same effect is Raz's mention of "weighing of metal on scales and its transfer from buyer to seller . . . or walking along the borders of the land bought." See Joseph Raz, Practical Reason and Norms 100 (1999).

[86] *Smith v Smith* (1734), 2 Str. 955.

section, insisting on the delivery requirement. Immediately following the passage I quoted, the court continues:

> This case stands unchallenged and in no way qualified by any other decision; but there are authorities shewing what constitutes delivery. All the cases shew that, while delivery may be symbolic (e.g., by delivery of the key of a warehouse where goods were stored . . .), it must be such as to give complete dominion over the property to the donee.[87]

Leaving to one side the verbal gymnastics here,[88] the right way to read that passage is as saying that, in fact, delivery is not required, and that a completed gift is one that is sufficiently public and meets the formal requirements of irrevocability.[89] This has been rendered even more formal and legalized through the mechanism of the deed: a deed is a communication that, by being under seal, is deemed to be sufficiently public as to act as the relevant indication of the rights of the parties to the transfer. The operation of wills is to the same effect: a will is basically a deed that is treated as communicated, and thus as a deed, by the law only upon the death of the testator, and a will whose testator is living is juridically equivalent to an uncommunicated subjective intention, since all wills are revocable until death.

Three final points. The first is about the donative intent. It is a mistake to think that subjective intention to make a gift is a part of what constitutes gift giving. There is some controversy about this in the law, but to the extent that there are cases that require subjective intent as a matter of the actual *ratio* of the decision (which is not totally clear), those cases must be understood to be wrongly decided.[90] The second is about contracts, sales, and so on. There are, of course, a wide variety of contractual doctrines dealing with situations in which a contract involves a transfer of property from one person to another. Sometimes when I sell you something it can become yours upon signing the contract and sometimes it can become yours when you receive it. The contractual (and statutory)

[87] *Kingsmill v Kingsmill.*

[88] A delivery of a key is not, in idiomatic English, a delivery of the thing it unlocks. The court here thus really qualifies its earlier claim about delivery by showing that, sometimes, *not* delivering a thing "constitutes delivery" of it.

[89] The pure version of this point applies to part of the law we have not yet discussed, namely, intangible rights such as choses in action, some of which are transferred through a mere communication of the intention to do so, since any physical notion of delivery is unavailable. See Sarah Worthington, Equity 60–61 (2d ed 2006). Worthington suggests that this rule is "designed to meet the commercial needs of modern society," but it seems to me that the better explanation is that the converse is true, which is to say that older rules requiring actual delivery were designed to meet the (commercial and noncommercial) needs of pre-modern societies, where only actual physical delivery could sufficiently manifest the intention to transfer with sufficient publicity.

[90] For discussion, see Hyland, Gifts at 148–70. In some jurisdictions, donative intent is not a matter of subjective motivations, but a mechanism to distinguish gifts from loans or other transfers.

overlap complicates those cases to the extent that I cannot deal with them, because the ideas that constitute this body of law are sophisticated enough to allow for various deviations from the picture I draw here while maintaining a more fundamental consistency with the basic commitment as it applies to the contractual context. The third is about testamentary disposition. I take testamentary disposition to be a species of alienation and justified on the same grounds as other alienation.[91] However, I am attentive to the concern that testamentary disposition is a cause of significant inequality. This could easily be understood as an instance of the sort of structural problem I discussed in §§3.2–3.3. I mention the question of how to address this in §6.1.

4.5 Shared Ownership

The doctrines considered in the last four sections might be thought of as something like elaborations of the basic and necessary ways in which parties interact through the idea of yours and mine. I mean "basic and necessary" in the sense that a system of property could operate with only those doctrines (and could not operate without them). However, as I noted in §1.5, property is importantly a mechanism for the exercise of moral creativity, as we manipulate the idea of yours and mine to create new ways to act and relate to others. We can now turn to some doctrines that can be understood as the result of the exercise of such creativity.[92] These doctrines are optional in a quite specific sense: an institution of property might exist without anyone in it ever having invented them. There is nothing in the idea of yours and mine that counsels against inventing them, but if and when the subjects or officials of a system do invent them, as the subjects and officials of the common law invented various kinds of shared ownership, tenancies, and servitudes, the idea of yours and mine applies, which is to say that the doctrines must be structured to ensure that they allow parties to relate to one another on terms of equality.

A wide swathe of property doctrines can be usefully thought about as different instances of a broad, abstract, and inclusive idea of shared ownership.[93] Joint tenancy and tenancy in common (along with their American relatives, tenancy by

[91] For an argument to the same effect, see Paul Miller, "Freedom of Testamentary Disposition" in Simone Degeling, Jessica Hudson, and Iret Samet eds, Philosophical Foundations of the Law of Express Trusts (2024).

[92] H L A Hart refers to the elements of a category like this one, where the law allows its subjects to "realis[e] their wishes, by conferring legal powers on them to create, by certain specified procedures and subject to certain conditions, structures of rights and duties within the concrete framework of the law," as "amenities." See H L A Hart, The Concept of Law, 27–28, 96 (2d ed 1994).

[93] For a similar thought, developed rather differently, see Gregory S Alexander, "Governance Property" 160 University of Pennsylvania Law Review 1853 (2012).

the entirety and community property, which I will not mention outside these parentheses) are instances of ownership which is shared concurrently.[94] In these cases, two (or more[95]) people are both at the same time owners of the land in the sense that they both have what is called a "present possessory interest," so that they can concurrently exercise all the elements of ownership discussed so far. That is, they can both make claims in trespass, extend licences to third parties, and so on. There are rules about how such arrangements are created, and in particular about whether one or another of them has been created in a given instance. These rules need not detain us here; the core idea in the creation context is a requirement of publicity of notice, such that all affected parties can relate as equals with respect to what is going on in terms of the creation of these interests, know what they have and what others have, and so on. Importantly, by "all affected parties," I mean the co-owners themselves, since an important feature of all forms of co-ownership is that they are (as I will put it) opaque to third parties, in the sense that a third party's rights with respect to co-owned property are not affected by the fact that it is co-owned: co-owners are "*vis a vis* the outside world, one single owner."[96] This is of course important from the point of view of ensuring that any co-ownership arrangement is consistent with the equal standing of these third parties: it would not be acceptable for a group to be entitled to subordinate third parties by creating some co-ownership arrangement for themselves.

The interesting question about concurrent ownership is about how the parties relate to one another. If you and I are concurrent owners, we each have the right that others not enter our land without a licence. But I do not have that right against you, and you do not have it against me. Generally speaking, you and I can each use our land for whatever purposes we like, just as a sole owner does. But the law insists on the reciprocity of the relationship and preserves it by ensuring that neither you nor I may use the land in a way that amounts to a dispossession or, as the law says, "ouster" of the other, which is to say by using it in a way that is inconsistent with the other's status as owner. Importantly, this is a legal, rather than factual idea, so that, for example, one co-owner installing locks on the door to keep out third parties does not count as ousting the other, unless and until they keep the other owner out.[97] And it is a high bar, in the sense that, if I choose

[94] See, e.g., *Hansen Estate v Hansen*, 2012 ONCA 112.

[95] Co-ownership can be iterated to allow for more than two owners. To keep things simple and clear, I'll discuss only the two-party cases. But everything I say can be applied, *mutatis mutandis*, to cases with three or more co-owners.

[96] *Hammersmith & Fulham LBC v Monk* [1992] 1 AC 478, 492 (HL).

[97] *Jacobs v Seward* (1872), LR 5 HL 464; *Daly v Brown* (1907), 39 SCR 122. The same rules apply to co-owned objects: *Rourke v The Union Insurance Company* (1894) 23 SCR 344. What precisely amounts to ouster is not possible to describe in the abstract, but will require a reasonability standard akin to the one we saw in nuisance.

not to use the land because I no longer want to see you, you will not be said to have ousted me; instead you need to take some positive step to dispossess me in order to be liable for ouster.[98] That said, if I use the land to generate profits, then you have a claim against me to a share of those profits. These rules, it seems clear, are meant to ensure that neither you nor I can subordinate the other with respect to our co-owned property, so that we can relate as co-owners of it on terms of equality. This egalitarian relation between co-owners is the central feature of co-ownership understood as a development of the idea of yours and mine along the lines introduced at the start of this section: once legal systems allow for any form of co-ownership, such a form must be egalitarian in this sense.[99]

A different kind of co-ownership is co-ownership across time.[100] The law allows you and me to both be owners of the same bit of land consecutively rather than concurrently, so that you can be present owner and I future owner. In such a scenario, I have no present right to enter or use the land—if I did so without your leave, it would be a trespass—but nevertheless, as we can put it, I am *now* the owner of the-land-in-the-future.[101] If you promise to sell me land, then we can predict that in the future I will own it and I might even in some circumstances have a legal right that at some point in the future you make me its owner. But in the cases that are now our target, I am already the owner of the-land-in-the-future.[102] The problem of your and my relation here is different than in the concurrent ownership case. You, as present owner, are permitted to use the property as if it were yours, and such uses might extend to using it in a way that damages or even destroys the object, so that when my time to be present owner comes along, there is nothing left for me to own. The law here imposes a rule—and has done so since the twelfth century—that you may not "waste" the property. The doctrine's insistence on an egalitarian relation between successive owners can almost be read off of its face: you must not cause damage that is excessive or unreasonable to the property, either affirmatively (i.e., by intentionally damaging it) or

[98] *Wiseman v Simpson*, [1988] 1 WLR 35.

[99] For a more general discussion about co-ownership that is egalitarian in this way, see Yara Al Salman, "Independence in the Commons: How Group Ownership Realises Basic Non-Domination" in Michael Bennett, Huub Brouwer, and Rutger Claasen eds, Wealth and Power: Philosophical Perspectives 207 (2022). As Al Salman's discussion makes clear, there are important overlaps between private forms of co-ownership and public ownership, in particular in the egalitarian form of relation that is appropriate to each. However, public ownership has other important features to be discussed in chapter 7.

[100] For a similar line of thought developed differently, see Yael R Lifshitz, Maytal Gilboa, and Yotam Kaplan, "The Future of Property" 44 Cardozo Law Review 1443 (2023).

[101] *Stuartburn v Kiansky* (2001), 155 Man R (2d) 35 (QB).

[102] It is this element of the common law's system of future interests that brings it within the purview of this part of the chapter. Of course it's necessarily true that someone will own any land I own after I own it: the land isn't going anywhere and eventually (or ultimately) I am. But it's not necessary that they own the land-in-the-future *now* or that there's any connection at all between present and future owners. Only with such a connection do the considerations in the text become relevant.

permissively (by failing to perform reasonable repairs or otherwise unreasonably letting it fall into disrepair). The notion of reasonability is best understood here, as it was in nuisance law, precisely as saying that your obligations are just those that are consistent with your and my being able to relate on terms of equality as owners of the same thing.[103] One image that strikes me as helpful arises by noticing that, viewed abstractly, the idea of reasonability in the law of waste is just a temporal version of the spatial idea of reasonability in the law of nuisance, so that we can view our successors and predecessors in title as our neighbors in time. It may also be helpful to notice here the empirical asymmetry of this relation: the future owner, of course, cannot do anything to affect the present owner. Nevertheless, we can understand the relation as egalitarian in the sense that the present owner is not entitled to use what is theirs (i.e., the land now) in a way that subordinates the future owner's use of what is theirs (i.e., the land in the future). This is a helpful reminder that the idea of an equal relation that is present in the idea of yours and mine is an idea of nonsubordination that applies even in asymmetric contexts (as in the relation between the propertied and the homeless).[104]

This relates to one final point about concurrent ownership, especially as realized in its more developed forms, such as condominiums,[105] co-ops, and so on. Some of these forms involve express rules about the use of the property by co-owners, and from time to time the contents of these rules might appear to give one party power over others, as in a condominium corporation's board. I doubt that this is a problem for three reasons. First, the mere fact that one person has legal control over another's use of a space is not inegalitarian: as I have argued, if the terms structuring the relationship are sufficient, it can in fact be egalitarian in an important sense. Second, the law will restrict the contents of these kinds of rules in order to ensure that they never become subordinating in a problematic way: a condominium board, say, could never give itself the power to enter and use the units of other members of the corporation at will. Third, co-ownership in the common law has always included an as-of-right option to exit the co-ownership agreement through some form of partition, allowing a co-owner to

[103] See Robert Megarry et al, Megarry & Wade: The Law of Real Property 3-090*ff* (7th ed 2008). For an interesting discussion, see Thomas W Merrill, "*Melms v. Pabst Brewing Co.* and the Doctrine of Waste in American Property Law" 94 Marquette Law Review 1055 (2011). There are further questions about so-called ameliorative waste, which is about actions by a present owner that improve the value of the property while changing its character. I leave them to one side here.

[104] Another illustration of this is in its application to riparian rights cases: water flows in one direction and so the upstream owner is in a position to subordinate the downstream owner but the reverse isn't true. Nevertheless, the law applies an idea of equal (as nonsubordinating) relations to the situation in the riparian right.

[105] For general discussion of condominiums that fits the picture in this section, see Douglas C Harris, "Condominium: A Transformative Innovation in Property and Local Government" in Nicole Graham, Margaret Davies, and Lee Godden eds, The Routledge Handbook of Property, Law, and Society 113 (2023).

become a sole owner of some share of the co-owned property.[106] This means that any substantive rules are importantly optional and voluntary so that the equality of the parties is conserved.

4.6 Tenancy

This model of co-ownership can help us to frame another important part of property law, namely, landlord-tenant law. A tenancy is, in effect, a special kind of co-ownership arrangement: the paradigmatic feature of a tenancy at common law is that the tenant has a property right in the lease,[107] which is to say that they have more than a right that the landlord allow them to stay there. Rather they have a right to exclusive possession against the world for a determinate time, akin to the right of an owner, that allows them to bring claims in trespass and nuisance and exercise the power to license entry.[108] In short, it is very plausible to think that a tenant can say of the leased space, "this is mine" in a way that is quite similar to the way that an owner can do so. At the same time, the landlord retains a property right of their own, called the reversion: because an essential feature of a lease is that it comes to an end, the existence of a lease necessitates the existence of the reversion. The tenant can say "this is mine" for the period of the lease and the landlord can say "this is mine" for the period after the lease ends. (And they can say that during the lease: the reversion is an example of the idea of the thing-in-the-future that I introduced in §4.5.)

A helpful way to think about the lease is therefore as what we will call an *artificial res*. We saw, in §4.2, how the law of nuisance works in part to constitute the legal boundaries of what we own, and there we introduced the idea of the res to give a name to the kind of legal object so constituted.[109] The creation of the

[106] See, e.g., *Partition Act*, RSO 1990 c P4.

[107] The granting of a lease is "properly a conveyance of any lands or tenements . . . for a less time than the lessor hath in the premises,"2 Blackstone 317, cited in 1 Tiffany, The Law of Landlord and Tenant at 159 / §16. So a lease is not merely a contract. A lease can be created gratuitously (1 Tiffany, The Law of Landlord and Tenant at 164 / §16) and, in fact, while almost all leases require rent as a matter of fact, the law does not seem to require rent. For example, Queen's Park, the park on which the Ontario Provincial Parliament stands, which is across the street from my office, is actually owned by the University of Toronto, and leased to the City of Toronto at a nominal rent for 999 years. See *An Act to authorize the Senate of the University* ***of*** *Toronto to appropriate certain Lands for the purposes of a Park, and to include the same within the limits of the City of Toronto, and to extend the Police regulations of the said City to the University Lands adjacent thereto* SC 22 Victoria Cap CX 1858. And for general discussion see Ben McFarlane, The Structure of Property Law 656–707 (2008), and Thomas W Merrill, "The Economics of Leasing" 12 Journal of Legal Analysis 221 (2020).

[108] *Lane v Dixon* (1847) 136 ER 311 (CP). Hiram H Lesar, "The Landlord-Tenant Relation in Perspective: From Status to Contract and Back in 900 Years?" 9 Kansas Law Review 369, 370 (1961): "Once the tenant for years had secured the benefit of ejectment, his position was as good as that of the owner of any estate in land."

[109] I will elaborate the idea of a res in much more detail in §5.4.

lease divides a single res, a single *this* to which an owner can refer in saying "this is mine," into two, the "leasehold" res that is the tenant's and the "reversion" res that is the landlord's. This phenomena helpfully illustrates the way that the res, the subject matter of the property right and the idea of yours and mine, is artificial not in the sense of fake, but in the etymological sense of a work of artifice, created by law. Without landlord-tenant law, there could be no such thing as a lease. I said already that the operation of the law of property means that even in the case of natural objects and spaces, ownership is fundamentally a legal matter, so that the legal object or legal space is not necessarily coextensive with the natural. Here the point is starker: the res is entirely a creation of law in a more robust sense. There is such a thing as an avocado absent property law. So the legal res that the avocado's owner has is a matter of law, but also closely based on the physical object that is owned. Here, since there is no such thing as a lease absent property law, the res is even more robustly a legally created entity, whose boundaries are much less dependent on the physical. One illustration of this point is the fact that leases can be granted for specific uses, so that a tenant may not have complete control over the leased space, but may instead only be permitted to do certain things there; "an exclusive right of occupation of the land, though subject to certain reservations or to a restriction of the purposes for which it may be used," is sufficient to create is a lease.[110]

This artificiality of the lease, we should note, is a neat illustration of the way in which property allows us to exercise our moral creativity. While property is a necessary constituent of a society of equals, leases are not. A society in which nobody ever thought of the idea of a lease could in principle be a society that achieved the ideal of a community of yours and mine. So leases are, in that way, optional. At the same time, we can see quite obviously why people did in fact think of the idea of a lease, why it might sometimes be helpful to be able to have a property right in a space for a limited time. Once this thought does arise as a result of an exercise of moral creativity, the egalitarian basis of the idea of yours and mine applies to it in two ways. The first is that the exercise of moral creativity itself must be permissible, because to disallow it without any reason would be to subordinate those who believe it to be helpful. That is, the open-ended nature of the idea of yours and mine is important in allowing each of us to use what is ours in whatever way we see fit as long as doing so does not subordinate others, and in this way creating a lease seems no different than making guacamole in the sense that it should be allowed in principle.[111] But the second way that the egalitarian

[110] *Glenwood Lumber Co Ltd v Phillips*, [1904] AC 405, 408 (PC).

[111] There's an objection looming here, roughly that the *numerus clausus* principle limits the creation of property interests. In short, in most legal systems, there seems to be a more or less explicit norm that limits the capacity of individuals to create new forms of property right. So our capacity to exercise moral creativity in that way is, after all, limited. I think this is easy enough to explain, along the lines of the now well-known explanation offered by Smith and Merrill (see Thomas W Merrill and

basis of property applies is by conditioning the possible legal realization of the idea of a lease to ensure that actual leases do not result in the subordination of the parties to them. This has important doctrinal implications.

The first, which we saw already, is that a tenant is in a position very similar to an owner vis-à-vis third parties. For a tenant to be able to use the property as their own, they need to have the same rights in trespass and nuisance as owners: in short, "probably the most important attribute of a lease from the tenant's perspective is the transfer of in rem rights associated with ownership for the duration of the lease term."[112] This is the reason that a lease is, in the common law, fundamentally distinguished from a licence. A licence is a merely personal right whereas a lease is a property right. If a friend lets me stay at their home as a licencee, then I have no claim against you if you enter without permission, because my licence does not create a property right; it is a merely personal relation that affects only me and my friend. By contrast, if my friend leases me their home, it becomes, as far as you are concerned, my home, so that it is up to me whether you may enter. A more limited version of the same point applies if my friend transfers the property (voluntarily, through gift or sale, or involuntarily, through death or insolvency) to another: their successor-in-title is bound by the lease but not the licence. This is all explainable in terms of the idea of the artificial res: the lease creates two different objects of property, and my friend the lessor only has the reversion, and so can only pass the reversion to a third party, and vis-à-vis third parties, I as tenant can say that the leased property is mine during the term of the lease and thus that what happens to it is up to me. None of this is available in the case of the licence. These implications[113] are why the common

Henry E Smith, "Optimal Standardization in the Law of Property: The *Numerus Clausus* Principle" 110 Yale Law Journal 1 (2000)). In short, allowing individuals to create new forms of property off their own bat has the potential to make it too difficult for others to know what property rights are out there and, therefore, what obligations they have. As we saw in considering first possession, the relation between the way that property is good against the world and fair notice imposes requirements that the creation of new property rights be at least knowable to everyone. And a system that allowed new forms of property to be created willy-nilly would be in significant tension with these ideas. How precisely easy or difficult it turns out to be to create new forms of property and how many forms there should be—that is, questions of "optimal standardization"—turn on a variety of contingent factors that differ across societies, which is why some societies have more forms of property than others.

[112] Thomas W Merrill and Henry E Smith, "The Property/Contract Interface" 101 Columbia Law Review 773, 822 (2001).

[113] And others: for one, thing, most contemporary jurisdictions have tenant protection legislation that applies to tenancies but not to licences. For another, the fact that a tenancy is a property right has implications in tort law. For a case that illustrates the importance of this point by misunderstanding it, see *Canadian National Railway Co v Norsk Pacific Steamship Co*, [1992] 1 SCR 1021, a classic relational economic loss case. The defendant negligently damaged a bridge owned by a third party that was habitually used by the plaintiffs. On the classic—and correct—approach to the question, the plaintiffs had no claim, since they had merely a contractual licence to use the bridge and thus no *in rem* right in it that could ground a claim against the defendants, who were not a party to their contract. In her judgment, at 1138, Justice McLachlin dismissed the classic approach in part by dismissing the crucial distinction between a lease and a contractual right: "Someone who invests in

law insists on a stark division between lease and licence. The law's basic test here is just the application of the idea that a lease is exclusive possession for a term. That is, if the arrangement granted exclusive possession, it is a lease. If not, it is a licence.[114] Importantly, the law here tends to impose a relatively formalistic account of this distinction. What matters is not the words used by the parties but rather the actual legal rights created by their agreement. This important aspect of the law can be understood as an elaboration of the idea that what matters, again, is what is public as between the parties to the arrangement, and thus protective of the possibility of equal relations between them.

The requirement that leases be realized in a way that is consistent with the basic commitment also has important implications for the relation between landlord and tenant. One of these has to do with the kinds of implied terms, including the warranty of habitability, that play an important role in much contemporary residential tenancy law. The well-known decision in *Javins v First National Realty Corp* illustrates the idea:

> The assumption of landlord-tenant law, derived from feudal property law, that a lease primarily conveyed to the tenant an interest in land may have been reasonable in a rural, agrarian society; it may continue to be reasonable in some leases involving farming or commercial land. In these cases, the value of the lease to the tenant is the land itself. . . . in the case of the modern apartment dweller, the value of the lease is that it gives him a place to live. The city dweller who seeks to lease an apartment on the third floor of a tenement has little interest in the land 30 or 40 feet below, or even in the bare right to possession within the four walls of his apartment. When American city dwellers, both rich and poor, seek "shelter" today, they seek a well-known package of goods and services—a package which includes not merely walls and ceilings, but also adequate heat, light and ventilation, serviceable plumbing facilities, secure windows and doors, proper sanitation, and proper maintenance.[115]

Here I think the court gets things approximately right: the point of an apartment is to be "a place to live." Property is meant to allow us to relate on terms of

a bridge in order to use it cannot be distinguished from someone who leases a bridge in order to use it. If the bridge is lost they have both lost something of value: the use of the bridge." Ignoring the fact that leases have *in rem* effect where licences do not on the basis of vague allusion to "value" is quite difficult to reconcile with large swathes of private law doctrine. For a defense of the classic view, see Peter Benson, "The Problem with Pure Economic Loss" 60 South Carolina Law Review 823 (2009).

[114] See *Street v Mountford* [1985] UKHL 4. For a critical, but still very clear, review of the common-law categories, see Note, "Tenant, Lodger, and Guest: Questionable Categories for Modern Rental Occupants" 64 Yale Law Journal 391 (1955).

[115] 428 F2d 1071, 1074 (DC Ct App 1970, note omitted).

equality with respect to space and tangible objects, and when it comes to residential space, having "a place to live" that is protected by the law of property as set out here—the law of trespass, licences, nuisance, and so on—is what is required to relate to others on terms of equality.

So we should understand the creation of a residential lease in these terms, and thus we should understand such leases to include implied covenants of habitability and quiet enjoyment as a matter of landlord-tenant law.[116] In *Javins*, the court insists that

> In order to reach results more in accord with the legitimate expectations of the parties and the standards of the community, the trend toward treating leases as contracts is wise and well considered. Our holding in this case reflects a belief that leases of urban dwelling units should be interpreted and construed like any other contract.[117]

While it is true that important terms of a lease can be understood as implied terms of the contract that created the lease, to think of the lease as purely contractual (as the *Javins* court does) strikes me as going somewhat too far, because among the central and most important features of a lease is precisely that it is not merely a contract. A contract is an *in personam* relation, like a licence, and a lease creates a property right. We saw earlier in this section that, since a lease involves the creation of an artificial res, successors-in-title to the landlord and tenant are bound (at common law) by the terms of the lease.[118] This matters practically because, were the terms of the lease merely contractual, successors-in-title to the original parties would (at least in many important situations) not be bound by them. To ensure that the lease terms can continue to protect tenants and to allow the parties to relate as equals through the idea of yours and mine, they need to be seen as terms of the conveyance.

To be clear: the claim here is not meant to denigrate the capacity of contract law to imply terms that are necessary to ensure that the parties to contracts can be said to relate as equals. The problem is broader than contract law can handle,

[116] *Javins* is still among the best discussions of the warranty of habitability. On quiet enjoyment, see *Southwark London Borough Council v Mills and others*, [1999] UKHL 40. And for an early application which accords very well with the analysis here see *Dyett v Pendleton*, 8 Cow 727 (NY 1826). I should also note that the argument in these pages can be extended to the case of commercial leases, with something like "making use of the space for human activities" substituted in for the idea of having a place to live. To the extent that there are genuine substantive differences in the law as between residential and commercial leases, they can be understood as developments of that basic difference.

[117] *Javins* at 1075.

[118] This is not quite right. The lease contract may include terms which, because they do not touch and concern the leased land itself, are merely personal contractual terms and so do not run with the land. But we can set that point aside, because the lease also contains terms which do run with the land and bind future landlords and tenants.

since it is possible for a landlord and tenant to end up in such a relation through noncontractual means, as when either party comes to hold their interest through insolvency or a testamentary disposition. In such a context, the parties would not be in contractual privity, so no contractual warranty of habitability could be implied. So the contents of the warranty of habitability need to be implied into the substance of the artificial res—the leasehold interest—itself. The permissibility of residential tenancies in a system of property understood as the realization of the idea of yours and mine requires the imposition of an implied warranty of habitability understood not merely contractually but as a part of the res that is created by the lease.[119]

There is another set of worries about the consistency of the landlord-tenant arrangement with the egalitarian basis of property law, circling around the fact that a lease necessarily ends and so can result in the eviction of a tenant who may have no other place to stay.[120] Some jurisdictions impose rules that protect tenants against no-cause evictions and give an automatic right to renew a lease. These are laudable and necessary: for a tenancy to do the job it does, the tenant must be a tenant, not a mere licencee. But the idea of a lease does bring with it the possibility of eviction at the end of the term, and so the possibility that a tenant may be evicted entirely unproblematically and left with nowhere else to live. This problem is structural in the sense I set out in §3.1, so we will postpone discussion of possible solutions until §6.5, when we discuss the public law of housing.

4.7 Servitudes

The central question of landlord-tenant law revolves around the difference between a lease, which is a property right, and a licence, which is not. A similar dynamic arises in a different set of contexts, too, where two owners enter into an arrangement in which each maintains possession of their own land while modifying the rights that they have *inter se*. This is the law of servitudes. Sometimes one owner will want a right to enter or use another's land in a way that

[119] John Gardner makes a somewhat similar claim, that we ought not to let the contractual relation between landlord and tenant crowd out the noncontractual relation. The worry, he says, is that "by giving succour to the idea that the [landlord-tenant] relation is *merely* a contractual one, [the law] has invited erosion of the distinction between [tenancy] and its absence. It has invited the exploitation of the plasticity of contractual relationships to create hybrid arrangements, some of them designed to subvert or evade the law's residual uses of the [tenant/licencee] distinction." See John Gardner, From Personal Life to Private Law 45 (2018). In the actual text of this passage, Gardner is talking not about landlord-tenant law but about employment law; the bracketed insertions are mine, taking a claim he makes about employer-employee relations and changing it to a claim about landlord-tenant relations, but it's clear from the text (e.g., at 44) that he sees employment as an instance of a broader phenomenon which also includes tenancy.

[120] Matthew Desmond, Eviction (2016).

they otherwise would not be allowed to do, say, to walk across it: such a right can be created as a personal right (a licence) or it can be created as a kind of property right, in which case it is called an easement. In a different kind of case, one owner might want a right that the other not use the other's land in a way they otherwise would be able to, say that the other not paint their house a certain color: again, this can be created as a personal right (typically a contract) or it can be created as a property right, in which case it is called a restrictive covenant. In both cases, the property-right version of the arrangement parallels one of the dynamics we saw in the tenancy context, in that the arrangement "runs with the land," which is to say that it continues to bind successors-in-title to the original parties even though they are not parties to the original (personal) agreement. In this section we will examine these doctrines. Before we proceed, a bit of terminology: in both kinds of servitudes, the land that benefits from the arrangement is called the "dominant tenement" and the land that is burdened by it is called the "servient tenement."

The essential feature of servitudes—that they run with the land—is what makes them an interesting topic of discussion. When you and I are neighbors, we each have some space that we can think of through the idea of yours and mine, and as we have seen, this means that we each have certain rights against the other (and others) that are realized through trespass, nuisance, licences, and so on. Moreover, the idea of yours and mine brings with it an idea that there is something, a res, that we can apply it to, something about which we can think "this is mine" or "this is yours." So we think about the space of my land as mine and the space of your land as yours. But we cannot simply think in terms of space; we need also to recognize the legal dimensions of the land, the way that nuisance (for instance) helps to determine what precisely we own when we own land. When we create a servitude—an easement or a covenant—what we are doing, I will now argue, is transforming the subject matter of our ownership: we are changing what it is that we own.

Take a right of way as an example. A right of way—the right for one landowner to cross another's land—is a familiar kind of easement. When you and I are neighbors, you normally have a right that I not enter your land without a licence. But if we create a valid right of way from my land across yours, then you no longer have that right. Instead, I am free to walk across your land along the path defined by the right of way. Your land, before the easement existed, included as a matter of law the right that I not enter it but, once the easement comes into existence, your land does not include the right that I not enter it (in that way, on that path[121]); conversely, my land, before the easement existed, does not include as a matter of law any privilege to walk across your land but, once the easement comes into existence, my land includes such a privilege (as well as a right that

[121] Questions arise about the scope of easements, about when the dominant tenement holder is or is not going beyond the right provided in the easement. These are important but not generally difficult, so I leave them aside here.

nobody, including you, unreasonably interfere with my exercise of the privilege[122]). The fact that a valid easement runs with the land and binds successors-in-title makes this point even clearer: your successor-in-title also does not have the right that I not walk across what is now their land, because when the land passed from you to them, it passed without that right, since that right is no longer part of the legal res that is the subject matter of the ownership of what we roughly think of as the land (and was the subject matter of the conveyance of property from you to them). This is a (rather long-winded, I guess) way of articulating the traditional idea that an easement must be appurtenant to the dominant tenement. An easement is not a free-standing property right, but rather needs to be understood as part of the dominant tenement, consistent with the idea that we transform both the dominant and servient tenement through its creation.[123] The same is true of covenants: a covenant requires some land that benefits from it. So where a lease creates a new res, a servitude reshapes a res (actually two res) that already exists.

The creation of a servitude legally reshapes the affected parcels of land by changing the rights associated with them in a way that affects not only the individuals who create the servitude, but everyone else, including, importantly, successors-in-title. This idea generates the two most prominent sets of rules in the law of servitudes. The first involves notice: because a servitude affects not only those who created it but also successors-in-title, there is a requirement that such successors be at least able to know about the servitude. How precisely that requirement is operationalized is pretty complicated and depends on a lot of details: there are different rules for easements and covenants, and for holders of dominant and servient tenements, and for different remedies (legal or equitable), and depending on whether (in the case of easements) the servitude came into existence as the result of some explicit agreement, or implicitly as part of another agreement, or through a process of prescription. Suffice it to say that these rules can be understood as different realizations of the same abstract

[122] An interference with the exercise of an easement is a nuisance: John Murphy, The Law of Nuisance 71–72 (2010).

[123] Failure to see this point can lead to all sorts of confusion, as when property theorists make claims about easements being a kind of property in the sense that an easement is a kind of thing one can own, just like land (or foxes or whatever) and thus a kind of counterexample to a Blackstonian view of property on which the essence of property in land is the so-called right to exclude, on the grounds that an easement is the right to use someone's land and not the right to keep anyone off. Moreover, the argument goes, "even if a right to be free from interference in the exercise of an easement were counted as an instance of the right to exclude"—which, I've gotta say, it definitely, definitely should be—"the role of that protection is clearly peripheral and secondary. The heart of the right-of-way is the simple freedom to cross" the other land (see James Y Stern, "The Essential Structure of Property Law" 115 Michigan Law Review 1167, 1187–88 (2017)). If an easement were considered to be a stand-alone right, this analysis would make some sense. But an easement is not like that at all: it isn't a free-standing thing that can be owned, but appurtenant to the ownership of some land.

notice requirements seen several times already as required by the idea of yours and mine.

The other doctrinal idea is more interesting here. In both kinds of servitudes, we find a kind of substantive restriction on validity. An easement cannot run with the land and affect the rights of future owners—and thus be comprehensible as transforming the substance of their rights as owners—unless it "accommodates" the dominant tenement.[124] And to the same effect, a covenant cannot bind successors-in-title unless it can be said to "touch and concern" the land in question, which is to say that it must "either affect the land as regards mode of occupation or it must be such as per se, and not merely from collateral circumstances, affects the value of the land."[125] The rough idea in both cases is that a servitude must be about the land, rather than merely about the persons who happen to inhabit it. One might think that this is simply a requirement that servitudes be impersonal, but the test is more demanding. An easement that allowed its holder to enter a popular attraction (a zoo, say) for free would increase the value of the land to which it was attached and so be of impersonal value. But it would not accommodate the land because it would be a benefit to the owner in their personal capacity rather than their capacity as owner. The point is even easier to see with covenants: a right that someone else not do something is always valuable to anyone, since at the very least it could generate a price to allow the other to do the thing.

Instead of being about personal vs impersonal, the requirement is more closely connected to the idea of yours and mine, in that it insists on a connection between the servitude and the res, the subject matter of the property right. The law looks to a kind of legal recognition of the value of property in land as a distinctive mode of relating to others, and requires that the servitude be connected to that. We can understand this as the recognition of the independence of the res from particular persons, of the idea that the subject of the property right exists independently of particular interactions between particular persons. So a servitude's validity turns on the possibility of our thinking about the new property-plus-servitude res as independent in that sense, and the law interprets this condition through a recognition of the social context in which we are taken to be able to understand that there is something that a piece of land is for *as such*, that there are rights associated with land as such.[126] It is those sorts of rights that can be the subject matter of a servitude.

[124] *Re Ellenborough Park*, [1956] 3 WLR 892 (CA).

[125] *Rogers v Hosegood*, [1900] 2 Ch 388, 395. See generally *Galbraith v Madawaska Club Ltd*, [1961] SCR 639.

[126] This point parallels the one we saw in discussing nuisance, that part of what the law does there is help to construct the contents of a legal idea of what the res is: in the *Fearn* case for instance, the court seems, with the *Javins* court, to recognize that part of what land is (at times) is a place to live, and so purely intangible effects that interfere with the possibility of using land in that way can be nuisances. In these doctrines, the law is constructing a legal notion of what property in land is that is not necessarily coextensive with the physical notion of land.

Notably what satisfies this test will be a matter of some socially determined contingency. Historically, as we saw in discussing leases, English law tended to see land as being primarily about economic benefits, and so rights of "mere recreation" were said to be unable to qualify as easements.[127] More recently, the UK Supreme Court relaxed this requirement by noting that "recreational and sporting activity . . . is so clearly a beneficial part of modern life that the common law should support structures which promote and encourage it, rather than treat it as devoid of practical utility or benefit."[128] Among the many good things property allows us to do—far beyond merely participate in economic activity—is engage in recreation, and so the addition of the use of a servient tenement's recreational facility can, we now think, be said to make a dominant tenement a better piece of property.[129]

I should briefly discuss one other issue here, namely, the question of discriminatory covenants. This is something that receives a lot of attention in the literature on restrictive covenants. And basically everyone agrees that a discriminatory covenant—one that purports to prohibit transfer of property to a particular class of persons—is invalid. The question is why. I think there are (at least) two different things going on. The first is that, as the Supreme Court of Canada's leading case on the question makes clear, discriminatory covenants are not valid because no servitude whose content involves the personal characteristics of individual persons can be valid.[130] Such personal characteristics cannot have the requisite degree of independence for them to be able to form part of the construction of a res: the whole point of servitudes is their impersonality in precisely this sense. The second thing that is going on is more diffuse: there seems to be a commonality between a concern about a discriminatory covenant and, say, a concern about a discriminatory contract (that does not involve property at all), the latter concern evidenced by various contract law doctrines of public policy. That is, there is a concern about the discriminatory exercise of any number of private law powers. But there is a range of plausible explanations of this latter concern, ranging from a moral prohibition on discrimination to a concern about the "honor of the court" asked to enforce them, and beyond. Exploring all of these would take us too far afield, especially given that the more basic explanation I just mentioned is sufficient to address the actual problem.

[127] *Ellenborough Park.*

[128] *Regency Villas v Diamond Resorts,* [2018] UKSC 57, [81].

[129] There are some kinds of easements that seem almost per se valid and don't require anything like the sort of social inquiry familiar from *Ellenborough Park* or *Regency Villas.* If one parcel of land is subdivided into two, with one of the new parcels completely surrounding the other, the law will imply the creation of a right of way from the inside parcel across the outside to a public road, to ensure that the owner of the inside property can come and go.

[130] *Noble et al v Alley,* [1951] SCR 64.

5
Property within Private Law

5.1 Me and Mine

In this chapter, we will turn to a different set of questions about property law—questions about the place of property within private law and about the relations between property and the other departments of private law. Where chapter 4 showed how understanding property as the realization of the idea of yours and mine can illuminate the basic doctrines of property law, my task in this chapter is to show how the same notion can illuminate these somewhat more abstract questions. In §2.2, I said that we can think about an institution of property as the law of yours and mine: here that same form of words has a slightly different meaning. It allows us to distinguish property rights from personal rights and from contract rights. Later on, we will also see how to think about so-called novel property claims, cases in which a court is asked to determine if someone has a property right in a context where property has not been previously recognized.

My core thesis will be that property rights, distinctively, are realizations of the idea of yours and mine. In slightly more depth, the thought will be this: as we have seen, the idea of yours and mine brings with it the requirement of a res, that is, the requirement of a subject matter with a kind of independent existence. As the House of Lords put it in a well-known case, property "has an existence independent of a particular person."[1] This independence cuts in both directions. There is independence from the holder. When I point to some *this* and say "this is mine," I am employing a form of thought that commits me to understanding that this might be yours: there is nothing special about me. In this way, property rights can be distinguished from personal rights. But there is also independence from those who owe corresponding duties. When I say "this is mine" to you, I assert a claim that does not depend on there being any transaction between you and me giving rise to my claim: there is nothing special about you (or perhaps better, about us). In this way, property rights can be distinguished from contractual (and other *in personam*) rights.

We will begin, in the next couple of sections, by thinking about the difference between property rights and personal rights, the rights I have over my person or, if you like, over what is me. We have already encountered some familiar such

[1] *OBG v Allan* [2007] UKHL 21, [309].

Property Law in the Society of Equals. Christopher Essert, Oxford University Press. © Oxford University Press 2024.
DOI: 10.1093/oso/9780197768952.003.0006

rights: for instance, we each have a right that others not touch us without consent, protected by the tort of battery. My rights to my person are necessarily always *my* rights to my person, whereas there is a clear sense in which my property rights are merely contingently mine and in which those rights would persist unchanged were they to become your rights instead. As we have seen, first in §1.5 and then several times since, in the case of property this contingency is based on the fact that the idea of yours and mine requires that there be *something* that is mine, some subject matter independent of me to which the idea can attach. The independence is associated, too, with the contingency of our holdings. As we saw in §4.3, property needs to be acquired. Your explanation for why it is that you have a right that I not interfere with this particular avocado always rests on a story about why it is *you* who has that right, since it might have been me or her or him or anyone else whose avocado it was. And as we saw in §4.4, the contingency of your acquisition is closely related to the contingency of your continued ownership: what is mine today might be yours tomorrow. By contrast, in thinking about personal rights, there is no such independent subject matter, the question of who holds the personal rights to a particular person just does not come up in the same way, since the subject matter of the right is the right holder itself.[2] The main legal upshot of this notion is the idea that we can alienate property, whereas our personal rights are inalienable. Notably, when such alienation takes place, the character of the rights acquired is just the same as the character of the rights alienated: they are simply the rights of the owner, and the only difference is the identity of the person to whom that label attaches.

Notice how, although it often tracks familiar empirical categories, this distinction is a legal one, and so one that cannot be reductively explained by reference to empirical factors. While we can get some grip on the way that the avocado I am handing you is different in an important sense than the hand I hand it to you with, it is relatively easy to think of cases that blur this line: while my hair is part of me, I could cut if off and sell it to you (as a wig, say) at which point it would be your property, no different, legally, than an avocado. (More on cases like that in §5.2.) I think it is not obvious that outsourcing the legal question to experts in the metaphysics of human bodies (or some such thing) will help with that case or more difficult cases like it. Moreover, it is not obvious that this would be the right move from the point of view of legal theory. The difference between property rights and personal rights is fundamentally a legal difference. And so it is a difference that we can and should understand by reference to the role that these two different kinds of rights play in our legal system and, through it, our social world.

[2] For intricate discussion of some of the ideas in this neighborhood, see Sean Aas, "(Owning) Our Bodies, (Owning) Our Selves" 9 Oxford Studies in Political Philosophy 213 (2023).

At this point, my story about property as the solution to the Problem of Yours and Mine should be familiar enough. So think for a moment about a parallel story we might tell about our personal rights, a story that would, you might say, tell us how those rights are a solution to the Problem of You and Me. Without these most basic rights to our own persons, such as rights that others not use our bodies without our consent, it would be impossible for us to relate as equals with respect to anything. Every interaction would simply be a matter of strength, of might rather than right. Relating as equals with respect to our persons means participating, on terms of equality, in those activities and relationships grounded on each having a right to their own person. These activities and relations are even more pervasive than those requiring property, since they involve everything we do—we literally cannot act except through our person. As Shiffrin puts it, a conception of the social world without this type of control over our persons would "render (morally) impossible real forms of meaningful human relationships and the full definition and recognition of the self (not to mention making medical and dental care cumbersome, dangerous, and awfully painful)."[3]

In the property case, we understand an idea of the independence and (thus) the alienability of the res to be inherent in the idea of yours and mine and inquire as to how it can be consistent with the basic commitment to equality. By contrast, we do not understand these more personal activities and relationships to presuppose any such notion of alienability or independence of right holder and subject matter. In fact, something close to the opposite is true: we take equal relations with respect to our persons to be important and valuable precisely because we understand the rights that constitute them to be inalienable. I do not—indeed, I think I *cannot*—understand my own person as something that exists independent of me: I am my person.[4] By contrast, I am not what I own and what is mine today might be yours tomorrow without anything else changing at all, and the possibility of that transfer is part of the point of having property.[5] Again, though, this is not a nonlegal point, but a point about the very justification of these different kinds of rights: I need to be able to give my property to others in order for property to do the thing it is meant to do, whereas I need to be unable

[3] Seana Valentine Shiffrin, "Promising, Intimate Relationships, and Conventionalism" 117 Philosophical Review 481 502 (2008). I also think this basic story can explain the heart of negligence law. I defend this thought in "The Value of the Neighbour Relation" in Haris Psarras and Sandy Steel eds, Private Law and Practical Reason (2023) 297.

[4] "We do not 'have' a body, rather we 'are' bodily": Martin Heidegger, *Nietzsche* 99 (David F Krell trans, 1961/1991). The difficulty of imagining one's own whole person as independent of one seems to me to parallel, in some way that I can't quite pin down, Freud's claim that "it is indeed impossible to imagine our own death; and whenever we attempt to do so we can perceive that we are in fact still present as spectators." Sigmund Freud, "Thoughts for the Times on War and Death" (1915).

[5] Notice the word "possibility": surely it's true that some rights that are independent of their holders in the relevant sense are not alienable because of some constraint imposed upon them, but that does not mean that they do not count as property.

to give my rights over my person to others for those personal rights to do the thing that they are meant to do. Again, the point is not merely that the value of our rights to our persons is not grounded in alienability; the point is that it is grounded in inalienability. The activities and relationships that we enter into with others on terms of equality with respect to the control that each has over their person matter to us precisely because we are our own persons, there is no "space" or independence as there is between owner and res, so each has that control over our person in an inalienable way.

Here is perhaps a simpler way to put the point. We saw in chapter 2 that the possibility of property's being consistent with the basic commitment required property rights to be alienable, so that they can satisfy the requirement that, as a position conferring rights over others, they be "open to all under conditions of fair equality of opportunity."[6] An institution that allowed some but not others to have rights in property, that limited the way that such rights were transferable from one to another, would seem straightforwardly to be a caste system—as literal a system of "haves" and "have-nots" as could be conceived—and, therefore, clearly inconsistent with the basic commitment.[7] But in the case of our personal rights, the basic commitment works in just the opposite way: rather than seeing the "position" of "holder of the rights over my person" as open to all, we need to see it as open only to me, because allowing any other person to hold it would (in light of the kinds of creatures we are) give them a kind of control over me that is radically inconsistent with the basic commitment. Allowing one person to have "property" in another's person is the most egregious form of subordination humans have invented. To say that one person could own another, to say that the one could have complete control over the other as the master has over the slave, would be to propose an arrangement as radically inconsistent with the basic commitment as could be conceived. Property in persons could thus never be permissible in a system of property in a society of equals.

Now I want to develop the thought that the inalienability of personal rights is, to adopt (and adapt) a different Rawlsian catchphrase, legal rather than metaphysical. In saying that, I want to situate my view between, on the one hand, arguments that see a complete determinate account of inalienability as in some way provided by our concepts or our metaphysics independent of the law, and, on the other, arguments that see it as an unstructured and unconstrained "policy" choice. The latter contrast is easier to see. There are those who think, often under the influence of a kind of law-and-economics-gone-wild, that the inalienability of personal rights is merely a contingent matter, and that, were certain facts

[6] The phrase is (still) from John Rawls, A Theory of Justice, rev ed 266 (1999).

[7] To the same effect, Singer locates a central part of the value of property in what he calls an "antifeudal principle." Joseph William Singer, No Freedom without Regulation: The Hidden Lesson of the Subprime Crisis (2015).

about people's preferences, transaction costs, or whatever slightly different, we might think ownership of entire persons to be permissible.[8] This is just not at all a reasonable view. It is more like a *reductio* of that way of thinking about legal rights.[9] As I just noted, the prohibition against slavery is as close to an axiomatic part of a democratic legal system as we could imagine, and to say that it is a contingent matter that depends on the aggregated preferences of individuals is to fundamentally misunderstand the entire point of a legal order.

On the other side of the aisle, some have thought that denying the "policy" argument requires committing to the view that inalienability of personal rights is metaphysical (in a non-legal sense). There is something to this thought, but it needs to be developed carefully, to ensure that it does not turn into a view on which the law simply takes as given some nonlegal account of the distinction. Beings constituted as we are could not treat their entire bodies as alienable, such that you and I could exchange bodies; our bodies just lack that sort of independence from us. Still, that is not enough on its own to explain why I could not be the one to determine how your person (along with my own) is to be used. Slavery is wrongful but (given that it is actual) it is not impossible. Put differently, we can agree that persons are not ownable, but it seems like that agreement is grounded on the basic commitment (or something very like it), not on the nonnormative metaphysics of persons, or on the features of the concept *person*.[10] That is, I doubt that any amount of reflection on non-normative, nonlegal metaphysics or concepts is going to generate an account of the scope of our rights in our persons or a conclusion that property rights and personal rights are different.[11]

[8] Guido Calabresi and A Douglas Melamed, "Property Rules, Liability Rules, and Inalienability: One View of the Cathedral" 85 Harvard Law Review, 1089, 1111 (1972).

[9] Margaret Jane Radin, "Market Inalienability" 100 Harvard Law Review 1849, 1865–66 (1986).

[10] The contrast here is with James Penner, who claims that there is a "conceptual criterion" that marks a boundary between property rights and personal rights. He goes on to say that it is "impossible to conceive of certain rights as property rights," because "one cannot conceive of how such rights could be *separated* from one—they are the constitutive rights that being a person entails having." See James E Penner, The Idea of Property in Law 113–14 (1997). G A Cohen accuses Kant, in arguing that we do not own ourselves, as "trying to pull a normative rabbit out of a conceptual hat." Self-Ownership, Freedom, and Equality 212 (1995). To the same effect is Jeremy Waldron, The Right to Private Property 33 (1991). In fact, Kant's argument that slavery contracts involve a kind of conceptual confusion is, as Ripstein puts it, "an implication of the moral nature of rights," which is to say that it's a legal argument in the sense I am articulating in the text (although it's also metaphysical in Kant's sense). See Arthur Ripstein, Force and Freedom: Kant's Legal and Political Philosophy 134*ff* (2009); and Kant, The Metaphysics of Morals 6:241 (1797). One way to characterize things to which I am sympathetic is to say that slavery is juridically or morally impossible. See, for instance, Ernest J Weinrib, Corrective Justice 142 (2012).

[11] The opposition between those who think about inalienability in purely conceptual or metaphysical terms and those who think about it in legal or moral terms is found in the case law around the possible ownership of professional degrees or licences. Such cases typically involve one party claiming on divorce that their spouse's MBA or dental licence is marital property to be divided upon dissolution of the marriage. Generally, courts have refused to endorse claims of this type, on the grounds that the licence is inalienable. Some courts seem to have viewed this as a conceptual claim, whereas others have seen it as more akin to the legal/moral argument about slavery in the text. For the former view, see *Caratun v Caratun*, 10 OR (3d) 385 (Ct App 1992); and for the latter, see *Severs v*

5.2 Bodies and Their Parts

We arrived at the thought that we have inalienable personal rights to our persons, which contrast formally with our alienable property rights. This inalienability is the legal implication of the fact that, in the property context, the right is with respect to a res that is independent of its owner, whereas, in the personal rights context, there is no such independence between person and right holder. So far, I have concentrated on the very core case of personal rights, which is to say the right that each of us has in their whole integral person: to say that this right is inalienable is to say that I cannot make myself someone's slave, that I cannot make myself into property. We will turn now to some more difficult cases, cases about the possibility of ownership of particular bits of individual bodies.

As we proceed, we should remember that, although we will need to engage in some casuistry, it will be structured by the distinction between the abstract categories. That is, while "there will be hard cases the courts need to adjudicate, . . . the moral concepts themselves are capable of doing" an important part of the work in that adjudication.[12] We need to understand the borderline cases under the guise of the abstract distinction between the two categories. And that abstract distinction allows us to clearly articulate an explanation for classifying a given case in one or the other category. Indeed, the indeterminacy of the borderline cases is interesting not because there is nothing to say about what category they should fit into, but rather because there is often a compelling case to be made for each of the two categories.

In law and morality, we tend to think of our bodies as integral wholes, which is just to say that my right to my person protects all the parts of my body not as parts but just as "my person". That means that a wrongful interference with any attached part of me is a wrongful interference with me. I do not have my hands or hair or kidneys. Instead, they (together with all my other parts) constitute my person (in law). As the House of Lords put it, in holding that someone who committed a robbery with his hand positioned within his pocket to create the appearance of a handgun did not commit robbery in possession of an imitation firearm, "One cannot possess something which is not separate and distinct from oneself. An unsevered hand or finger is part of oneself. Therefore, one cannot possess

Severs, 426 So. 2d 992 (Fla Dist Ct App 5th Dist 1983). While this contrast is interesting, in my view, as I suggest in the last paragraph of §5.5, these licences are not property for a different reason, which is that they do not provide a right to determine the permissibility of others' conduct. Instead, they are (Hohfeldian) liberties to do things which would otherwise be prohibited, and as such cannot ground relations through the idea of yours and mine. Thus even alienable licences, for example to operate a taxi service or radio station, or to fish, do not count as property rights.

[12] Arthur Ripstein, "Embodied Free Beings under Public Law: A Reply" in Sari Kisilevsky and Martin J Stone eds, Freedom and Force: Essays on Kant's Legal Philosophy 183, 190 (2017).

it."[13] What goes for hands goes for hair or kidneys or any other part. While these things are unseparated parts of our bodies understandable as integral wholes, they lack the requisite degree of independence to count as a res, so our rights to them are personal and not proprietary.[14] The legal upshot of this is that they are protected by those torts that protect personal, rather than property rights. Someone who sneaks up behind you and cuts off part of your hair and runs off with it has committed a battery rather than a trespass.[15]

More interesting and difficult questions arise when we ask about things that once were, but no longer are, parts of integral human bodies. Discussions of our subject matter here often focus on emerging technologies—we can do live donor transplants of kidneys, livers, and many other body parts and tissues—but the practice of one person taking and using a part of another person's body is nothing new: wigs have been made of human hair for thousands of years.[16] By contrast with our full, integral bodies, detached individual body parts on their surface look and act, from the point of view of the law, like any other tangible physical object. There is no difference in the legal treatment of a wig made from human hair and a wig made from synthetics. Or, for that matter, a hat. In any of these cases, we can point to an object—the wig, the hat—and unproblematically employ the forms of thought grounded on the idea of yours and mine. I can say "that is my wig," or "would you like to borrow my wig?" It is something that I own because I acquired it, and that I could give to you such that your relationship to it would be just the same, in terms of its legal character and justification, as my relationship to it was when it was mine.

So it is possible for us to relate to one another through the idea of yours and mine with respect to objects that once were, but no longer are, parts of human persons. The way we relate with respect to these objects is essentially no different than the way we relate with respect to any other tangible objects. Once detached, my hair, which was a part of me, is no longer a part of me, and so merely mine (or yours). It is also possible to illustrate this contrast in terms of the way that the wrong in property can sometimes be seen as a kind of deprivation, or perhaps taking. By contrast, in the personal rights case, the idea of deprivation seems less directly applicable: I can act inconsistently with your rights over your person but it not clear that in so doing I deprive you of anything. Notice that, while the legal distinction seems to turn on an empirical distinction, the empirical distinction is not directly grounding the legal distinction. Rather the particular distinction is

[13] *R v Bentham*, [2005] UKHL 18 at [8].

[14] For a different view, see Amitpal Singh, "The Body as Me and Mine: The Case for Property Rights in (Attached) Body Parts" 66 McGill Law Journal 565 (2021).

[15] Recall from §4.1 that I won't distinguish among intentional property torts.

[16] J S Cox, "The Construction of an Ancient Egyptian Wig (c.1400 BC) in the British Museum" 63 Journal of Egyptian Archaeology 67 (1977).

grounded on a legal argument concerning the abstract distinction between two sorts of rights, which abstract distinction is then brought to bear on the particular empirical facts to draw the line in the case. As we will see, the legal distinction need not be exactly coextensive with the empirical.

One question that arises pretty quickly from acceptance of these points is about what we might call "the transition." The hair that makes up the wig and thus the subject matter of a property right was at some earlier point hair that was part of someone's body and thus the subject matter of a personal right. How did it get here from there? The obvious answer is this: when my hair was detached from me, it ceased being a part of my person. In fact, I think that is correct, but not for the reasons it seems to be. To see why, consider a different case: while rebuilding the garage, I cut my finger off with a table saw. My finger is thus detached from me. Suppose you happen upon the scene and grab the detached finger and run off with it. Have you committed battery (a personal wrong) or conversion (a property wrong)? The answer, I want to say, is not obvious.[17] I have a strong intuition that the finger is, although detached, still a part of me. One important fact that grounds that intuition is that, as I am imagining the case, the finger might be reattached to me, and thus once again be part of the integral whole that is my person. By contrast, the hair that is cut off my head can no longer be reattached. Even if I were to gather the hair and make the wig myself, styling it so that, once I put the wig on, I looked just the same way that I did when the very same hair was attached to my head, my relationship to the hair is not the same as it was when it was growing out of my head. Then it was me, now it is mine.

Sticking with the hair case for a moment, saying that the hair enters the world of property because it cannot be reattached still does not provide a complete account of the transition, because we do not yet know *how* it does so. I am inclined to think that the cutting off of hair is, to the law of property, analogous to the birth of a wild animal or the landing on earth of a meteorite: it is a physical process by which something ownable comes into existence. Before this fox was born there was nothing to catch and so nothing to own; after its birth whoever catches the fox owns it. Similarly, before the hair is cut off there is nothing to be owned, but once it is, the hair becomes an ownable object, acquirable according to relevant norms of acquisition.[18] How and when exactly this happens cannot, like much of the subject matter here, be stated determinately in the abstract. There seem to be two options. One treats the hair as what we might call utterly

[17] In thinking about what follows, I've been immensely assisted by Japa Pallikkathayil, "Persons and Bodies" in Kisilevsky and Stone, Freedom and Force 35.

[18] There is a line of thought in the English law, I suspect traceable to a confused reading of Locke, that requires that biological material be modified by "work and skill" before it can count as property: see *Doodeward v Spence* (1908) 6 CLR 406. But this can't work: surely the wigmaker's boxes (bags? bushels? buckets? bales?) of raw materials are his property just as much as the completed wigs are.

unowned, so that whoever satisfies the relevant test of first possession (as in §4.3) becomes its owner. Here, if I pick your hair up off the floor of the barber shop, it becomes mine. The other option gives the person whose hair it was a kind of right of first refusal, so that prima facie it is presumed to be their property.[19] This right is then paired with a recognition of the role of abandonment, so that most of the time we are properly understood through our treatment of hair, fingernail clippings, and so on, to be communicating an intention to abandon any property right we might have.[20] As for which option to prefer, the question seems to be a matter of institutional discretion. Note, importantly, that either view is easily able to account for the wrong in the well-known case of Henrietta Lacks or the *Moore* case.[21] The fact that a detached body part is ownable does not mean that wrongfully detaching it, or detaching it without the right kind of consent, can have no implications for the relationship of the detacher and the person whose part it was. Performing an operation with the intention to use removed tissues without the relevant consent is (at least) an instance of battery, the remedy for which should be tied to the use of the parts after they are removed.

Let us return to the more abstract question about the transition. The treatment of the hair and finger cases might make things seem like they turn on the single question of the possibility of reattaching the part to the body of which it was originally a part. But even that is too simple. Consider the case where you experience kidney failure and I agree to—notice this word!—donate one of my kidneys to you. I assume that, once the relevant medical operations are complete and the (alien) kidney is inside you, we will want to say that it is protected by your right to your person, that it is not yours but rather a part of you. So the kidney that was part of me (but not mine) becomes part of you (but not yours). What about during the transfer? When the kidney is moving through space in the operating room from my body to yours, should it be regarded as property? Here, again, I think things are not obvious. It is possible to say that the kidney is not property in this case, that it went from being part of my person to being part of yours without ever passing through the law of property, so that a wrongdoer who burst into the operating room and took the kidney would be committing

[19] Notice the way this relates to the discussion of acquisition in §4.3: there I claimed that there is nothing a priori about the rules of first possession that we have. Here I am articulating the possibility of a case in which the rule for acquisition is different than it is in the basic case. In both cases, the different rules are answering the same very abstract question about how to get a particular thing into the system of property, and answering it in different ways based on the particular context.

[20] Simon Douglas and Imogen Goold, "Property in Human Biomaterials: A New Methodology" 75 Cambridge Law Journal 478, 498–502 (2016). I'm much indebted to the excellent treatment of English law in this article. But for skepticism about abandonment, see Konstanze von Schütz, "Keeping It Private: The Impossibility to Abandon Ownership and the *horror vacui* of the Common Law of Property" 66 McGill Law Journal 721 (2021).

[21] See Rebecca Skloot, The Immortal Life of Henrietta Lacks (2010); *Moore v Regents of the Univ of Cal*, 51 Cal 3d 120 (1990).

battery, rather than trespass. To make sense of that claim, we would need an account of whose person they were wronging that took account of where in the medical procedure we were, since *ex hypotheosi* the kidney is at one point part of me and then part of you. That might be hard, but the alternative view, on which the kidney is someone's property during the transition, needs to answer a parallel set of questions. Indeed it looks like on that view there are as many as three transitions (me->mine->yours->you) instead of one (me->you).

I think the same analysis holds for the detached finger: as long as it can be reattached to my hand, it should be regarded as a part of me rather than something that I own or possess.[22] We would most reasonably understand this situation as one in which the finger was not properly thought of through the idea of yours and mine. We do not think, that is, that you would wrong me by interfering with my capacity to participate in the kinds of activities and relations with others that are paradigmatic of property—including sharing, selling, and so on. We would not think, about the detached finger, that the finger is mine and it is up to me whether and under what circumstances to give or sell it to you, and that by taking it you acted in a way that was inconsistent with that. Rather we would think you interfered with a part of me. But you might think that things are different in the kidney case, that the wrong lies precisely in the interference with my attempt to make a transfer. Again, I think this is a plausible view, and all that is required here is that we settle things one way or the other as a matter of positive law. And so I think that nonlegal philosophical discussion here, about commodification and so on, is best understood to be about the reasons to settle things one way rather than the other. I take no position on that; my goal is merely to understand the private law structure.

One upshot of all of this is that we might properly regard some things that once were but no longer are parts of our integral person as nevertheless protected by our personal rights. This suggests the important point that our persons might extend beyond our bodies. How far can this principle stretch? Consider another case: *Yearworth*.[23] The case is about a group of men who, during the course of chemotherapy treatments which had the potential to harm their fertility prospects, had stored their sperm in the defendant's hospital facility for future use. The defendant negligently allowed the sperm to be destroyed. The men claimed for damages, and, simplifying slightly, the law of negligence requires plaintiffs in their position to show that they have some kind of right—either personal or property—that was infringed by the defendant's negligence in order to recover damages for the loss.

[22] According to this view, the claim from *Bentham*, that "an unsevered . . . finger is part of oneself" is true, but underinclusive: a severed finger might also be part of oneself.

[23] *Jonathan Yearworth and Others v North Bristol NHS Trust* [2009] EWCA Civ 37.

The English court considered both of the options. It noted that, in German law, the plaintiffs would have been held to have had a personal right in their sperm. That is, their personal rights would have in this case extended so far beyond their bodies as to include frozen biological materials stored in a location that could have been quite distant from the plaintiffs themselves. I do not find that position to be insupportable. The sperm is understood by all the relevant parties to be intended for reproductive use, which use in the "traditional," that is, non-technologically assisted, case has a legal character quite like the kidney transplant, where biological material goes from being part of one person to part of another (to, eventually, part of yet another) without ever being anyone's property. It is easy to think through a sequence of increasingly elaborate interventions in the reproductive process that might involve biological material spending some time not being a part of anyone's integral body (from at-home artificial insemination through intrauterine insemination [IUI] through live embryo in vitro fertilization [IVF] through frozen-embryo IVF, etc.), and it is not obvious that any of those cases is sufficiently distinct from the previous member of the sequence to mark the distinction that warrants the interposition of property law. (The English court glossed the German law as saying that reproductive tissues in cases like this "retained a functional unity with the body" of the person whose tissues they were.[24]) It is also worth noting that the German approach heads off the worry that denying property protection to tissues removed from the body means that they would be unprotected by law, simply by showing us that other forms of protection are available, at least in theory.[25]

Instead of taking the German route, the court rejected (as "a fiction") the idea that the plaintiffs could have a personal right in the sperm,[26] and took the other route, holding that the sperm was the property of the plaintiffs. In *Yearworth*, one of the men involved had died before the suit, and so his wife was suing in her capacity as the executrix of his will. But slightly modifying the facts so that the husband had died before the sperm was destroyed, we might wonder if a wife should be able to sue for the loss of a deceased husband's sperm in her own capacity, that is, as owner of the sperm (with plans to use it). Here, we cannot say that the damage infringes the husband's personal rights (as he has no such rights after death), and we clearly cannot say (yet) that the sperm is part of the wife's person, but we might think that the husband ought to have been able to

[24] *Yearworth* at [21].

[25] For an expression of that worry, see Simon Douglas, "Property Rights in Human Biological Materials" in Imogen Goold et al eds, Persons, Parts and Property, 89, 98*ff* (2014).

[26] *Yearworth* at [23]. I take it that the English court's assumption is that there is some fact of the matter, existing pre-legally, according to which the sperm could not be thought of as a part of the plaintiff, and so treating it that way amounts to doing something intentionally but permissibly false (i.e., fictional). As I note in the text, that's what I (and the German court) deny: we are making the determination of what the person is in deciding this case.

give (testamentarily) the sperm to his wife. That kind of giving requires treating the sperm as property.[27] Moreover, the justificatory story for that treatment is not entirely implausible: many people seem to view certain of their biological materials as res, as suitable subjects for sharing and giving, and would want to view their interests in those materials once removed from the body in those terms. That suggests a property treatment might be appropriate, although the questions about commodification and so on would need to be dealt with. This is a serious concern but it is not insurmountable. The law has the capacity to make certain goods giftable but not saleable, for example.

Another point is worth mentioning. These cases, taken together, suggest a variety of ways in which the line between personal rights and property rights is not, at least automatically, drawn in the same place as the line between our bodies and (if you like) the world. In particular, the German treatment of the *Yearworth* facts, and kidney transplant and severed finger cases suggest that our rights to our persons might extend beyond our integral bodies. Indeed, the German court based its decision on the idea that, with respect to the right to the person, "It is not the physical matter as such that is protected . . . but rather a person's entire area of existence and self-determination, which is materially manifested in the body,"[28] the idea that, at least in some circumstances, the control over our own persons that is necessary for equal relations with respect to our persons can extend beyond our physical bodies. The sperm in *Yearworth* was intended to be used not as an object distinct from the claimants but rather in just the same way that nonpreserved sperm is used, and so the German court's view is that it ought to be protected in that way.

How powerful is this idea in general? Notice that we can integrate things that are not parts of our bodies, as we might put it, under the cover of our personal rights. This was what happened in the kidney transplant. But it is also what happens when we have a pacemaker implanted, or, for that matter, whenever we eat. You commit a battery by removing my pacemaker because you need to open up my chest to do so. We might want to think the pacemaker counts as part of me when it is inside me, so that your interfering with it would be a battery even if done without otherwise interfering with the rest of my person. (Assume the existence of some philosophically conveniently arranged electromagnetic waves that could do this.) We can push things further. Consider the use of prosthetics or of other mobility-assistance devices such as mechanized wheelchairs.[29] We might want to view these objects as part of the person of those

[27] See also Imogen Goold and Muireann Quigley, "Human Biomaterials: The Case for a Property Approach" in Goold et al, Persons, Parts and Property 231, 252.

[28] Bundesgerichtshof (Sixth Civil Senate) 9 November 1993, BGHZ 124, 52, trans Snook (at https://germanlawarchive.iuscomp.org/?p=157).

[29] Or, more speculatively, certain culturally or religiously important clothing or accessories.

whose objects they are, even when not physically in contact with them, so that taking the wheelchair or prosthetic leg when its user was asleep would count as something more like battery than theft. Doing so seems, at least plausibly, more consistent with the best social understanding of these objects, as being more like the bodies of their users than like their property, in that they are not objects that are regarded by their users (nor should be regarded by the rest of us) as independent from them in the way that the subject of a property right needs to be, as something that might be theirs today and someone else's tomorrow, but instead as something necessary for participation by their user in essentially any action or relation with another.[30] Moreover, part of the explanation for this is the fact that were we to treat these things as property, we would be creating a problematic distinction between those who need prostheses and those who do not, such that those in the first category would not be able to understand their own embodiments as protected parts of their persons but rather as merely things that they happen to own.[31]

5.3 In Rem and In Personam

Recall that our project in this chapter is understanding the distinctiveness of property rights vis-à-vis other private law rights. The fact that my property rights have a certain independence from me, that the property I have is contingent, in a way, helps to draw the line between property rights and personal rights. But we need now to confront a different set of questions, because the rights that we have in contract and with respect to debts seem similar in that way: what contracts you have entered into or what debts you are owed are, like what property you own, contingent matters. So we need a different way to distinguish these rights from property rights. The familiar idea that is normally employed here is that property rights are *in rem*, whereas contract rights and rights arising out of debt (and perhaps other private-law rights) are *in personam*.

We can explore this. We have seen that when I own something, I have a right that nobody else interact with it in certain ways. My right to my avocado, as the expression goes, is "good against the world." By contrast, when you and I enter into a contract—say for you to sing a song about avocados in exchange for my dying your hair—the contract does not change the legal rights of others: nobody else has to sing me a song, nobody else is wronged if I choose not to dye your hair, and so on. Our rights are governed by the idea of privity of contract. The

[30] A lot might turn on that "essentially," and one might argue that its applicability could determine the right way to understand a particular case of this sort.
[31] Again, see Pallikathayil, "Persons and Bodies." See also Aas, "(Owning) Our Bodies."

in rem–in personam distinction also applies within property law. Most prominently, recall the distinction between leases and licences, discussed in §4.6. An important part of the law there is the way that licences are *in personam*, that is, not property rights, and leases are *in rem*, that is, a form of property. What do these terms mean, and how can they help us?

There is a huge volume of literature about this question. But I am going to try to avoid getting into its details, and instead just identify some very broad themes. Historically, the distinction traces back to some intricacies of Roman law and then, more specifically, to medieval England, when the law was governed by very strict procedural requirements associated with a system of "forms of action."[32] Roughly, in these contexts, there was an important distinction between cases in which one would bring a(n *in personam*) claim against a person for having done a wrong and cases in which one would bring a(n *in rem*) claim in respect of some specific object, like a cow.[33] Because of this, it is sometimes said that the Latin expression *in rem* means "against a thing," but as we shall see, that is probably not quite right.[34]

Moreover, in the nineteenth and early twentieth centuries especially, there was a move away from identifying *in rem* rights with things toward characterizing *in rem* rights in terms of the way in which they are good against the world. This view, among whose prominent proponents were Austin and Hohfeld,[35] notices the contrast between the way that *in personam* rights like contract rights bind

[32] F W Maitland, Equity, Also the Forms of Action at Common Law (1913).

[33] Avocados not yet having been introduced to Europe.

[34] Still, this kind of historically oriented view quite obviously can connect to an account of the nature of property rights on which a property right must be a right to a thing, so this is a good place to say why I reject such a view. The idea of property as distinctively about things has two versions. One, which claims that property is about physical objects—as in Simon Douglas and Ben McFarlane, "Defining Property Rights" in James Penner and Henry E Smith eds, Philosophical Foundations of Property Rights (2013) 219—is just not plausible. It attempts to answer a legal question by outsourcing it to a question about the physical characteristics of a subset of the area of analysis selected for no reason other than empirical familiarity. The other view—as in Henry E Smith, "Property as the Law of Things" 125 Harvard Law Review 1691 (2012)—sees a "thing" somewhat in the way that I see a res here: as the kind of independent subject matter that can be owned. (For more on this sort of view, see also *infra* note 47.) One problem with that view as it is developed is that it rests on an overly narrow normative grounding for the entire institution, as argued, from a point of view not far from mine, in Joseph William Singer, "Property as the Law of Democracy" 63 Duke Law Journal 1287 (2014). (For more general criticism of thing-based views, see my "Property in Licences and the Law of Things" 59 McGill Law Journal 559 (2014).) I think Singer's view, in its way, lacks the resources to properly account for the distinctiveness of property rights and property law. (I am sympathetic to the idea that all law is the law of democracy: see Seana Valentine Shiffrin, Democratic Law (2021).) Because the idea of yours and mine is an idea that generates both the kind of egalitarianism that Singer associates with democracy and the notion of a res (or thing) that Smith uses to distinguish property from other parts of the law, the claim that property is the law of yours and mine can capture the advantages of both Singer's and Smith's view.

[35] See John Austin, Lectures on Jurisprudence: Or the Philosophy of Positive Law 252–53 (1874/2014); Wesley Newcomb Hohfeld, "Fundamental Legal Conceptions as Applied in Judicial Reasoning" 26 Yale Law Journal 710 (1917).

only certain specific people whereas *in rem* rights seem to bind everyone in the world. Hohfeld's treatment was particularly influential, and led to a small subindustry developing and refining his view.[36] One thing Hohfeld clearly has correct is the idea that all private law rights are rights against private persons, so that the distinctiveness of property rights needs to be conceived in a way that is consistent with that idea. Rather than saying that property rights are rights to or against things, Hohfeld recognizes that both property and contract rights are rights against persons, but claims that they are against different classes of persons. He uses the (totally normal and conversationally familiar) words "paucital" and "multital" to refer, respectively, to rights that bind fewer and more duty bearers, and basically argues that contract rights are paucital rights because they apply only against the counterparty whereas property rights are multital rights because they apply against everyone (or almost everyone) else. Again, there is a lot to say about all of that, but I am not going to say it, because Hohfeld's approach seems to me to miss an important element that needs to be taken into account in thinking about private law rights. The problem, I think, is that the development of the Hohfeldian idea has tended to cluster around trying to identify descriptive or nonjustificatory characteristics of the form of property rights, like the numerosity or generality of the duty bearers.[37] But my account of property so far has been justificatory through and through: to understand property, I am arguing, we need to understand the way in which it is a solution to the Problem of Yours and Mine.

So, rather than hoping to settle the matter of *in rem* and *in personam* by reference to facts that are entirely descriptive, we should instead turn to thinking about the distinction through the lens of justification.[38] That is, we should ask *why* there is a distinction between rights *in rem* and rights *in personam*. As it was in the case of the distinction between personal and property rights, the thought is going to be that the explanation lies in the different reasons for which we have institutions providing rights of this form: some institutions, to do the thing we

[36] For one strand of that, see Penner, Idea of Property in Law; my critique in "The Office of Ownership" 63 University of Toronto Law Journal 418 (2013); Penner's reply in "On the Very Idea of Transmissible Rights" in Penner and Smith, Philosophical Foundations at 244; and my response in "The Office of Ownership Revisited" 70 University of Toronto Law Journal Supplement 2 287 (2020). Penner also elaborates a more comprehensive (and, to me, largely effective) critique of Hohfeld's picture of property in his Property Rights: A Re-Examination (2020).

[37] See Albert Kocourek, "Rights in Rem" 68 University of Pennsylvania Law Review 322 (1920). Another problem arises out of a point we saw in §4.7. Some servitudes apply, in a sense, only to one other person: a covenant really only binds the holder of the servient tenement. That could in principle be anyone but at any given time it's likely to be only one person. And yet a servitude is almost universally agreed to be a property right and *in rem*.

[38] For a similar view of this issue, see Pavlos Eleftheriadis, Legal Rights 137 (2008). And see generally Grégoire Webber, "Asking Why in the Study of Human Affairs" 60 American Journal of Jurisprudence 51 (2015).

want them to do, to solve the moral problem that needs solving, require *in rem* rights, whereas others require *in personam* rights to do their job.[39]

The Problem of Yours and Mine arises when we cannot relate to others through the idea of yours and mine. The Problem itself has a kind of *in rem* form: for me to be able to enter into valuable activities and relations with respect to avocados on terms of equality with each other member of my society, I need to be able to relate with respect to the avocado to each other member of my society through the idea of yours and mine. The idea of yours and mine does not tell us merely that what is mine is not yours, but more broadly that what is mine is not *any* other person's.[40] Indeed, that is part of the point: there is nothing special about you in virtue of which I have a right against you with respect to what is mine. That is, the identity of the duty bearer is immaterial to the application of the idea of yours and mine: my capacity to determine the permissibility of others' actions with respect to what is mine does not depend at all on anything about those particular others. My claim is "this is mine," and it has the same force regardless of who I say it to. There is thus an independence of what is mine not only from me—distinguishing property from persons—but also from everyone else. This independence manifests legally in the *in rem* form of the rights.

And that is how it needs to be: if my avocado were mine only vis-à-vis some and not others, the Problem would not be solved. Property rights are *in rem* because they solve a problem about equal relations that arises not because of any special relationship between right holder and any particular duty holder or holders, but precisely because of the lack of any special relationship. The account of property as the realization of the idea of yours and mine (and consistent with the basic commitment) relies, in part, on the impersonality of the idea of "each other person": there is nothing special about being any particular nonowner in virtue of which we say that that person, who happens to be a nonowner, is subordinate to the owner. This is the complementary point to the one about the impersonality of the owner (as opposed to the connection between a person and their personal rights): just as my rights as owner have nothing special to do with me beyond the fact that I happen to be owner, your duties (indeed, everyone's duties) as nonowner have nothing special to do with you beyond the fact that you happen to be nonowner. The relation between right holder and duty ower is mediated by the idea of yours and mine and thus is impersonal and independent of the particular identities of the parties to it on both sides.

So the justificatory considerations relevant to thinking about property require property rights to be *in rem*. Making the parallel version of the claim for *in*

[39] The thought is that differences in legal form track underlying moral or justificatory differences. For a development of this idea, see Larissa Katz, "Legal Forms in Property Law Theory" in James Penner and Michael Otsuka eds, Property Theory: Legal and Political Perspectives 23, 28–31 (2018).

[40] As we saw in §4.5, co-ownership is not inconsistent with this.

personam rights is a bit harder. For one thing, there is some dispute about what, precisely, are the parts of private law that have *in personam* form: most will agree that contract and debt are *in personam*, but beyond that things get a bit blurry in a way that I cannot here explore, in particular with respect to the law of unjust enrichment[41] and various fiduciary relations. For another thing, and because of the first thing, it is not totally obvious how to classify an overarching idea of when *in personam* rights are appropriate. (Nor is it obvious that all *in personam* rights are grounded on the same considerations; it seems rather more likely that they are not, just as property and personal rights, neither of which are *in personam*, rest on different justificatory considerations.) Finally, even if those problems were easily soluble, this is a book about property, not a book about "*in personam* rights," so there is only so much detail I should go into. However, I think I can say something both sufficiently general and sufficiently helpful to our present topic to be worth saying.

The *in personam* rights we have in our private law can all be said to arise out of what I will call a *transaction* between right holder and duty bearer. The basic idea is that a transaction—a particular, datable, legal interaction between two particular, identifiable people—is the ground of the right (and duty). You have a contract right against me because and only because you and I entered into a contract, and our entering into that contract explains why you and only you have a right against me and only me. The right does not preexist the transaction but is instead created by it. By contrast, in the property case, my right that you not touch my avocado does not arise out of any transaction between us, but preexists it. (One way to see the contrast is by seeing the way that the two kinds of rights interact in a familiar contractual setting: my *ex ante* position is constituted in part by my property right in the avocado I want to sell you, but your right to delivery of the avocado arises only out of the transaction.) Because this transaction is between two individuals and happens at a particular time, and because the rights that arise out of it arise entirely out of it, we can see how the transaction gives rise to rights that are *in personam* in the sense that they bind only the parties to the transaction. Indeed, legally, the entire point of the transaction can be seen to be just the creation of these rights. And it should be easy enough to see how you might tell a story about how *in personam* rights like this are needed to solve a certain kind of moral problem, about the possibility of doing certain kinds of things together in a way that is consistent with the basic commitment.[42]

Here we can see more clearly a really important point I mentioned already: the fact that property rights are *in rem* as opposed to *in personam* is, in an important

[41] For a recent discussion of unjust enrichment emphasizing its connection to property, see Charlie Webb, Reason and Restitution: A Theory of Unjust Enrichment (2016).

[42] One might say more here but I think I should keep this as thin as possible because different views of contract are going to cash this out in different ways.

sense, the mirror image of the way that property rights differ from personal rights. In that case, as we saw in §5.1, property rights are distinct from personal rights because of the way in which they are independent of the right holder. I can determine the permissibility of your interaction with what is mine because it is mine. But what is mine might be yours. And, if it were, you would in just the same way be able to determine the permissibility of my interaction with it. By contrast, only I will ever be able to determine the permissibility of your interactions with me. In this case, the right I have against you in the *in personam* contractual context is a right that depends on something special about you, namely, the fact that you and I, through our contractual transaction, brought the right into existence. In the property case, things are different: my right that you not touch my avocado does not depend on any transaction at all, and so does not depend on you or your identity. In other words, as an *in rem* right, my property right is independent of the (identity of the) duty-bearer in a way that mirrors how, as an alienable right, it is independent of the (identity of the) right-holder.

The next thing to say about the *in rem—in personam* distinction is that there is a range of important classes of cases that seem in various ways to blur it. These are cases that seem, from one point of view, to involve *in rem* rights and, from another point of view, to involve *in personam* rights. I am thinking here about corporate shares, debts, mortgages, trusts, and the like. I will explore those cases in detail in §5.6. But before we can do that, we need to take a bit of a detour to further develop the notion of a res and its application in various kinds of intangible contexts.

5.4 The Res

I have employed the notion of the res a few times now. A res is the subject matter of a particular property right, the *this* I refer to when I say "this is mine." I have already suggested that a res is a legally constituted entity: what is mine in any particular case is a matter of the law, of the nature and scope of the legal rights I have, of what it is with respect to which others' actions are up to me. It is time for me to say some more about this notion of a res. It will be helpful to begin by connecting it to the points made so far in this chapter, to see how the way that the idea of yours and mine generates the independence of property from both right holder and duty owers illuminates the notion of a res. Then we will be in a position to employ the notion to help us understand the possibility of property rights in intangibles, by seeing how the law can construct a res in certain intangible contexts, allowing us to think about them through the idea of yours and mine, which is to say to think about them as property. In this way, we will be able to use the idea of yours and mine to draw the boundaries of property within private law.

I said that the independence of property is an implication of the idea of yours and mine. So think back to the Problem of Yours and Mine. We saw that, even in the negative community, it would be possible to have rights with respect to our persons and also that it would be possible to have other legal rights arising out of particular transactions with others, like promises. The Problem is that these rights are insufficient to allow us to meet the basic commitment, because there is a huge and important part of the social world that is grounded on interactions between persons that involve more than merely our persons and particular transactions. This is the sphere of property law: property rights are those that allow us to relate as equals in situations where our interaction is about some subject matter that is independent of our persons (i.e., in which personal rights are inadequate) and independent of any particular transaction (i.e., in which *in personam* rights are inadequate). The core cases of property—spaces and physical objects—cast light on the form here. Spaces and objects have an existence independent of persons, and the Problem of Yours and Mine arises because these things are just *there* and so we need to figure out a way to relate with respect to them that is consistent with our relating as equals.

More abstractly, the Problem of Yours and Mine arises when the possibility of equal relations consistent with the basic commitment requires that the idea of yours and mine has application. Such application requires that there be something that is, or could be, yours or mine. Think about an uncontroversial case of property, such as the property that I have in my avocado. And focus again on what it is about my right in the avocado that marks it out as different than other private law rights that I have. Important insight arises from highlighting the way that my right to the avocado is independent of me. As Baroness Hale put it in *OBG*, "The essential feature of property is that it has an existence independent of a particular person."[43] There is a range of different forms of thought and talk that seem more or less apt to capture this idea: we think about the avocado that my right in it has nothing in particular to do with the fact that it is *my* right in it; we think that the rights in the avocado would be essentially unchanged were it your avocado rather than mine or perhaps that the right persists unchanged in the transition from me to you; we can think of the wrong with respect to the avocado, at least sometimes, in terms of my taking something that is yours from you, in the sense of depriving you of it; we can be drawn to think that the rights to the avocado seem to attach to it even before anyone acquires it, so that the acquisition of the avocado is the acquisition of a preexisting, prepackaged set of rights; we might say that, when the avocado becomes mine, I "step into the shoes" or perhaps "take up the office" of owner, in the sense again that the legal entitlement associated with ownership exists without me, and so again that when I transfer

43 *OBG* at [309].

it to you, I stop and you start being "owner," where "owner" is a status or position cognizable independently of your identity or mine. At the same time, this independence from me or you, this independence from the right holder, is importantly mirrored in the independence of the ownership of the avocado from the myriad duty bearers. You owe me a legal duty not to interfere with my avocado, and that fact does not depend on anything special about you; were I to give (i.e., legally transfer, not just physically pass) the avocado to you, I (and everyone else) would owe you just the same duties not to interfere with the avocado that, before the gift, you (and everyone else) had owed to me. By contrast, the duties you owe me in contract rest directly on the fact that it was you who entered into the contract. The duties others owe to me or you when the avocado is mine or yours exist entirely independently of any particular transaction between duty bearer and right holder.[44]

This set of ideas leads us to affirm the basic idea with which we began this part of the account, namely, that the sphere of property law is defined by those cases in which we have private law rights with this form, where the subject matter of the right has the relevant kind of independence both from the right holder (to ground the right's alienability) and from the duty bearer (to ground its *in rem* structure). But the independence we are reflecting on generates more than merely the divisions between departments of private law. Notice again the quote from Baroness Hale: "The essential feature of property is that it has an existence independent of a particular person." I take it that the meaning of the word "property" that is the referent of "it" in the second clause in that sentence is some generic particular property right. The claim is that for any given property right, that right has this independence. This thought seems to presuppose that a property right has some independent subject matter or, to put it in different terms, that when we employ the idea of yours and mine (or any of the property law concepts that depend on it), we presuppose that there is *something* that is yours or mine.[45] For it to be possible to say "this is mine" or "this is yours" there must be subject matter to which the "this" refers.[46] This subject matter needs to have, as Baroness

[44] I take Swadling to make the same point as the one here when he says that "the hallmark of a property right is its ability to bind strangers to its creation" (William Swadling, "Property: General Principles" in Andrew Burrows ed, English Private Law 4.03 (3d ed 2013).

[45] "The statement 'I own' is meaningless if not followed by a description of what you own." Sjef van Erp, "Ownership of Data: The *Numerus Clausus* of Legal Objects" 6 Brigham-Kanner Property Rights Conference Journal 235, 250 (2017).

[46] I won't go into a lot of detail about this claim but what I say in the text is, I think, sufficient to show why pure nominalism about property, as in Arnold S Weinrib, "Information and Property" 38 University of Toronto Law Journal 117, 129 (1988) ("the word 'property' as applied to *any* property rights recognized by law is also an unanalysed expression of certain secondary consequences of the primary fact that the law makes some rudimentary requirement of good behavior"), isn't an adequate view: we can't apply the concept unless we can locate a subject matter with the features I identify in the text to which to apply that concept. See also *infra* note 47.

Hale says, a kind of independence from any particular person, an independence that can explain both how the right can have the same legal character regardless of the identity of its holder and how it can preexist any particular transaction between right holder and duty bearer.

This subject matter is the res. So the idea of yours and mine applies to an interaction whenever there is some res with respect to which the parties are interacting. As I said, the res is a legal construction. I have made some remarks about that already, and I will elaborate upon them in a moment. But before I do, I need to spend a couple of paragraphs being precise to the point of pedantic, because there is an obvious potential *mis*understanding of these ideas that I need to close off here. The misunderstanding is that when I say that for the idea of yours and mine to apply there must be *something* that is mine, you hear me to be saying that for the idea of yours and mine to apply there must be *some thing* that is mine; the misunderstanding is reinforced by the common translation of the Latin word "res" into the English word "thing." For reasons I will give now, though, I think we need to resist equating the res with a thing, and, recherché though the word is, maintain a clear focus on the idea that property requires a res, even if it does not require a thing.[47]

[47] My view here is in certain respects not *so* different from the view that property is the law of things. (See on this point also *supra* note 34.) I want at the same time to express sympathy for the common thought, which I recall hearing on the very first day of my first-year property course, that property is about "rights not things" and for the seemingly contradictory view on which when we own property we own "things," as long as we recognize that such things are themselves determined by the law of property itself, so that property law is in part a matter of "defining things": Henry Smith, "Economics of Property Law" in Francesco Parisi ed, The Oxford Handbook of Law and Economics: Volume 2. Private and Commercial Law 148, 149 (2017). So I should say a bit more about property theory and "things". In brief, property theory through the twentieth century largely coalesced around the idea that property is about rights, not things; one motivation for this view (among others) was that we seem to think and talk about property in contexts where there is not, at least not obviously, any *thing* to be owned. For discussion, see Charles A Reich, "The New Property" 73 Yale Law Journal 733 (1964), Thomas C Grey, "The Disintegration of Property" in J Roland Pennock and John W Chapman eds, Property: NOMOS XXII (69) (1980), as well as Kenneth J Vandevelde "The New Property of the Nineteenth Century: The Development of the Modern Concept of Property" 29 Buffalo Law Review 325 (1980). More recently, an important literature has emerged to provide a contrast to that view, and to argue that property is, as this literature puts it, the law of things. For instance, see Smith, "Property as the Law of Things". This new literature recognizes, for the most part, that there can be property in the sorts of situations that do not involve spaces or objects, the presence of which motivated the original rights-not-things move, but insists that we can nevertheless understand these cases in terms of an idea of a thing (and that we should do so, in order to solve the problem that we are presently facing, namely, the problem of how to draw lines between property rights and other kinds of private law rights). This is fine, as long as we remember that the "thing" I own will always be defined by the egalitarian structure of the law. My suggestion in the text is that using the word "res" in place of the word "thing" will make the remembering easier. Substantively, Smith's view differs from mine here primarily in that he thinks that the basic justificatory criterion is a kind of cost-benefit analysis that focuses on information costs, so that things are determined by reference to what would minimize information costs. Indeed, we should be clear that a theory of property that is as robustly normative as mine does need to provide an account of what a given owner owns in a given case. (See Christopher M Newman, "Using Things, Defining Property" in Penner and Otsuka, Property Theory 69.) (The drafters of the forthcoming Restatement (4th) of Property, of whom Newman is one, and Henry Smith is chief, set out the idea that a res or a "thing" is defined by the purposes of the law, when they

One objection to talking about property as being about things rests on a concern about the term "thing," a concern that, notwithstanding the subtlety with which the idea of a thing has been employed by proponents of the law-of-things view, there is a risk of simplification so that the view reduces to something like the view that property is only about tangible objects and spaces.[48] This strikes me as legal theory by definitional fiat, and, more importantly, very strongly at odds with our actual legal practice which recognizes (quite plausibly, as we will see) many kinds of intangible property rights. By contrast, the term "res" is sufficiently unusual that this slippage is easier to avoid: you are probably carrying much less pre-theoretic baggage about what might or might not count as a "res" than you do about what might or might not count as a "thing". Moreover, and conversely, certain Kantian or legal usages aside, it seems rather plausible to say that a person is a "thing," and yet (as we saw) a person cannot be property (i.e., cannot be a res). Another reason for concern is that the term "thing" leads not merely to an assumption that only tangibles can be property but also or instead to the assumption that, when it comes to tangibles (which surely can be property), the legal conception of the thing is coextensive with the physical conception of it. We have already seen (in particular in the discussion of nuisance in §4.2) that this is not the right way to think about property in land; I will say some more about this point later in this section.

A res is not a thing. Rather, a res is the subject matter of a property right, and, as such, it is a legal construction. For what it is worth, it turns out that the Latin term *res* actually has an etymology that is distinctly apt for this task. The word was originally a legal word, a word about legal proceedings, whose original meaning seems to have been something like "the affair . . . about which there was a deliberation," something that "existed precisely as the objection of interactions between different actors," and it eventually "came to designate . . . the asset about which there was a trial. But the asset was only the *corpus* of the affair, and the same word *res* referred to both, the litigious situation and, by extension, the asset in dispute."[49] In other words, the res is the thing about which parties to a legal

write: "But the function served by property interests requires them to be readily identified and understood by numerous unrelated actors, and so in practice the law at any given time has recognized only a standardized menu of enumerated property interests. . . . Existing legally recognized interests have arisen out of some felt need and embody established groupings of legal relation fitted to serve a functional role in some recurring context familiar to legal actors and courts." Their view of the law's purposes is different than mine, but on this point, I agree.)

[48] For this view, see, e.g., Douglas and MacFarlane, "Defining Property Rights."

[49] See Claudia Moatti, "The Notion of *Res Publica* and Its Conflicting Meanings at the End of the Roman Republic" in Catalina Balmaceda ed, in *Libertas* and *Res Publica* in the Roman Republic 118, 122–23 (2020). The deeper history here is pretty intense and pretty interesting. At least one etymological dictionary defines the older or original sense of "res" as something like "goods" or "possessions" or "interest in something" or, particularly helpfully (or unhelpfully?) "property": see Alfred Ernout and Antoine Meillet, Dictionaire étymologique de la langue Latin: Histoire des mots 571 (1985). And etymological research that goes even further back seems to connect the Latin *res*

dispute are disputing. Legal disputes are about legal rights, or perhaps about the subject matter of legal rights. When I make a legal claim based on the idea of yours and mine, I am making a claim about what is mine. And what is mine is legally constructed, even if it is associated with some physical thing: what is mine is the res, and the res is what is mine.

In summary, a res is the subject matter of a particular property right, the *this* or *that* to which the idea of yours and mine applies in a given context. To have a property right, it must be possible that there is some res to which the idea of yours and mine can apply, about which the holder of the right can say "this is mine." A res must be understood as being independent of any particular person. This independence fits well with the points made in §§5.1 and 5.3. First, a property right can be distinguished from a personal right because of the presence of the res, a subject matter that exists independently of the owner, where the subject of a personal right is necessarily tied to the person whose right it is. We need property rights to relate as equals with respect to any given res because our innate rights to our persons are incapable of doing that. Second, a property right can be distinguished from an *in personam* right because of the presence of the res, a subject matter that exists independently of and thus antecedent to any particular transaction between right holder and duty bearer, whereas the source of an *in personam* right is precisely such a transaction. We need property rights to relate as equals with respect to any given res because the form of protection that is required cannot be created through *in personam* rights. (An *in rem* right cannot be composed out of *in personam* rights.[50]) Two further points can add to this analysis. First, notice the idea of something's being *res nullius*, unowned. Whatever the contours and legal implications of the idea, it presupposes something like independent existence: it is the idea of something existing without an owner. By contrast, there is no sense at all in which *in personam* rights like contract rights exist independently of the particular persons who enter into the transactions that bring them into existence. A contract is not waiting there (where?) to be entered into in the way that an avocado is waiting there to be picked. A related point can be made about licences to enter land and their treatment in the version of the bundle of rights view of property known as the "bundle of sticks" view: a licence for you to enter my land simply does not exist before I grant it to you (as an

to a proto-Indo-European word that means something like "wealth" or "goods": Michiel de Vaan, Etymological Dictionary of Latin and the other Italic Languages 520–21 (2008). As I note in the text, I am not resting the argument or the definition of the term in this book on the etymology. But it's interesting, at least, to see that the Latin word did not seem to mean, primarily, something like "object" or "entity" in the more general sense of the English word "thing."

[50] This is a version of a point we saw in the text accompanying chapter 2, note 11: the *in rem* right applies to every possible person, and with new people arriving all the time, we cannot construct an *in rem* right out of actual *in personam* rights.

in personam right), the implication of the bundle of sticks view that it does exist and is waiting to be granted to you is one of that view's deep confusions.[51]

The notion of a res is very closely connected to the idea of yours and mine. The form of the Problem of Yours and Mine can guide us to seeing how our property rights need to have the (*in rem* and alienable) form that they have. A different way to say this is by saying that the Problem of Yours and Mine exists when there is a res with respect to which we need to relate as equals. The basic case of the Problem is the one we have concentrated on up to now, the one where the res is the legal realization/translation/version of some nonlegal thing, like an avocado. But there are other cases, too, cases in which the res is not the legal version of some nonlegal thing, but is instead an entirely legal entity, a subject matter that, to relate as equals with respect to, we need the idea of yours and mine. This suggests why it is also important, to coin a phrase, not to reify the res. A res is not a thing, and a right to a res is not simply a right to a thing. In the context of (actual, physical) things, the res should not be confused with the thing: my avocado in law is not my avocado in botany or physics or food science. The thing has an existence independent of the law and we can sometimes helpfully think, in rough terms, about the physical object being mine or yours. But the rights I have in a thing that is mine cannot be determined except through authoritative legal processes, which is why we need the law to set the (legal) boundaries of the res, conceding of course that the empirical boundaries of the thing will often be quite helpful in setting the legal boundaries of the res.

This last point can be helpfully illustrated by tying together some strands from chapter 4 about the scope of property rights in land. Recall, first, the *ad coelum* rule, discussed in §4.2, about the vertical boundaries of property in land. We saw in that context that the boundary is legal or relational, in the sense that the question "how high does my property go?" really only has legal meaning when it is read as "is there a height above which your entry does not count as trespassing?" So the "top" and "bottom" of my property are determined legally, by asking a question about when you might wrong me. We expanded the discussion by thinking about nuisance, where, I argued, the scope of the res in a piece of land is partly constituted by the rights that the owner has that others not unreasonably interfere with its use and enjoyment, so that the res might plausibly be said to extend, in that way, beyond the physical boundaries of the space to give the owner control over the rights of their neighbors. But our discussion of nuisance also started to help us to see that the law may in some cases construct the res in a more nuanced and specific way. The *Fearn v Tate Gallery* case held that certain kinds of overlooking can interfere with the use and enjoyment of a plaintiff's home as such, and thereby

[51] See J E Penner, "Potentiality, Actuality, and 'Stick' Theory" 8 Economic Journal Watch 274 (2011). The precise claim is that the res has an existence independent of a particular transaction between two parties, not an existence independent of the law, as the next paragraph will make clear.

constitute a nuisance. Here the Court might be understood to be constructing a more specific res, a home or residence as opposed to merely property in land considered independently of its character. Such a notion of property in a home fits well, as we saw in §4.7, with the development of the accommodation requirement in the law of easements over the last seventy-five years, as courts, in cases like *Ellenborough Park* and then *Regency Villas*, began to recognize how certain kinds of amenities could make a home better as a home. (A garden or tennis court does not make land better as land, but it makes a home better as a home.) We can understand the development of the warranty of habitability in landlord-tenant law (§4.6) along the same lines. In all these cases, the law has come to recognize that the way in which homes—residential property—are required for us to relate as equals means that we require a more nuanced understanding of the scope of the residential res than the (perhaps more historically prevalent) notion of land as merely a space. (To repeat one part of the argument from §4.2, insisting that the res in a case like *Fearn* extends only to giving a right against physical emanations would miss out on the important ways in which intangible nuisances can subordinate their victims and thus compromise the realization of the egalitarian idea of yours and mine in the residential context. The Supreme Court's recognition of this point in the *Fearn* decision is an important step forward in understanding property law.) Conversely, there remains a range of ways in which property in land does not prevent others from making any use of the space at all: reasonable invasions of smoke, smells, and noise; taking photographs; and other such uses of the land are not wrongs, and thus not properly thought about as interferences with the res. We see, even in the basic case of land, how the contents of the res—the contents of the *this* implicated in "this is my home"—are separated from the contents of the physical space (the thing), because they are legally constituted and based on the egalitarian justification of this sort of property right.

And so we can see that the legal constitution of the res allows us to move beyond the context of the physical to start thinking about property in contexts where there is no obvious nonlegal physical thing to which the idea of yours and mine can attach. Sometimes circumstances can arise in which the possibility of equal relations requires us to ask if the law ought to create a novel kind of res out of whole cloth. To have property, we need to be able to think—and to legally realize—the idea of yours and mine. This means that to have a property right in a particular context, we need a res to which the idea of yours and mine can apply. Now let me remind you why questions about the distinctiveness of property rights are not merely an idle academic concern.[52] The law is rife with cases

[52] Quine said that disciplinary distinctions are are a matter for deans and librarians: W V O Quine, Theories and Things 88 (1981). But as the text explains, at least the disciplinary distinction I'm discussing here has real legal consequences.

in which quite specific legal questions turn on what counts as property. Some of these are internal to property law, as we saw with the difference between a lease and a licence. And some are at least partly about other areas, as in bankruptcy law (where a bankrupt's *property* is treated in a certain way) or family law (where upon divorce a couple's *property* is divided), as well as cases in which a more general kind of question arises, in particular where a plaintiff claims a right against some defendant that is neither personal nor *in personam*. In these cases, we need a general account of what property rights are in order to decide the specific question of whether the case in question involves a property right. The most interesting such cases are those in which there is no obvious prelegal "thing" about which a plaintiff can say "this is mine." Nevertheless, in these cases we are often drawn toward proprietary thinking, toward talking in the language of yours and mine. Our question is about how to know when such thought and talk is appropriate.

The short answer will be that it is appropriate to think and talk about property just when it is appropriate to think and talk using the idea of yours and mine. This will mean that we need to locate, in these cases, some res that can be understood as the subject matter of a property right, and to show that, absent property in that res, we would have a problem with a yours-and-mine form. By "problem with a yours-and-mine form" I mean just that: a problem that has the same form as the Problem of Yours and Mine, a situation in which the possibility of relating as equals consistent with the basic commitment requires property. (I am using this new terminology to allow me to reserve the capitalized usage of "The Problem" to the subject of Part 1.) In the rest of this chapter, I will discuss two slightly different sorts of cases (although this classification is merely expository). One involves situations where, as we might put it, new interactions require new rights: these are cases where, as our social world develops, we invent new contexts in which problems with a yours-and-mine form arise. This class will be further subdivided: in §5.5, I will discuss rights arising out of various market relations, and in §5.6, I will briefly discuss some of the considerations arising out of the idea of property in information. The other kind of situation arises where the legal and social treatment of some *in personam* relation develops so that we can come to think of that relation itself (or a place in it) as a res, in a way. So in §5.8, I will discuss cases where law (or equity) has created *in rem* protection for *in personam* rights through the trust and through certain kinds of security interests, and other similar kinds of situations.

Throughout these cases a thematic point will be one I introduced earlier (in §4.6) in discussing the lease. As I noted, a res is sometimes property in a natural object or space: while my avocado in the legal sense is not directly coextensive with my avocado in the physical or biological sense, the former is clearly based on the latter and our experience of it. But sometimes, a res can be a purely legal creation, it can be *artificial*. A leasehold (along with its associated reversion) is a bit like this: a lease is a res that is created by the lease conveyance, although even in that case its underlying content is derived from the physical existence of the space in question. In the cases we are about to discuss, the artificiality is even more evident: as we shall see, legal relations can in various ways generate a kind of res that, although it can be understood as independent of any particular person or interaction in the relevant sense, seems to lack any nonlegal existence. This artificiality should not stop us from thinking about these cases using the idea of yours and mine.[53]

5.5 Property and Market Relations

One of the most obvious candidates for a right that counts as a property right even though it involves no physical thing is a trademark. In this section I will defend the idea that trademarks are a form of property, by showing that we can think of the mark as a res, as a subject matter to which we can apply the idea of yours and mine and, in doing so, solve a problem with the yours-and-mine form. This will be a simple illustration of the idea I just introduced about how to think about intangible property. We will begin with the problem to which trademark law is the solution. It is a problem about the possibility of competing in the free market on terms of equality.

Look at how the basic structure of the law of trademarks resembles the basic structure of property in spaces and objects. If I sell a product in the market and affix to it a mark—a symbol, a word—that consumers associate with my product, I can gain a right that you not sell other products with the same or a similar mark affixed to them in a way that will confuse consumers, which is to say will lead them to think that the product you are selling is my product or is made by me.[54] If you use my mark or a mark similar to it, you commit a private wrong against me, much in the way that you commit such a wrong if you use my avocado. Notice that I have already used the idea of yours and mine in setting out this basic idea: it seems utterly natural to think about the mark as something that is mine. The mark is the res: it is the subject matter of the idea of yours and mine and hence the subject matter of my property right. There are two further elements

[53] A rather bizarre but helpful illustration of the importance of a res for our thinking about property comes from the phenomenon of a nonfungible token (an NFT). An NFT is, in essence, a kind of property-like registry without a referent. A holder of an NFT gets the right to claim ownership of the NFT, but such claim brings with it nothing but the bare claim itself. There is no "this" about which the holder can say "this is mine." An NFT is, if you like, a solution to a nonproblem. There is no problem with yours-and-mine form that NFTs are needed to solve. Rather, the phenomenon uses the form of a property right to no valuable end at all.

[54] I am simplifying a lot here, because all we need is the basic idea of trademark.

to this story. First, notice that the mark—the res—is legally constructed in the following sense. My right is not simply a right that you not use a specific series of markings or letters; rather it is a right that you not affix to the product you are selling anything that will lead consumers to confuse your product with mine.[55] That means both that you might not be able to use different words or a different symbol if doing so would confuse consumers and that you might be able to use the same words or the same symbol if doing so would not cause confusion.[56] So the scope of the subject matter of the right—the boundary of the res—is determined legally, by reference to the nature of the legal relationship, by reference to the subject matter that is in dispute between us, namely, whether or not your product confuses consumers with respect to whether or not it is my product. Thus any mark that, taking into account "all of the surrounding circumstances"[57] would tend to confuse a reasonable consumer will infringe, since the relation between competitors is a relation of competition for consumers, so that confusion itself precisely will determine whether or not we compete on terms of equality.

Second, this idea of confusion is directly traceable to an idea that you and I must, to be able to compete for customers as equals, be able to offer products that our consumers will be able to tell apart. In the context of tangibles, the property rights in avocados are those that allow us to relate as equals (in a wide range of ways) with respect to the avocado; here, we need a property right that will allow us to relate as equals with respect to our competition for customers. Without a right such as this, we could not compete as equals since questions about what marks each of us could use, and how we could use them to compete to attract custom, would lack a basis on which to be resolved other than considerations of strength and weakness. We would be in a world akin to the world without property—the negative community—for the subject matter of trademark law. The point of trademark law, understood as a kind of property, is to realize a

[55] *Hanover Star Milling Co v Metcalf*, 240 US 403 (1916); *Mattel, Inc v 3894207 Canada Inc*, 2006 SCC 22.

[56] See Frank Schechter, "The Rational Basis of Trademark Protection" 40 Harvard Law Review 813 (1927). A very good illustration of the egalitarian structure of reasoning here is in *American Waltham Watch Co v United States Watch Co*, 173 Mass 85, 53 NE 141 (1899), where the court held that, where one company was manufacturing watches in a town called Waltham using a trade name "Waltham Watches," another company could use the name of the town since they were manufacturing watches there but not the specific name of the plaintiff company.

[57] *Mattel, Inc, passim.* Justice Holmes, in *Waltham Watch* at 142, essentially makes the same point when he says "in cases of this sort, as in so many others, what ultimately is to be worked out is a point or line between conflicting claims, each of which has meritorious grounds and would be extended further were it not for the other."Again, these ideas are indeterminate and require the application of judgment to particulars in order to decide cases. So it is true that, in the nineteenth century, "The terms 'trademark' and 'trade name' were tied to the concept of property and like the concept of property they lost their power to determine results." But it is not true that (see Vandevelde, "New Property of the Nineteenth Century" at 348) these concepts have no meaning, or that they can provide no assistance in our thinking through particular disputes, or that such disputes are thus amenable only to considerations of "policy."

regime of equal relations between competitors. The scope of the right is determined by reference to that framing idea. So we can see how the right protects you against using your mark in a way that leads to confusion and at the same time protects my own entitlement to use my own nonconfusing mark, since I need as your equal to be able to compete on fair terms and to attach my own mark to my own products in just the same way that you attach your mark to yours. This kind of way of looking at trademark law—as the law's creation of a new kind of res, a legal subject matter to which the idea of yours and mine applies in order to allow for egalitarian relations with respect to certain market dynamics—can be extended to think about some other kinds of liminal property cases.

Consider (as it is called in the United States) the right of publicity or (in Canada) the right protected by the tort of misappropriation of personality. Infringement of this right is a wrong that has, from one angle, a lot in common with the wrong of trademark infringement. The wrong arises when a defendant uses a plaintiff's image in a way that would lead the reasonable consumer to think that the plaintiff had endorsed the defendant's product. The basic case is a kind of false endorsement case. The relationship between the wrong and the idea of participation in the market as equals should be clear: in effect here, the plaintiff's image is like a trademark for the plaintiff themselves, associating the goodwill that consumers attach to them with the product being endorsed, so something like the analysis here, to the effect that a problem with the yours-and-mine form obtains, could apply to this context. The tricky question is whether or not the plaintiff's image (or perhaps we should say "persona"[58]) can be considered a res in the relevant sense: does this image have the requisite degree of independence from the plaintiff to count as their property rather than as a personal right? I am not actually sure what I think about this question, but the ideas here can help to structure an approach to answering it.

To start, one might think that your image is so closely related to yourself that only you could be the person with a right to determine how that image is used. Such a view of the right as personal seems to be in tension with the fact that the right is (in both Canada and the United States) alienable and descendible, so that a celebrity can transfer control over the right to a corporation,[59] or a celebrity's heirs can continue to exercise a right over the celebrity's image. But it might be quite plausible to think that this is merely a feature of some unsettled questions about private law and death, so to think (contrary to what we saw in our discussion of the idea of a res in §5.4) that the right lacks the requisite degree of

[58] Given that the wrong need not be visual, nor need it involve actual use of the plaintiff, but merely an act by the defendant that would lead the reasonable consumer to infer that the plaintiff had endorsed the defendant's product, two points most clearly illustrated in *Midler v Ford Motor Co*, 849 F2d 460 (9th Cir 1988).

[59] As did Tiger Woods, for instance: *ETW Corp v Jireh Publ'g, Inc*, 332 F3d 915 (6th Cir 2003).

independence from its holder, that it has a quite different character indeed when it is in the hands of the heirs than it did when it was in the hands of the person whose image it protects.[60] According to this view, it seems odd to think of the right as something that one can be deprived of rather than something that others can infringe without deprivation, like the right against battery. Still, one might press harder on the analogy with trademark, and think that the image can be detached from the person whose image it is, and that this detachment can ground the requisite degree of independence, and thus ground our thinking about the image as a res and thinking about the right as a property right.[61] Indeed, deprivation does seem possible, since if the right can rightfully be transferred to another, it seems like it could be wrongfully transferred, which is what deprivation or taking is. Here the legal alienability would be contrasted with the inalienability of other closely related rights to one's image, in particular the right that protects against the dissemination of private images:[62] those private images are too personal to be property, whereas one might have a different view about images involving endorsements.

The trademark setup can also help us think through what is probably the most famous case that centers on an inquiry into the nature of property, the US Supreme Court's decision in *INS v AP*.[63] In stylized form, the case is about competition between news organizations. The plaintiffs functioned as a normal news-gathering and reporting organization, sending reporters into the field and then publishing their stories. The defendants did the same thing, but would also take the stories from the plaintiffs' newspapers and publish them in their own as if they had actually gathered those stories. The plaintiff claimed, in effect, that the defendant was stealing its news. The court, saying that the case is about the "general question of property in news matter,"[64] held for the plaintiffs, employing strikingly proprietarian language:

[60] Andrew Gilden, "Endorsing after Death" 63 William & Mary Law Review 1531 (2022). See also Jennifer E Rothman, The Right of Publicity: Privacy Reimagined for a Public World (2018).

[61] *Gould v Stoddart Estate*, (1996) 30 OR (3d) 520 (Gen Div).

[62] See Restatement (2d) Torts §652. For discussion of the other cases, see Lisa M Austin, "Enough about Me: Why Privacy Is about Power, Not Consent (or Harm)" in Austin Sarat ed, A World without Privacy?: What Can/Should Law Do 131 (2014), Anita L Allen, "Natural Law, Slavery, and the Right to Privacy Tort" 81 Fordham Law Review 1187 (2012).

[63] *Int'l News Serv v Associated Press*, 248 US 215 (1918). As Henry Smith put it to me in conversation, there are probably as many theories of this case as there are property theorists. For some of the more prominent, see Richard A Epstein, "*International News Service v Associated Press:* Custom and Law as Sources of Property Rights in News" 78 Virginia Law Review 85 (1992); Shyamkrishna Balganesh, "'Hot News': The Enduring Myth of Property in News" 111 Columbia Law Review 419 (2011); Henry E Smith, "Equitable Intellectual Property: What Is Wrong with Misappropriation?" in Shyamkrishna Balganesh ed, Intellectual Property and the Common Law 42 (2013). I am not going to aim to show other theories are wrong, just to show how one could think about the case under the guise of the idea of yours and mine.

[64] *INS* at 234.

> In doing this, defendant, by its very act, admits that it is taking material that has been acquired by complainant as the result of organization and the expenditure of labor, skill, and money, and which is salable by complainant for money, and that defendant, in appropriating it and selling it as its own, is endeavoring to reap where it has not sown, and by disposing of it to newspapers that are competitors of complainant's members, is appropriating to itself the harvest of those who have sown.[65]

There are many strands to the decision, and examining all of them would take us too far afield. I mostly want to highlight the relationship between the idea of a res and the Court's famous (or should I say infamous) employment of the expression "quasi-property."

Start by noticing the way that the passage relies on the idea of yours and mine: INS, says the Court, is "taking material that has been acquired by [AP, and then] appropriating it and selling it as its own."[66] This passage, I think, shows us the way to seeing what the res is in this case, by showing us how the Court is thinking about there being something that belonged to AP and that was wrongfully appropriated by INS. The independence of the res from AP—the fact that the right is not a personal right—is a simple matter. AP's report of the news is, quite obviously, not AP. It is true that AP created the report, but that act of creation can be understood as just that, as the bringing into the world of a new res. And INS's dealing with that res can be straightforwardly understood as a kind of trespass, since what INS does is use AP's res—the news as reported by AP—in a way that is inconsistent with its status as AP's. The important factual point here is that INS was publishing the news that AP had reported as if it was INS rather than AP that had done the reporting. This misrepresentation can be understood straightforwardly as an instance of INS using AP's res.

The Court did not want to recognize this res as the subject of a property right, because it thought that doing so would be inconsistent with the right of the public to discuss the news.[67] There are two problems with this line of thinking. In order to see the first problem, the idea that a res is legally constituted is quite important indeed. As I emphasized earlier, there is no reason to think—none—that to have property with respect to a res is to have absolute control over some nonlegal thing. So it is entirely possible to think that AP has a property right in a res—"the news as reported by AP"—that gives AP rights over certain uses of the

[65] *INS* at 239–40.
[66] *INS* at 239.
[67] *INS* at 236 ("we may and do assume that neither party has any remaining property interest as against the public in uncopyrighted news matter after the moment of its first publication").

res while not giving it rights over all uses.[68] This is a really basic thought, one that I have emphasized several times. Your right in your home gives you a right that I not enter it but not a right that I not draw a picture of it or use its shadow to cool down in, and as we just saw, your right to your trademark gives you a right that I not use your mark in a way that would confuse your customers but not a right that I not use it in a nonconfusing way. Similarly, here, AP's right in its news report gives it a right that INS not use that news report to compete unfairly, but not a right that others (including INS) not discuss the news in noncompetitive ways, like around the water cooler, or a right that they not report the same facts on their own with their own reporters, or a right that they not use AP's report to track down sources and report the facts themselves. The right is certainly narrower here than in other contexts, but that is a difference in degree rather than in kind, and not a reason not to recognize the right in hot news as property.

And this leads us to seeing the second problem with the Court's quasi-property formulation. The Court seems to think that the right arises only out of the relation between the parties. But that is a mistake: the res can be understood to be required independent of any particular person. INS and AP have no preexisting *legal* relation that is relevant to the right that AP has in its news, and so its right in its news is independent of any transaction (in the sense defined in §5.3) between the parties in the way that it needs to be to count as property.[69] Anyone who did what INS did with AP's news would commit just the same wrong that INS did: the right is good against the world, *in rem*, because it is a right to a res. That is, the right does not arise out of a transaction, but rather arises independently of any such transaction, in a way that is recognizably akin to the process of initial acquisition of a tangible object like a fox. So the entire idea of quasi-property that emerges so famously from the case is just an unnecessary detour that could have been avoided with a clearer understanding of the nature of *in rem* property rights.

Now, as I said, property rights are responses to problems with a yours-and-mine form. It will be helpful to say a little bit about how that point matters here. The considerations in the previous paragraph are an important part of the story. As in the case of trademark, market competition is not a legal relation, and so

[68] *INS* at 239 ("The right of the purchaser of a single newspaper to spread knowledge of its contents gratuitously, for any legitimate purpose not unreasonably interfering with complainant's right to make merchandise of it, may be admitted, but to transmit that news for commercial use, in competition with complainant—which is what defendant has done and seeks to justify—is a very different matter.").

[69] They had a preexisting *factual* relationship, sure: they were competitors. But the Court's pointing to this nonlegal relation (e.g., *INS* at 239, where the Court says that the case must be decided by "considering the rights of complainant and defendant, competitors in business, as between themselves") is just not the right kind of argument. The fact that only INS was factually in a position to infringe AP's right is no more relevant here than the fact that I happen to be the only person around who can trespass on your land is to our understanding of your property right in land.

the right that AP has in its news against INS is not one that arises out of any legal transaction between them but instead is one that is based on the res that preexists their legal interaction. And we can draw a link between such a res and the problem with the yours-and-mine form to which the right is a response. Absent the right to hot news, news organizations would compete entirely on the basis of who could publish a report first and not on the basis of their status as news-gathering organizations. Plausibly this would allow stronger organizations always to prevail in such competition in a way that seems inconsistent with these organizations' competing (relating) as equals.[70] So it makes sense to talk about AP having a property right against INS because that right can be understood as an *in rem*, alienable right to determine the permissibility of certain of others' interactions with a res, a right that solves a problem with a yours-and-mine form and allows AP and its competitors to relate on terms of equality. Those who want to use AP's news reports can now do so subject to AP's leave, and the use of those reports will be determined by considerations of right rather than by considerations of strength.[71]

[70] You might think this point isn't that plausible. That's fine, actually. I am not wedded to the view that the Court in *INS* got it right. The point of what I am doing in the text is to show how the Court's reasoning can be fitted into a broader understanding of what property is.

[71] The analysis here may be clarified by contrasting *INS* with the decision in *Victoria Park Racing & Recreation Grounds v Taylor*, [1937] HCA 45, a contrast that is often made in Canadian law school property classes. The case involved a plaintiff who operated a horse racing track. The defendant, who was the plaintiff's neighbor, erected a tower on his property, at the top of which was a viewing platform. From there the defendant was able to observe the plaintiff's races and, in addition, to broadcast a live commentary over the radio. The commentary proved so popular with local racing fans that live attendance at the track began to suffer. The plaintiff sued for nuisance and for misappropriation of the property in its spectacle, incidentally, indicating a parallel between nuisance and unfair competition. The Court in *INS*, at 241, also invoked that connection by claiming that INS acted "in violation of the principle that underlies the maxim '*sic utere tuo*,' etc." The *Victoria Park* court held for the defendant. There was no nuisance, because (see chapter 4, note 36) the defendant's overlooking had no impact on the use of the plaintiff's land *as* land, even if it had an effect on the profitability of the plaintiff's activities. (This fact is what explains the UK Supreme Court's distinguishing *Victoria Park* in *Fearn v Tate Gallery*, [2023] UKSC 4, [184].) In reaching its decision on nuisance, the court also noted that the plaintiff could not have a right that the defendants not open their eyes and see what they see; I think that this means that even if the kind of interference in this case could have been a nuisance, it would have been a matter of give and take, live and let live, and so not actually a nuisance on the facts. If we think about the possibility of the spectacle of the race as a res, we see something similar. My rights to my res cannot include a right that you not disclose true publicly available information about it. That is, I cannot prevent you from using your eyes and acting on what you see, as the court puts it. Reports about my product are different products, even if the former depend on the latter. There was no misrepresentation in *Victoria Park*, and, indeed, it is hard to know how there could have been. No matter how talented the radio announcer was, it would never be possible for his listeners to mistakenly think they had entered the racetrack itself. Thus the slightly different factual context of the case meant that the defendants' radio broadcasts of the races in effect automatically included an attribution of their source, a giving of credit to the plaintiff. (The contrast also helpfully clarifies the relevant idea of competition, and in particular the way that it is not *merely* an economic idea. While it's true that a given consumer might on a given day choose to stay home to listen to Angles' broadcast instead of attend the race, that fact on its own does not make the competition unfair.) On this reading, the result in *Victoria Park* makes sense in light of *INS*. Indeed, the Australian court's suggestion that, even if the plaintiffs had property in a spectacle, such a property right would not necessarily mean that

The considerations about the idea of yours and mine and its application to a res can also help us to think through some other prominent cases which inquire into the possibility of property rights in certain market contexts. These are cases in which a party has a government-created or -granted right to participate in a profession or activity that those without the licence are prohibited from doing. I am thinking about taxi licences, fishing licences, or radio-frequency licences, as well as licences entitling the holder to practice a certain profession, like law or dentistry.[72] Some of these cases seem to turn on a version of the question about the difference between property and personal rights, as when a court inquires into whether or not a certain licence is sufficiently independent from its holder to be a res.[73] While those cases often include interesting discussions of that narrower question—and can be as helpful as the body parts cases we saw in §5.2 for our thinking about it—in fact, all these cases fail to be cases of property for a more basic reason: they are not cases where the idea of yours and mine has any application at all. A licence is, as courts sometimes say, a right to do something that would otherwise be prohibited, so it does not give its holder any control whatsoever over the permissibility of others' actions. And such control is at the heart of the idea of yours and mine and at the heart of property.[74] Just one more

others could not describe its subject, fits well with my analysis: you can in general describe others' property, and, were INS to have reported AP's news as "AP's news," there is a clear sense in which they would have been describing AP's news, rather than misappropriating it.

[72] See Katrina Miriam Wyman, "Problematic Private Property: The Case of New York Taxicab Medallions" 30 Yale Journal on Regulation 125 (2013); Anthony Duggan, "In the Wake of the Bingo Queen: Are Licences Property?" 47 Canadian Business Law Journal 225 (2008); R. H. Coase, "The Federal Communications Commission" 2 Journal of Law & Economics 1 (1959). For an earlier treatment of these issues, with which I am still mostly on board, see my "Property in Licences and the Law of Things" 59 McGill Law Journal 559 (2013), and for penetrating criticism of one of its elements with which I am no longer on board, see Newman, "Using Things, Defining Property."

[73] See *Caratun v Caratun* and the discussion in note 11 *supra*.

[74] For a very clear and cogent statement, see *Illinois Transp Trade Ass'n v City of Chicago* 839 F3d 594 (7th Cir 2016). This is a judgment of Richard Posner, suggesting a pretty broad-based support for this idea. What I am offering here that is distinctive is an explanation of the idea. For a case that gets this precise point very, very wrong, see *Saulnier v Royal Bank of Canada*, 2008 SCC 58. I don't want to discuss *Saulnier* in too much detail, but it's noteworthy how the Court's conclusion that a fishing licence counts as property (for the purposes of statutory insolvency law) turns on a bad analogy. The court says that the licence, because it allows the holder to engage in an activity (fishing) that would otherwise be prohibited while at the same time allowing the holder to get a property right in the results of that activity (fish) is like a common law *profit a prendre*, which is essentially an easement giving the dominant tenant the right to take something (like fish or lumber) from the servient tenement. The problem with the analogy—and it is, to be fair, just an analogy, the Court is clear that it isn't saying that the licence is in fact a *profit*—is that a *profit* is a property right in the same way that an easement is a property right: interference by third parties is a wrong, a nuisance: Megarry and Wade, The Law of Real Property 7th ed §29-005. But in the fishing case, there is no parallel third-party protection, an unlicensed fisher is committing no wrong against a licensed fisher. The fishing licence really is more like a common law licence to do something on another's land that might involve getting a property right in some object acquired on that land; in this way it's like a ticket to a baseball game, where you might (famously, see *Popov v Hayashi*, WL 31833731 Cal 2002) become the owner of a ball hit into the stands. But the ticket is not a property right, it is an *in personam* licence good only against

thought about these cases: the reason that there is no property here is the form of the right, rather than the fact that they are statutory or sometimes that they are understood as aimed at promoting certain public policy goals. It would be possible to create a statutory licence aimed at allowing participants in some market to compete as equals and, were this licence created with a yours-and-mine form, it would make sense to think of it as a res that could be owned.[75] But for the most part the actual cases that exist do not have this form.

5.6 Some Considerations about Property in Information

There is a range of rather different issues treated under the heading of "property in information." I will not here purport to touch on all of them, but will just raise a few abstract points that are relevant to our thinking about them.

First, it is helpful to begin by noticing a question about the idea of property in information. The question is this: what is the res? What could the content of such a right be, what kinds of activities of others would be subject to its holder's control? When it comes to tangibles, as we have seen, the core of property rights involves notions of physical interactions. But when it comes to information, such physical interactions are (obviously) impossible. So we can approach the question by noticing that a broader idea, applicable even in the tangible context, is that of using: a holder of a property right has, at least to a certain degree, the capacity to determine how others may use what is owned. But what is it to use information? Some ways to use information are more readily understandable as species of broader genera which are not themselves directly about information. Take the *INS* case: the right in *INS* is, in a way, about the information reported by AP in its newspapers. But as I argued, the claim is really one about unfair competition, and the information in question is just the means by which INS is competing unfairly with AP.

To focus the analysis, we can think about ways in which information is used distinctively and specifically as information. One thought might be that you use information in that special way whenever you have certain cognitive attitudes with respect to it: when you know it or believe it or something like that. We

the issuer, and provides no third-party protection at all, so that if I counterfeited your ticket and took your seat, you would have no claim against me, although you might have a claim against the stadium if they failed to admit you, and the stadium would have a claim against me.

[75] For a proposal in the radio context, see Jora R Minasian, "Property Rights in Radiation: An Alternative Approach to Radio Frequency Allocation" 18 Journal of Law & Economics 221 (1975). For a discussion of the way that Los Angeles used to regulate taxis by providing medallion holders with something much more like a property right in my sense, see Ross D Eckert, "The Los Angeles Taxi Monopoly: An Economic Inquiry" 43 Southern California Law Review 407 (1970).

should immediately head off any suggestion that the owner of information could have a right that others not know or believe that information. Knowledge and belief are not under our control in the required sense: I cannot make myself believe or not believe something in the same way that I can make myself touch or not touch some object,[76] so I could not govern my activities according to any such right.[77] Here is a more promising line of thought: the sharing of information is a central feature of human lives and our social world. So perhaps it is the sharing of information to which the law ought to direct its attention. This thought is, I think, at least implicit in much of the discourse in this area, where it is repeatedly suggested that property rights in information are rights with respect to disclosure or publication.[78] And disclosure or publication are the sorts of actions that are under our control in the relevant way.[79] So let us consider the possibility that a property right in information is a right that others not publicize or disclose that information (without the consent of the right holder). Importantly, however, not every right that has that substance is a property right. Seeing why will help, once again, our more general thinking about the nature of property rights, by reflecting on the application of the more abstract ideas we have been considering in the last few sections.

Notice next that some rights with respect to disclosing information are not property rights, because they are *in personam* rather than *in rem*. Here it is most illuminating to reflect on the distinction between rights to confidential information and rights arising out of a relation of confidence. It is not remotely controversial to say that you and I could enter into a contract in which you promise not to publicize a certain piece of information that I convey to you, say, the number of different kinds of mustard in my fridge. If you publicized that information, you would breach the contract and I would have a claim against you. My right in that case is *in personam*, since it arose entirely out of the contract. Other kinds of legal relations that you and I might have could, in noncontractual settings, give rise to similar duties on you not to publicly disclose certain information.[80] These duties are known as duties of confidence, and are normally said to arise out of an explicit or implicit undertaking, and so are *in personam* in the sense articulated in §5.3. But can we imagine circumstances in which it seems like you owe me a duty not to publicly disclose some information without having undertaken such

[76] Pamela Hieronymi, "Controlling Attitudes" 87 Pacific Philosophical Quarterly 45 (2006).
[77] *R v Stewart*, [1988] 1 SCR 963. An important element of the rule of law, of course, as well as, arguably, the basic commitment is that we cannot be liable for things that are not under our control.
[78] It is, for instance, thematic in Samuel D Warren and Louis D Brandies, "The Right to Privacy" 4 Harvard Law Review 193 (1890).
[79] For a broader account of some of this section's subject matter that fits within the overall framework of this chapter, see James Grimmelman and Christina Mulligan, "Data Property" 72 American University Law Review 829 (2023).
[80] For discussion, see *Cadbury-Schweppes Inc v FBI Foods*, [1999] 1 SCR 142.

a duty? For the duty to be *in rem*, we would want to think about such a case as one in which the information was a res, and so anyone who came upon the information would be bound by the relevant duty.

Suppose, for instance, that you wrote down the information about my mustard preferences and then a third party came upon that information and publicized it. You would not have breached our contract, but we might wonder if I ought to have a claim against the third party. And courts have recognized that someone in my position in such a case could have a claim that would necessarily lack the *in personam* character of the duty based on an undertaking.[81] Indeed, there is recognition that the same logic would apply even in cases where a stranger came upon confidential information without any connection at all to the person whose information it is, as "where an obviously confidential document is wafted by an electric fan out of a window into a crowded street."[82] There is some controversy in the law and commentary as to whether such a right should be called a property right,[83] although much of that controversy is based on and beset by confusions about what is distinctive about property. On my account, we ask whether it makes sense to employ the idea of yours and mine here, and whether we can think of such a right as a response to a problem with yours-and-mine form. I return to that question in a moment. For now, we can see that the common law has recognized a distinction between *in rem* and *in personam* rights that determine the permissibility of others' disclosure of specific information, which is an important part of the possibility of thinking about property in information.

A third part of the story should thus come as no surprise. To think about property in information, we need to be able to think about that information in terms of a res that could be yours or mine. The difference between duties of confidence and duties with respect to confidential information illuminates the way to think about the independence of that res from those who owe the duty. So now we need to think about the independence of the res from the person who holds the right. Again, we can help to illuminate the target of our investigation by contrasting it with some other kinds of rights. The basic form of those contrasting rights here will be rights, good against the world, that some information not be disclosed or publicized but where somehow the information seems specially connected to a particular holder, so that we would not think of the information as something that the holder has but rather as somehow part of the holder. In other words, we are thinking about rights to information that are personal as opposed to proprietary.

[81] The clearest and most authoritative statement is found in Lord Goff's speech in *Attorney-General v. Guardian Newspapers (No 2)*, [1988] 3 All ER 545.

[82] *Guardian Newspapers* at 658–59.

[83] *Guardian Newspapers* at 659.

One candidate to fit into such a category might be copyright. We cannot explore copyright in detail here, given its immense complexity. But on what seems to me to be the most compelling account of the subject matter, copyright protects the right of an author to speak in their own name, and so the right is really closely connected to its holder in a way that makes it a personal right in the relevant sense.[84] According to this view, the wrong of copyright infringement is not interacting with some res that is independent of the author, but rather forcing an author to speak when they would have chosen not to do so. And while I will not defend this view, notice that even setting it out clarifies our bigger target, in that it shows how a view of copyright as a property right would need to demonstrate how the work protected could be thought of as a res independent of the author. In fact, that might be the way to think about patents. Patent law, like copyright, is another area that is far too rich and complex to discuss here. Patents do not seem to have anything like the close connection to their holders that copyrighted works do. And the law of patents as a whole does seem to have the same kind of egalitarian structure that trespass and nuisance law give to the law of (tangible) property: each patentee has rights over their invention that are structured and limited by doctrines (including nonobviousness and novelty, the doctrine of equivalents, and the rules about the relation between the contents of the specification and the scope of the monopoly[85]) best interpreted as realizing the demand that they be consistent with others having the same right, so that patent holders can relate to one another as equals. However, the commercial context in which patents operate—limited as they are to subject matters that are, arguably, tied to something like commercialization or industrial application[86]—might make the rights granted by patents akin to those granted in *INS v AP*, that is, rights with respect to information that are not really about information but are instead about constituting relations of equals among market participants. Exploring all this would take us too far afield and will need to wait for another day.

The problem of thinking about rights to information as personal or proprietary appears again in the context where rights to information are, these days, most salient, namely, rights with respect to what's usually called "data." Warren and Brandeis' famous article about the right to privacy helps us here: in that article, we find a variety of examples of information that we would plausibly consider personal in the relevant sense, information that is directly *about* me, so that any justifiable rights to it would need to be my rights in the way that rights to my body need to be my rights, as we saw in §5.1. Warren and Brandeis' examples might strike us as somewhat dated, but the contemporary world provides a

[84] Abraham Drassinower, What's Wrong with Copying? (2015).

[85] See *Tye-Sil Corp Ltd v Diversified Products* (1991), 35 CPR (3d) 350 (FC) on the first two and *Free World Trust v Electro-Santé Inc*, 2000 SCC 66, on the second two of those four doctrines.

[86] See, for discussion, *Amazon.com Inc v Canada (Attorney General)*, 2010 FC 1011.

multitude of examples of its own, including medical or genetic information or certain kinds of intimate information.[87] Any private rights[88] with respect to this information—rights that others not disclose it—would not be property rights and would not be alienable.[89] The suggestion I made that the value of such rights would lie in their inalienability is apposite here. The right seems intimately tied to the person whose right it is. As Anita Allen has suggested, "use of a man or woman's photo interferes with their freedom to limit the public gaze—a liberty so basic that without it one is, to that extent, a slave."[90] We value this control over our private information, that is, because it is our control and not anyone else's.[91] So a property right in information would need to be about information that lacks such a connection to its holder. The kinds of information that are typically protected under the guise of confidential information—things like trade secrets, customer or client lists, perhaps educational information like grades or exams—are more easily seen as proprietary in this sense. In these cases, we are more drawn to think that the information is separate enough from its holder—that

[87] This last is no idle theoretical point, as the disgusting contemporary phenomenon of "revenge porn" makes clear. In some jurisdictions, such activity is held to be a violation of a personal right. See, e.g., *Jane Doe 72511 v Morgan*, 2016 ONSC 6607. In endorsing that view, I don't deny that criminal law might be a more effective deterrent: see Danielle Keats Citron and Mary Anne Franks, "Criminalizing Revenge Porn" 49 Wake Forest Law Review 345, 357–59 (2014). For more see Lauren Scholz, "Private Rights of Action in Privacy Law" 63 William & Mary Law Review 1639 (2022).

[88] An important emerging question is about the ways in which a process of structural subordination might arise with respect to private rights in data, when nonwrongful uses of data over which private rights exist might accumulate to generate new forms of subordination. I will leave discussion of this problem to another day.

[89] The Restatement (2d) of Torts provides a right with respect to such personal information: "§652D: One who gives publicity to a matter concerning the private life of another is subject to liability to the other for invasion of his privacy, if the matter publicized is of a kind that (a) would be highly offensive to a reasonable person, and (b) is not of legitimate concern to the public." A subsequent section (§652I) clarifies that this right is inalienable.

[90] Allen, "Natural Law, Slavery, and the Right to Privacy Tort" at 1210.

[91] So, unsurprisingly, I disagree with those who think that the question of whether or not to protect privacy with a property right is a kind of pragmatic question that depends on the costs and benefits: the right could not be alienable, so it cannot be property. It's just off the table. For some treatments, see Jessica Litman, "Information Privacy / Information Property" 52 Stanford Law Review 1282 (2000); Pamela Samuelson, "Privacy as Intellectual Property?" 52 Stanford Law Review 1152 (2000); Paul M Schwartz, "Property, Privacy, and Personal Data" 117 Harvard Law Review 2056 (2004). Schwartz, incidentally, argues for a property right in personal data in part based on an utterly confused idea of what alienability is. He argues for what he calls a "hybrid" idea of alienability, which "would permit the *transfer* for an initial category of *use* of personal data, but only if the customer is granted an opportunity to block further transfer or use by unaffiliated entities. Any further use or transfer would require the customer to opt in—that is, it would be prohibited unless the customer affirmatively agrees to it." I hope that by this point in the book you'll see the confusion here: that is not, even a little bit or even in a "hybrid" way, what alienation is. That is just a licence, an exercise of the power to consent to something that would otherwise be a wrong, and involves nothing like the alienation of control to another that applies even against the transferor. When I permit you to use my body to practice cutting hair, the consent comes with an "opportunity to block further transfer"—you can't tell your sister that she can now cut my hair—and further use is prohibited unless I affirmatively agree to it—you can't cut my hair tomorrow without asking because I let you cut it yesterday. A right to prevent others from using one's information is quite readily understandable as a personal right and need not—and if Allen is right, *should* not—involve any notion of alienability at all.

the need to protect it is independent of the identity of its holder—that we can think of it as a kind of informational res and thus think of it through the idea of yours and mine. In a case where you misuse *my* trade secret, it seems plausible to think that you are wronging me in a way that is mediated by the idea of yours and mine, in contrast to a case where you misuse personal information, where my complaint is that you did something wrong to me, not that you misused or misappropriated information that just happens to be mine.

Let us put all of this together. To talk about property in information we need to remember first that any private right with respect to information cannot be a right that others not know or believe it but only a right that they not do something with it, and most likely a right that they not disclose it. Second, by carefully attending to the idea of a res and the associated independence of a property right from both right holder and duty bearers, we can notice how not all rights to information are best thought of as property rights. Only a right that, on the one hand, binds everyone and does not arise out of any transaction between right holder and duty bearer and, on the other, is not personal in the way that privacy rights are, could fit that description. Now add one more thought: in my view, a right only counts as a property right if it is a right that solves a problem with a yours-and-mine form. Are there such rights?

The right to confidential information seems like the best candidate here. Without going into too much detail, we can notice that (1) the fact that we need to communicate information to one another in order to live together as individuals,[92] paired with (2) the fact that important parts of our lives involve information that we seem to want control over the dissemination of, in a way that sometimes involves keeping it secret and sometimes passing it on,[93] might generate some situations in which a problem with a yours-and-mine form could arise with respect to certain kinds of information. Suppose I have some information that, in order to use, I need to be able to talk to others about. Without any right in that information, we might face the familiar problem about how to determine if you are using the information in a way that is consistent with our standing as equals, or if instead you might take the information and use it for yourself merely because you are (in some relevant sense) stronger than me. Some such situations might be better viewed through the lens of something like an idea of unfair competition, as I suggested about *INS v AP* and patent law. But we can imagine cases that are not about unfair competition,[94] and such cases might be plausibly thought of as cases in which, for the parties to relate as equals, we need property in information.

[92] A theme of Seana Valentine Shiffrin, Speech Matters: On Lying, Morality, and the Law (2014).
[93] Thomas Nagel, Concealment and Exposure, 27 Philosophy & Public Affairs 3 (1998).
[94] *Guardian Newspapers* might be such a case, although the facts there are complex in other ways.

5.7 Intangible Wrongs

Before we turn to a different class of cases, it will be helpful here to summarize some of the past few sections in a somewhat schematic way by reference to some ideas that have been, to a certain degree, suppressed. The idea of yours and mine is realized in the law through property rights. When I have a property right, I get to determine the permissibility of others' actions with respect to the subject matter of that right. When the subject matter of my right is a tangible object or a space, we seem to have a relatively intuitive way to understand the scope of the right, or, in different terms, to understand the words "with respect to" in that previous sentence. That is, when I own an avocado, I basically have the right that you not touch the avocado without my consent. Here "touch" includes both "intentionally physically handle" and also something like "negligently damage," because either of those can be understood to be inconsistent with my having the kind of control over the avocado that is required for us to be able to relate as equals with respect to the various activities and relations that we take ourselves to be able to enter into with avocados. When it comes to land, something similar is true, but we add the protection that is given by nuisance law, since a nuisance, by unreasonably interfering with my use and enjoyment of my land, is also inconsistent with the possibility of equal relations with respect to land.

Next recall the point, from §5.4, that when it comes to property in tangible objects, we need to keep distinct the nonlegal thing and the legal res. That point can be understood through the lens of these legal wrongs: what I have legally is a set of rights to the res, such that we can understand the res as constituted by the rights I have with respect to it. The legal boundaries of the res are not the physical boundaries of the thing. Of course, the legal boundaries of the res are set by reference to the physical boundaries of the thing in the following sense: the res is constructed by applying the idea of yours and mine to the thing, by asking how we could relate as equals with respect to the thing. When it comes to most tangible objects and spaces, the Problem of Yours and Mine demands rights against physical interferences (coming onto land, taking or using avocados); conversely, we do not tend to need protection against others' acting in ways that do not involve physical interaction with the object or space in order to relate as equals. (Although sometimes we do, as in the case of intangible nuisances.) So there are lots of ways that we can talk about others' using or interacting with the thing that are not wrongful. To repeat myself, drawing a picture of your avocado is not a wrong because we do not need rights against drawing pictures to relate as equals with respect to avocados; in fact, it must not be a wrong because a right of that sort would allow avocado owners to subordinate others. So when it comes to physical objects, the res is going to be close to (but not coextensive with) the thing because equal relations here are going to be primarily equal relations with respect to physical interaction with the thing. But—and I think this is the theoretically most important claim—the role of the physical is not basic but rather derived from the abstract relational egalitarian normativity of the idea of yours and mine.

When it comes to intangibles, the same abstract structure applies, but without the physical thing's being present to play the same role. So the res is more explicitly legally constructed or artificial in the sense that the law creates the res to ensure equal relations with respect to some particular form of human conduct. But the rights to the res in the tangible cases are those rights that are necessary to ensure equal relations in that context, and so the rights in the various intangibles case must be constructed in the same form. Some kinds of interactions with the res will be wrongs but others will not, and the line between these cases is drawn by inquiring into what kinds of rights are needed in order to allow for equal relations through the idea of yours and mine with respect to the type of res in question.

We can make this concrete. In trademarks, the possibility of equal relations between market competitors requires that I have a right that you not use my mark or another mark in a way that would be confusing. But you are free to use nonconfusing marks, because a right that I had that prevented you from doing that would give me too much control over our competition for us to be able to relate as equals.[95] The right is against certain uses of the res but not others. In the *INS v AP* case, we can discern a similar dynamic. The property right in the res—the report of the hot news—gives its holder a right that protects against some uses of the res but not others. Specifically, it gives AP a right that INS (or anyone) not use the news as reported by AP in a way that competes against AP's own use of the news, but it does not give AP a right that the public (or anyone, including INS) use that news in a noncompetitive way, for instance, by talking about it around the water cooler. The discussions from the §5.6 suggest how to think about these ideas in the context of information or data: a right holder might have (as in the case of confidential information, perhaps) a right that others not disclose the information but could not have a right that others not believe or think about the information. In all these cases, the scope of the right in the res is determined by the application of the idea of yours and mine: we ask, what kinds of rights in this res would be required to allow you and me to think about it using that idea and thereby to relate as equals.[96] And, of course, there is often a significant amount of indeterminacy in answering that question, which is why we need courts exercising judgment in the application of the abstract idea to the particulars of a given context.

[95] *Waltham Watch* illustrates this point: see notes 56–57, *supra*.

[96] There may be a worry about circularity here—since the boundaries of the res are grounded on the possibility of equal relations with respect to the res—but I think it can be managed. We need to start the analysis in any given case by noticing some pre-proprietarily constituted context in which a problem with a yours-and-mine form arises. In the case of tangibles, this is the context of relating with respect to the physical thing; in intangible cases, it is some other social or legal context. But this pre-proprietary context is just the starting point of our analysis, the res is the result.

One more thing: notice the way that the nature of the res can shape the application of the idea of yours and mine. That is, we think about what it means for this or that subject matter to be mine by reference to the nature of this or that subject matter. As I said, when it comes to tangibles, to think of something as mine is roughly to think of having control over physical interactions with it. The wrong in this case involves interfering with that control. When it comes to the market-relations cases, we apply the idea of yours and mine to think about having some kind of control over the way that others use certain elements of the business (the product or service), so that the wrong involves them taking control of "my mark" or "my news" or "my information" or what have you. But the important point is that "taking control" is in part a function of the nature of the res: how I take control of your mark is quite a different matter than how I take control of your avocado.

All of this might be summarized in the following table. The essential thought is that the form of property rights is not different for tangible and intangible rights. In all cases, property in some res exists in order to allow equal relations with respect to that res, and so the holder of the right can prevent activities that are inconsistent with such equal relations but not activities that are not.

Res	Content of yours-mine problem	Right to prevent	No right to prevent
Avocado	Physical uses: guacamole, avocado toast, paperweight	Interference with control over physical use by intentional use; damage preventing usability	Uses that do not interfere with owner's use: drawing, writing songs about
Land	Use as a space to do things on	Unauthorized entrances, damage, nuisances	Give-and-take interferences, most nonphysical uses
Trademark	Participating in competitive market	Confusing uses	Nonconfusing uses
Hot News	Participating in a competitive market	Commercial uses	Noncommercial uses
(Confidential) Information	Keeping information secret	Disclosure	Belief

Keeping this structure in mind will help us with a different class of cases.

5.8 In Rem Protection

The cases I discuss in this section do not have a unified name in our legal thought and talk, and they can be doctrinally quite far from each other. At a high level of generality, they are all cases in which we find operative in legal reasoning about the result both some considerations that seem to be about *in personam* rights, typically contracts or debts, and some considerations that seem to be more about property. Cases like corporate shares, transferable debts, mortgages, trusts, and other similar situations are all, in various ways, like this.[97] Without claiming to be exhaustive, I want in this section to try to provide something of a theoretically comprehensive account of this kind of case.

The basic idea is, roughly, this: sometimes, an *in personam* right creates for its holder a kind of vulnerability to interference by third parties, so that those third parties can (in various ways, which depend on the particular *in personam* right in question) interfere with the *in personam* relationship between the (*in personam*)

[97] You might say: hold up, there is a unified name for (many of) these cases and that name is "chose in action." What exactly this term of art means and what its extension is are matters of some dispute. Luckily—seriously, this is really very lucky—what a chose in action is need not concern us here, because, as I hope to show, we can just approach these questions head-on, as it were, without the need for this mediating category. For a helpful one among many overviews of the real morass about the nature of choses in action, see O R Marshall, The Assignment of Choses in Action 1–33 (1950). One point is worth noticing with respect to the overall argument of this book. In short, choses in action are generally distinguished from choses in possession (which latter category includes tangible objects) on the grounds that the holder of the latter, but not the former, can vindicate the right in question by physical possession, whereas the holder of a chose in action needs the assistance of the law (i.e., of a legal action) to vindicate their right. From this distinction it's a short step to the confused view that the law, in the case of tangible things, merely protects some notion of possession or use that is itself independent of the law. One important contribution to the literature on choses in action, for instance, argues that "there is much in property [in land and tangibles] which cannot be said to consist in right; which is, in a manner, independent of law," and contrasts with this "the nature of incorporeal things! [exclamation mark *sic*] They are mere claims to have things (in the primary sense) which others possess, or upon things, which others possess, or to have things or services rendered by others. They are claims which may be satisfied by acquiescence therein, but which, if disputed, can only be enforced by going to law." (See T Cyprian Williams, "Property, Things in Action, and Copyright"43 Law Quarterly Review 223, 225–26 (1893); the whole of pages 225–26 is worth reading because it is a clear statement of this confused idea.) As I've tried to stress throughout the book, this is just not right: even in the case of tangibles and spaces, property is about having, not holding, and thus "can only be enforced by going to law," because *what I have,* my res, is in a very important sense a legal construct. (Self-help is no objection to this claim, as all permissible self-help is itself legally regulated. Indeed, Williams himself seems to contemplate this, describing self-help as something that, in some cases, "the law leaves me free to exercise." For discussion of self-help, see Zoë Sinel, "De-Ciphering Self-Help" 67 University of Toronto Law Journal 31 (2017).) As I said, we can hold or manipulate objects without property, but we cannot without property have them as yours or mine and therefore cannot use them in a way that is consistent with the basic commitment. Therefore, whatever it is about choses in action that makes them a distinctive category, if a distinctive category they be, must be located in the *way* that they are legally regulated, and not the fact that they are "claims which . . . can only be enforced by going to law." For an expression of a view similar to mine in a prominent text, see Paul L Davies and Sarah Worthington, Gower's Principles of Modern Company Law 10th ed §23-1 (2016): using the term "chose in action" is "not helpful, for 'chose in action' is a notoriously vague term used to describe a mass of interests which have little or nothing in common except that they confer no right to possession of a physical thing."

right holder and the (*in personam*) duty bearer in a way that we could recognize as subordinating of the right holder, just in their capacity as holder of the *in personam* right, to third parties. In other words, a problem with a yours-and-mine form arises with respect to the *in personam* right; more colloquially if slightly imprecisely, there is a problem about deciding *who* has the *in personam* right vis-à-vis the *in personam* duty bearer. What the law does, in these cases, is protect the *in personam* right with an additional, distinct *in rem* right, and in so doing sees something like the position of the *in personam* right holder as itself a kind of a res. I know that is a mouthful and might in the abstract seem hard to grasp. As we proceed through a range of examples, the abstract idea should come into focus.

We can start with a sort of toy example. Think about a ticket to a sporting event. Such a ticket is a licence, which is *in personam*.[98] I have no claim against you if you somehow forge my ticket and use it to gain entry to the stadium: you may have wronged the stadium (in trespass or fraud) and the stadium may breach its contract by refusing to let me in. But the ticket does not give me any property in the event or the stadium. Now, traditionally, tickets of this sort are printed on pieces of paper, and the tickets are treated by their issuers as freely transferable in the hands of buyers, such that whoever holds the ticket is allowed to enter. The piece of paper, of course, is an object that is unproblematically ownable. But the piece of paper represents an *in personam* right, and so the value of the property in the paper is more properly understood to be the value of that *in personam* right—that is, the value of being able to enter the game. The *in rem* property right in the physical ticket thus works, in a way, to protect the *in personam* right embodied by the ticket.

This model can be used to think about a range of (arguably) more important cases, starting with corporate shares. The idea that a share is property seems for many theorists almost truistic.[99] But things are more complex than they appear.

[98] See generally §4.1 as well as, more precisely on this point, *supra* note 74.

[99] "Of course, it is true that shareholders own shares of stock." Julian Velasco, "Shareholder Ownership and Primacy" 2010 University of Illinois Law Review 897, 929. To the same effect see Davies and Worthington, Principles of Modern Company Law at §23-3, who claim that it is "clear" that shares are "recognized as objects of property." To be clear, the question here is about owning shares and not about owning the corporation. I won't deal with the question of whether or not the shareholders own the corporation. I'll just say this: for it to be the case that they do, we'd need be able to identify *the corporation itself* as a kind of res that is distinct from its shares or a right in its reputation or its business goodwill or its profits or its assets or . . . or the residual claim. I think that the best explanation for the common nonlegal thought and talk according to which someone can own a corporation is just that they own all or a majority of its shares, which, as I am about to explain, is a real (if limited) kind of ownership. For a similar skepticism about the idea of a corporation, applied to some particular questions in corporate law, see Edward Iacobucci, "Indeterminacy and the Canadian Supreme Court's Approach to Corporate Fiduciary Duties" 48 Canadian Business Law Journal 232, 235–36 (2009). And for an argument that a share is not property that depends on the kind of physicalist paradigm of property that I reject, see Arianna Pretto-Sakmann, Boundaries of Personal Property: Shares and Sub-Shares (2005).

A corporate share is, at heart, a kind of *in personam* right held by the shareholder against the officers and directors of the corporation to (in some combination according to competing views) being paid a dividend, having a vote in shareholders' meetings and in elections of directors, and some residual claim in the corporation's assets upon its dissolution.[100] This *in personam* right is transferable, in the precise sense that when I give or sell you the share, I give or sell the attendant *in personam* right I have against the directors (whatever its precise content) to you.[101] (When I own the share, I have certain rights, and then after I sell it to you, you have those same rights.) This transferability alone does not make this *in personam* right into property, because the nature of the right is distinctly tied to the identity of the duty bearer (the directors) and the transaction that gave rise to it (or the issuance of shares). But the fact that the *in personam* right is transferable allows for the possibility that a third party might effect a wrongful transfer, essentially usurping the place of the rightful shareholder. This introduces the possibility of thinking about shares using the idea of yours and mine.

How exactly this usurpation is effected depends on a range of details. So-called bearer shares are printed on pieces of paper and work the same way as the ticket described two paragraphs ago, in that the rights accrue to whomever has the piece of paper.[102] But most shares are not like that: whether printed or not, the holder of the share is listed on a register, and the *in personam* rights of the shareholder can be exercised by whomever is listed.[103] It does seem, however, that it is possible in various ways (too complex to detail here) to usurp the position of a particular shareholder on such a register. When that happens, we can use the idea of yours and mine to understand the nature of the wrong: someone who usurps the rights under "your" shares seems to take something from you. You would say to the person who took your vote, "that was my vote to cast,"[104] so the possibility of usurpation is a problem with yours-and-mine form. By granting a shareholder a right against such usurpation, the law can be understood to be that

[100] For this view of the nature of the *in personam* right see Larissa Katz, "Shares as Shares" in Ben Agnew and Sinéad Agnew eds, 10 Modern Studies in Property Law 107 (2019). The official definition of a share in, for instance, the Ontario legislation is to the same effect: see Ontario *Business Corporations Act*, RSO 1990 c B16, s 22(3).

[101] These days most shares are "uncertificated," and so transfer is effected by substituting the name of the old shareholder for the name of the new one in the corporate registry. See, for instance, OBCA s 100.

[102] Pretto-Sakmann, Boundaries of Personal Property at 111–13, 191.

[103] Most event tickets these days are not printed on pieces of paper either. But they seem to still have the character of a bearer share, in that entry to the venue is the right of whomever has the relevant QR code or NFC data. This suggests that someone who spoofs the venue's reader is not wronging the true ticketholder.

[104] *Pender v Lushington*, (1877) 6 Ch D 70.

the share, understood as the right to exercise whatever the precise contents of the *in personam* right are, is itself a kind of res.[105]

We can grasp this through the idea of yours and mine by seeing the affinity between the usurpation of my shareholder rights and the sense in which certain core wrongs in tangible property can be understood as themselves a kind of usurpation. This is, for instance, a common understanding of conversion: "the gist of conversion is the unauthorized assumption of the powers of the true owner."[106] Whereas the usurpation in the tort of conversion involves a wrongdoer using the object without the owner's determination that such use is permissible, in effect taking the decision out of the owner's hands, the wrong in the share case involves taking, roughly, the "shareholder decisions" out of the owner's hands. The important thing to see is that the *in rem* right is distinct as a legal matter from the *in personam* right constituted by the relation between the shareholder and the directors of the corporation. So we are not running together *in personam* and *in rem* rights, but rather seeing that the one generates the other.

This mention of conversion and usurpation in the present context might bring to mind the question, addressed by the House of Lords in *OBG*,[107] of whether or not a contract right can be the subject of a conversion action. The facts of the case are complex, but for our purposes it suffices to say that the defendant, through some insolvency proceedings, mistakenly ended up in a position to be the beneficiary of a contract that the plaintiff had entered into. The plaintiff's claim was thus, in a way, that the defendant had usurped the plaintiff's position in that contract, and that therefore (in effect), the defendant took something that was the plaintiff's. In dissent, Baroness Hale agreed with this claim. Her speech emphasized how the defendant "took control" or "took charge" not only of the plaintiff's tangible assets but also of the plaintiff's contract rights, and so could be seen to have usurped those rights in a proprietary way.[108] On

[105] How exactly the law does this is complex enough and involves specific statutory rules in different jurisdictions, so I can't go into much detail here. But See OBCA ss 248 and 250 and Ontario *Securities Transfer Act, 2006*, SO 2006, c 8, as well as §8-503 of the Uniform Commercial Code. The situation in England is more complicated, but it does appear that a shareholder has the right to have a share register altered if someone else has been mistakenly registered in their place: see Davies and Worthington, Principles of Modern Company Law, §23-3. Nowadays, most corporate shares are held by intermediaries—stockbrokers—so that much of the law concerns what happens when such a party mistakenly transfers shares from one client to another. See Ronald J Mann, Elizabeth Warren, and Jay Lawrence Westbrook, Comprehensive Commercial Law: 2019 Statutory Supplement 416–18 (2019), discussing UCC §8-503 in particular. For reasons involving the way that such intermediaries operate—sort of like banks, in that a client doesn't have a specific share or set of them but rather has the ability to get a certain number of shares from the intermediary—another way that the shares have a property-like protection is that clients have a kind of super-priority in insolvency over the intermediary's other creditors: UCC §8-511.

[106] Comment, "Conversion of Choses in Action" 10 Fordham Law Review 415, 415–16 (1941).

[107] For a helpful treatment, see Simon Douglas, "The Scope of Conversion: Property and Contract" 74 Modern Law Review 329 (2011).

[108] See *OBG* at [309], [311].

this reading of the case, conversion of a contractual right would require quite narrowly circumscribed facts, involving usurpation of the position of a plaintiff within an actual contract, as opposed to merely inducing that contract's breach.[109]

We can say something similar—but not quite the same—about debt. First, a reminder that, while many debts arise out of contract, debt is strictly speaking a distinct legal relation.[110] But debt is *in personam,* since debt arises out of some transaction, be it contractual, or wrongful (like a judgment debt). The crucial thing about debts is that they are measured in fungibles, like money or grain. This matters because when I loan you $100, I (now called the creditor) do not have a right to any particular hundred-dollar note, but rather a right that you (the debtor) pay me $100. In other words, there is no res to which I can point and say "that is mine." This fungibility has effects on the third-party status of debts. In the contrast case, when I lend you some specific thing, like an avocado, I create a bailment relation, and I still have rights against third parties with respect to that specific avocado if they take it from you: I can sue them to get it back. But when I lend you money, there is no res that is mine that I have given to you, and so nothing in virtue of which our relation could create obligations on third parties. So I cannot bring any action to get the money back. Moreover, the fact that they took it has no impact on your duty to pay me back. Another way to see this is through the idea of usurpation. Someone who fraudulently convinces you to pay them, rather than me, that $100 has not usurped my place in our *in personam* debt relation because the law is clear that their fraud does not affect that relation at all, and that you still owe me $100. By contrast, someone who takes my avocado and makes guacamole with it or votes my share is exercising rights that are mine to exercise. This is why, notwithstanding some common nonlegal

[109] There is a lot to say about the tort of inducement, which is discussed at length in *OBG*. But I don't know that going into detail here is required or helpful to the general argument. A couple of points are in order. There are some who take the inducement tort to "[treat] contractual rights as a species of property": *OBG* at [32]. See also Francis Bowes Sayre, "Inducing Breach of Contract" 36 Harvard Law Review 663(1923), and Peter Benson, Justice in Transactions 91–95, 354–55 (2019). It is true that the form of the tort fits, to some degree, with the form I am elucidating in this section in that there seems to be some kind of right, good against the world, protecting the position of the holder of the contractual right. But something else might be going on here. It is not clear as a general matter that the inducement tort involves usurpation in the relevant sense, since "the defendant may be liable for inducing breach without acquiring the promised performance": Jennifer Nadler, "Freedom from Things: A Defense of the Disjunctive Obligation in Contract Law" 27 Legal Theory 177, 199 (2021), but usurpation seems to require just such an acquisition. And, from a different direction, analyses which treat the tort as somehow about the defendant's failure to respect the plaintiff's status as a potential contracting agent—by treating the plaintiff's contract as a "nullity": Ernest J Weinrib, Reciprocal Freedom: Private Law and Public Right 80–82 (2022)—might be thought to make the claim personal rather than proprietary.

[110] A V Levontin, "Debt and Contract in the Common Law" 1 Israel Law Review 60 (1966). Also, let me say that this is not a book about law and finance, so I'm going to talk only about simple debts. But I believe that what I say here goes, *mutatis mutandis*, for many other more complicated financial instruments.

thought and talk, the law and clear-eyed commenters on it insist that a debt is not a property right, that it is a matter of (as it is sometimes put) owing rather than owning.[111] Again, to put the point in my terms, there is no idea of yours and mine in this basic case of a debt because there is nothing that you (a third party, not the debtor) can take from me, nothing I can (or need to) point to and say "this is mine" to justify a claim about how you may act.

However, things are a bit more complicated. While the core of the idea that debt is merely *in personam* is conditioned on the fact that third-party interference does not affect the creditor's claim, there is a situation in which that condition does not hold. That situation is insolvency: when a debtor is insolvent, they are (by definition) unable to pay all of their debts, and upon insolvency the creditor's claim abates, which means that they are as a matter of law no longer able to vindicate it. What they are entitled to is, at best, a pro rata share of the debtor's assets. But this share can often be a tiny fraction of the amount of the original debt. So upon insolvency, we might think of a problem with yours-and-mine form as having arisen among the creditors with respect to the debtor's assets. Secured debt is a kind of solution to this problem. Again, there are lots and lots of details here, but a secured debt is roughly a debt in which (for one or another reason), the creditor gains "priority" in the insolvency proceedings, allowing them to extract the value of their claim (typically through seizing an asset) from the insolvent debtor's assets rather than have it divided among other creditors.[112] This priority in effect gives the creditor a right against third parties upon insolvency. And this right does not arise out of any transaction between the creditor and those third parties, so we can think about the secured debt as a kind of res, through the idea of yours and mine, with accompanying *in rem* protection.[113]

[111] Sarah Worthington, Equity 62 (2d ed 2006).

[112] For helpful discussions of the law here, see, in brief, Worthington, Equity at 77–81 and at more length Lionel Smith, "Security" in Burrows ed, English Private Law 307. I also benefited from the discussion of security interests in McFarlane, Structure of Property Law and from chapter 1 of Gerard McCormack, Secured Credit under English and American Law (2004).

[113] Two further thoughts here. First, while, as I noted, a debt is not a contract, many debts arise out of contracts, and so what I said about the *in rem* protection of contract rights also applies to those debts. Cook recognizes this: "Alienability of Choses in Action" at 820n4. So does Worthington, Equity at 62n12: she claims that the inducement tort adds "to the armoury of protection" of choses in action in a way that "parallels the protection afforded to 'proprietary' rights," suggesting that the lines between the two classes are "becoming increasingly blurred." Second, Penner argues that debts have *in rem* protection because the debtor's assets—his "wherewithal," to use Penner's term—are protected against third parties because they are, let's assume, tangibles, and so the creditor has such *in rem* protection in an "indirect" sort of way. This account is, I've gotta say, genuinely clever. But it's dependent on Penner's otherwise very implausible understanding of the nature of the *in rem* right associated with property, according to which we all owe duties of noninterference to "the plurality of property holders." That view, which I've criticized at more length elsewhere, is just not a plausible way to understand property as a part of private law. For Penner's view here, see Penner, Idea of Property in Law at 131, 142.

These brief remarks about the idea of a secured debt let me make the following even briefer remarks about mortgages. While there is a rather wide range of rules across common-law jurisdictions, the basic idea of a mortgage is present in all of them.[114] That basic idea is that an owner of property can enter into an agreement with a lender, which gives the lender, now called the mortgagee, a kind of security interest in the mortgaged property—protected, *in rem*, in ways that parallel what I just said about secured debts—as well as a potential possessory interest upon a default on the loan by the mortgagor (the original owner). The history of mortgage law is complicated and encrusted with lots of detail, some interesting,[115] some less so. But there are three basic things to say here. First, much of that law, including the creation and maintenance of the idea of the equity of redemption, can be understood as a series of attempts to ensure that mortgagor and mortgagee relate as equals with respect to the mortgaged property, somewhat in parallel to what I said in §4.5 about various kinds of shared ownership. Second, as noted, regardless of the various name changes and different doctrinal regimes, we can and should understand the mortgagee's interest as a property right in the land.[116] Third, in their modern, financialized, guise, mortgages give rise to important and pervasive possibilities for structural subordination, and I will return to those in §6.5.

The final category I want to talk about in this section is a big one: trusts.[117] The law of trusts is an immense and magnificently complicated area of law, so that I simply cannot begin to say anything detailed about it here. However, I can note how the basic structure we have seen so far in this section can allow us to explain the idea that the beneficiary of a trust holds a kind of a property right. A trust is, at heart, an *in personam* relation between the trustee and the

[114] For the English law, see the discussion in Smith, "Security," and McFarlane, Structure of Property Law. In fact, in England now, the arrangement is called a charge, rather than a mortgage, and is statutorily recognized as a distinctive kind of property right. American law is more complicated, as different states have different conceptions of mortgages (the so-called lien theory, title theory, and mixed theory conceptions). On American law and its history, I find helpful Ann M Burkhart, "Lenders and Land" 64 Missouri Law Review 249 (1999). Canadian law is more like English law: see Joseph E Roach, The Canadian Law of Mortgages (3d ed 2018).

[115] Here are two cool facts. (1) The French word for a "pledge," is *gage*. About 1,000 years ago, there were two kinds of pledges one could make with respect to land in England. One involved the lender earning money from the land, and was called a living pledge, or *vif gage*, whereas the other did not, and so was called a dead pledge, or *mort gage*. (2) As I say in the text, mortgages developed to protect both the interests of mortgagor and mortgagee through the life of the mortgage, and one of the most important protections of the mortgagor's interest was developed in the Courts of Equity and hence known as the equity of redemption, from whose name we get the idea that a homeowner has a certain amount of *equity* in their home (and that that amount rises as they pay down the debt to the mortgagee), and, it seems, the idea that non-debt investment instruments are known as equities.

[116] As I said two notes ago, this is true statutorily in England. And for a more general discussion, see Yun-chien Chang and Henry E Smith, "Structure and Style in Comparative Property Law" in Theodore Eisenberg and Giovanni Ramello eds, Comparative Law and Economics 131 (2016).

[117] And in fact the category is even bigger than that. See *infra* notes 120–122.

beneficiary, which arises through a transaction (of some sort; there are different kinds of trust) between them. The trustee holds the trust property for the benefit of the beneficiary, putting the beneficiary in a position of vulnerability or subordination to the trustee; the fiduciary duty owed by the trustee to the beneficiary protects against this. But because the trustee is the legal owner of the trust property and has a right to deal with it, the beneficiary is also vulnerable to certain actions of third parties. If I hold this avocado on trust for you and give it to a third party, your *in personam* right against me will be insufficient to ground a claim against the third party to get your avocado back. This is a problem with a yours-and-mine form: there is quite clearly a sense (I guess I should call it the "equitable" sense) in which the trust property is yours, although there is also a sense (the "legal" sense) in which it is not yours. Since the avocado is not yours in the second sense, you do not have a straightforward legal claim to the avocado, because legally it is mine, not yours. But your claim against the third party seems to rest on some sense in which something that is yours was taken from you.

I think the way to proceed here is to say that equity allows us to see what's normally called "the beneficiary's interest in the trust" as a res that is protected, in certain ways, by an *in rem* right against third parties.[118] To see this, we need to notice that the *in rem* right is not the *in personam* right the beneficiary has against the trustee. The *in rem* right precisely protects the beneficiary against the sorts of third-party interference that the example illustrates, third-party interference that could be understood using the same idea of usurpation employed in this section. But as it was earlier in the section, it is crucial here to see that the beneficiary's right is not the same as the trustee's right. In particular, when the trust property is a physical thing, the trustee has (but the beneficiary lacks) a right that others not interfere with the thing physically.[119] The beneficiary's *in rem* right is grounded on the *in personam* trust relation, and protects the beneficiary against interference with their interest under the trust, that is, with their right against the trustee that correlates with the trustee's *in personam* duty to them.

Put differently, the beneficiary's *in rem* right is one that "derives from" and protects the *in personam* relation. In saying that I am trying to suggest that the core of the analysis of the trust in terms of "a right against a right" proposed by

[118] Maitland said that we could describe those bound by the beneficiary's rights in two ways. First, we could say that the beneficiary has rights "enforceable against any person who has undertaken the trust, against all who claim through or under him as volunteers (heirs, devisees, personal representatives, donees), against his creditors, and against those who acquire the thing with notice actual or constructive of the trust." Or, we could say, second, that his rights are "enforceable against all save a *bona fide* purchaser . . . who for value has obtained a legal right in the thing without notice of the trust express or constructive." See Maitland, Equity at 120. I take it that the second description is much closer to the way I am arguing that we ought to think about what is happening.

[119] See, for some discussion, Andrew Tettenborn, "Trust Property and Conversion: An Equitable Confusion" 55 Cambridge Law Journal 36 (1996).

McFarlane and Stevens is consistent with what I say here.[120] Of course, I part ways with them about the classification of these rights as property. McFarlane and Stevens want to deny that the beneficiary's right is a property right because it is not a right to a physical thing. But if we abandon that requirement, as I think we ought to do for the reasons set out earlier in this chapter, we can instead embrace the idea that a property right is a right to a res, but allow that the res is a legal (or equitable) construction, something that is created in order to solve a nonphysical problem with a yours-and-mine form. That is not to say, of course, that there is no value in identifying this kind of case as in important ways quite distinct from the core cases of property. The equitable context seems important and the category of "equitable property" seems like a helpful one to mark that distinction.[121] In invoking this term, I mean to suggest that there are probably other cases—including some of those I have discussed in this section—that fit this same mold, and many of them are the ones normally talked about as "equitable property." I cannot here take a stand about the nature of equity. There have been places in this chapter and the previous one where I have discussed equitable doctrines without identifying them as such. For my purposes here, not much turns on the distinction. The important point is that, however we mark the way in which equitable property is a distinctive kind of property, we recognize the possibility of property in a legally constituted res and mark it in a way that preserves the thought that equitable property is a kind of property.[122]

Before I leave this section let me remind you of the content of §5.7. There I said that an important upshot of the picture of property I have tried to articulate is that the scope of any property right should depend on the nature of the subject matter of that right, on the nature of the res. The cases considered in this

[120] Ben McFarlane and Robert Stevens, "The Nature of Equitable Property" 4 Journal of Equity 1 (2010). The words "derives from" in the previous sentence are a modification of a sentence on page 15 of McFarlane and Stevens.

[121] For more expansive discussion of equitable property that fits the basic model here see Worthington, Equity at 58*ff*, as well as McFarlane and Stevens, "Nature of Equitable Property," and Ben McFarlane, "Equity, Obligations, and Third Parties" [2008] Singapore Journal of Legal Studies 308. In a working paper, Henry Smith suggests that we can think about trusts as rights against rights or as "some other second-order structure in which a second layer of property is imposed on a more contractual structure," which is closer to the view in the text. My sense is that Smith is agnostic as between these two descriptions, which seems broadly right to me: "Property as a Complex System" at 22.

[122] Were I forced to say something, I would embrace an account for which what I said about the trusts in the text is a kind of model: equity involves rules with a common-law-like form, the need for which comes into the picture where the operations of common-law doctrines generate the potential for new kinds of subordination. This subordination is generated, importantly, by common-law rules that are themselves necessary as responses to problems about subordination (like the Problem of Yours and Mine). Somewhat in the same way as we are about to explore with public law, the problems to which equity is a response cannot be eliminated by "going back" and eliminating the common-law rule. So equity is in this way, as the previous note indicates, second-order in a way that allows us to see its distinctiveness. This account is a kind of a gloss on the one outlined in Jennifer Nadler, "What Is Distinctive about the Law of Equity?" 41 Oxford Journal of Legal Studies 864 (2022).

section need to be thought of with that idea in mind, since in each of these cases the scope of the right might seem in various ways narrower than the scope of property rights in tangibles. As I just said, there is no harm in thinking, perhaps on the basis of this narrowness, that these property rights are in certain ways different than other property rights. But I think they are all property rights. We could thus continue the chart from the last section to include the lessons of this one as follows:

Res	Content of yours-mine problem	Right to prevent	No right to prevent
Share	Exercise of rights of shareholder	Voting, dividends?	Misuse of assets of corporation
Contract?	Position of party to contract	Procuring breach? Conversion?	Causing breach
Secured debt	Access to creditor's assets upon insolvency	Division of secured assets	Interference with assets before insolvency
Beneficiary's interest in trust	Third-party interference with trust property	Interferences derived from trustee's right	Interferences not derived from trustee's right

This concludes Part II. I will not summarize everything from the past two chapters, because there was a lot of it. But the very short upshot is that I aimed to show how thinking about the private law of property as a realization of the idea of yours and mine can illuminate a variety of important doctrinal questions, ranging from the contents of the law of land and tangible property to questions about intangibles and the differences between property rights, contract rights, and personal rights.

PART III
THE PUBLIC LAW OF PROPERTY

6

Property and Regulation

6.1 From Private Law to Public Law

In Part II, we saw how the private law of property can be understood to allow us to relate to one another as equals through the idea of yours and mine. These interactions have the characteristic form of private law, in that they are pairwise interactions between private persons. As we saw in §3.1, though, the private law of property, standing alone, would be an incomplete realization of property as the law of yours and mine. While the private law of property's interactions are, considered on their own terms, egalitarian, the phenomenon of structural subordination means that the cumulative effect of these interactions can, in various important circumstances, have the result of generating new forms of subordination. Structural subordination arises out of the system of the private law of property, which means that it is the legal system itself—the source of the authority of private law—against whom the complaint about subordination is to be leveled. So it is the legal system itself that must address structural subordination. This is the role of the public law of property: to complete the egalitarian project of property law and strive for the fullest possible adherence to the ideal of the community of yours and mine, we need rights against the state to protect against structural subordination. This will be the subject of Part III, comprised of chapters 6 and 7.

While this is obviously not the place for a complete theory of the subject, I do need to make some general schematic remarks about the relationship between private law and public law, and their respective places within a conceptually sequenced justification. In other words, I need to say something about the way that public law completes, as I just put it, the egalitarian project of private law.[1] What I will say is, in effect, a kind of translation into familiar legal terms of the theoretical argument in Part I, and especially chapter 3. In conceptualizing the nature of a legal system and its role in constituting a society of equals, we must begin with the institutions of private law. The basic commitment demands that we organize our legal and political institutions to allow us to relate to one another on terms of equality rather than as superiors and inferiors. Our familiar

[1] On the nature and importance of sequenced thinking, see Ernest J Weinrib, Reciprocal Freedom, Private Law, and Public Right (2023).

Property Law in the Society of Equals. Christopher Essert, Oxford University Press.
DOI: 10.1093/oso/9780197768952.003.0007

private law institutions determine our particular interactions with each other as egalitarian in this way, by structuring various kinds of interactions to allow the parties to them to relate as equals. My account of property here exemplifies that understanding of private law: property solves the Problem of Yours and Mine by allowing us to relate as equals with respect to its subject matter. I have gestured toward parallel accounts of personal rights and contract. In all cases, these private law institutions are constitutive of and necessary for equal relations between persons in their respective spheres, so the basic commitment obligates us to create them.

But these private law institutions have the potential to generate, through the systematic effects of their operation, new forms of subordination. Structural subordination, to which I have already made reference, is a central case of this: sometimes, the effects of a set of egalitarian interactions can accumulate in a way that ends up subordinating some members of the society, even though no other members are subordinating them. Because this subordination is not the result of anyone's subordinating anyone else but rather emerges out of the systemic effects of the private law institutions, it is the institutions themselves that must address it. We cannot solve structural subordination or other systemic forms of subordination arising out of private law by eliminating private law, because we are obligated to have these private law institutions.[2] We must therefore solve it by creating a new kind of law: public law. Here public law is to be understood as the response to a need that emerges only in light of private law, and it is in that precise sense that private law and public law are comprehensible as steps in a conceptual sequence.[3]

The specific content of public law, at an extremely high level of generality, can be derived from its role in the sequence. Public law is the law that determines and regulates the state's exercise of its public powers for public purposes. These powers must be exercised with the aim of the state's public purposes of ensuring that its subjects can relate as equals, and in particular ensuring that its own institutions do not generate forms of subordination that are inconsistent with the basic commitment to equality that gives rise to the need for those institutions in the first place. The specifics of these public purposes will be elaborated out of a more comprehensive account of the nature of the state and the various ways that it must ensure that its subjects relate on terms of equality. Saying any more about that in general is beyond my scope. I will turn to the application of this idea to the context of property in a moment. Before I do that, though, let me say two things. First, this understanding of public law also generates its paradigmatic form, namely, the form of relations between individuals and the state, and claims

[2] We saw Rousseau's dismissal of this suggestion in the Introduction and in chapter 3 note 14.
[3] Weinrib, Reciprocal Freedom at 107, applies this line of thinking to workers' compensation law.

by individuals against the state. This is opposed to the form of private law, which is the form of relations between private persons. Second, I want to emphasize that this conceptual sequence should not be mistaken for a claim about normative priority or hierarchy. To say that we need to think about private law before we think about public law is not to say that it is more important. Neither private law nor public law can function without the other.[4]

We can now turn to applying these rather abstract ideas to property. We can helpfully think about (at least) three different ways in which this notion of public law becomes relevant in our thinking about property. These are, to be sure, ideal types, and many actual parts of public law will cross the lines I am about to draw. Nevertheless, the categorization exercise is helpful.

The first kind of public law is the broadest, but also the least relevant to this book. There is a lot of public law touching on our property—so much that we hardly notice it, it is like water to a fish[5]—and it can take a very wide range of forms. We have environmental laws that say I cannot pollute a river with my avocados, criminal laws that say I cannot throw my avocado at your head, consumer protection laws that say I cannot call my avocado an aardvark and offer it for sale, election financing laws that limit the number of avocados I can use in support of a particular political candidate or cause, and so on and so on. We can understand each of these as instances of the phenomenon just outlined, according to which the state needs to ensure that the systemic operation of private law does not generate new forms of subordination. But while property surely plays a role—perhaps through a slow succession of events—in the generation of these new forms of subordination, each of these cases is, at least in principle, comprehensible without reference to the idea of yours and mine. They are property-independent public purposes whose pursuit, as I will say, justifies external *limitations* on property rights. Because these public purposes are comprehensible independently of the idea of yours and mine, these parts of public law are not, in my view, part of property law. This is not to deny, even a bit, that these limitations are legitimate or important; surely many of them are among the most central pieces of the law of a society of equals. But they are beyond the scope of a book about property law.[6]

[4] Throughout this treatment of public law, I've been aided by Jacob Weinrib, "Maitland's Challenge for Administrative Law Theory" 84 Modern Law Review 207 (2021) and Jacob Weinrib, Dimensions of Dignity: The Theory and Practice of Modern Constitutional Law (2016).

[5] David Foster Wallace, This is Water (2005).

[6] One increasingly urgent field of public law that fits here is that concerned with climate change. Greenhouse gas emissions are caused, by and large, by the use of objects of property. Curbing such emissions is becoming among the most pressing tasks of law. Often, laws aimed at curbing such emissions will have the effect of constraining the uses to which private property can be put. Some of the benefit of such laws will be to allow for more use of property (we cannot live in houses that are underwater), but it seems as though the main goal of climate change laws will be to allow for the bare continuation of human life on earth as such. So it makes most sense to think about these rules primarily as limitations in the sense defined in the text (even if they do have some regulatory elements in the

The second kind of public law is exemplified by the phenomenon of homelessness understood as an instance of structural subordination with respect to the idea of yours and mine. As I gestured toward earlier and will elaborate at length shortly, while the homeless can relate on terms of equality in particular interactions with the propertied, because they are homeless they can be understood to be subordinated with respect to the idea of yours and mine by the system of property itself. The state therefore has an obligation to provide housing to the homeless in order to ensure that its system of property adheres to the greatest extent possible to property law's regulative ideal of the community of yours and mine. Here the relevant public purpose is internal to the idea of yours and mine and incomprehensible without it: the purpose is precisely to address structural subordination with respect to that idea. The public purpose here is a continuation of the justificatory force generated by the same normative notion—the idea of yours and mine—that explained the need for the private law of property. We do not need to appeal to any new (substantive) normative ideas to understand the problem: rather the idea of yours and mine is both necessary and sufficient to understand this kind of structural subordination. As such, we can consider this part of public law to be a part of property law, as it is a part of the complete realization of the idea of yours and mine. Because they are understandable through the lens of the community of yours and mine, which earlier I called the regulative ideal of systems of property, I will refer to these parts of public law as *regulation* of property.

A third kind of public law that is relevant here is the law of public property. The pursuit of any number of public purposes requires public space. (We need a place to have the public school, a place to have the courthouse, and so on.) In this way, public purposes are not unlike the various activities and relations that, as I argued in Part I, require property in order for us to participate in on terms of equality. The difference is that these public purposes are *public* purposes, which is to say, purposes that the state is obligated to pursue in order to ensure that its own institutions do not create forms of subordination that are inconsistent with the basic commitment to equality that explains the need for those institutions in the first place. These public purposes include those in both of the previous two categories. But here our attention is not on their matter but rather on the fact that they require spaces and objects. And the pursuit of these public purposes is inconsistent with the spaces and objects that they require being held as the property

sense defined in the next paragraph; as I noted, many or even most real-world instances of public law cut across the lines I am here drawing for illustrative purposes). On the specific question of how the need to curb greenhouse gas emissions should relate to the public law obligation to provide housing, see Christopher Essert and Olivia O'Connor, "Towards a Framework for Reconciling Climate Justice and Housing Justice" in Jutta Brunnée, Brenda Cossman, and Andrew Green, eds, Law in a Changing World: How Climate Change Is Affecting Law and What to Do about It (2024).

of private persons, since that would make the state's capacity to pursue its public purposes dependent on the will of those private persons. This is why the state must have public property, which is property that is not held through the idea of yours and mine. As this paragraph shows, the need for public property cannot be understood without the idea of yours and mine, not because public property is a realization of the idea of yours and mine but rather because it is a response to a kind of inevitable systemic inadequacy that would arise if all property were privately owned. Because of this internal connection to the idea of yours and mine, the law of public property is a part of the law of property.[7]

Before I turn to a more detailed exploration of the latter two members of that classification, let me elaborate a bit more on the classification as such. There are some property theorists who understand property law to encompass only the private law of property, and think of any public law regulation of property as somehow alien to it. And there are others who hold the converse view, on which all of property is public law, even the part that is nominally private law, since that part is just public law in disguise. Neither view is quite right, as neither can be said to carve the world at the joints, to draw lines at the most natural and illuminating places.[8] But neither is totally wrong. As I have indicated, the category "property law" crosses the line between private law and public law.[9] Property's complete realization requires both private law rights that allow individuals to relate to each other on terms of equality through the idea of yours and mine and the public law institutions that ensure that the systematic effects of the operation of private law rights do not generate new forms of subordination. Sometimes, as in cases of limitation, the public law rules do involve an imposition of externally motivated constraints onto private property rights. But other times the constraints are generated out of the idea of yours and mine itself. So when public law institutions are responses to structural or systematically generated forms of subordination that depend on the idea of yours and mine, we should understand them as part of the public law of property.

[7] One thing I will not discuss, which maybe some readers wish I would, is expropriation. Although I think that one could not offer an account of takings without an account of property, the converse does not seem true to me. Takings might more easily be understood in terms of the application to the property context of a more general idea that the actions of public authorities need to be carried out for public purposes subject to a requirement of proportionality, which requirement generates the obligation to compensate. And my suspicion is that an account of de facto expropriation can be derived from the idea of yours and mine, somewhat along the lines of what I said in note 32 of chapter 2, that regulation "goes too far" in Holmes' sense only when the regulated property can no longer be thought of by the owner as their own.

[8] Plato, Phaedrus 265e.

[9] Brudner sees this feature of property emerge most clearly in the discussion of takings: "the common-law takings rule is facially paradoxical in that it seems to view property as a hybrid concept—neither purely private nor purely public but somehow both in combination." See Alan Brudner, "Private Property and Public Welfare" in James Penner and Henry E Smith eds, Philosophical Foundations of Property Law (2013) 68.

One final point: this classificatory point is important not just for conceptual clarity—although I do think it's important to say out loud that property law is a category that includes both private law and public law elements—but also because it is crucial to grasping the egalitarian prestige of my account as a whole.[10] The law of property includes the public law of property, which means that the law of property includes public law rights against the state to the provision of adequate housing, to the protection against certain kinds of subordination with respect to homes, and to the provision of public spaces. These familiar egalitarian policies should be understood not as external limitations on the law of property that need an independent justification, but rather as part and parcel of the institution and grounded on the same justificatory considerations as private property rights. If you are committed to property, you are thereby committed to these forms of public law.

6.2 Thinking about Homelessness

Homelessness has some claim to being one of the most significant moral issues facing Western societies today. There are, on any given night, something like 500,000 people in the United States and 35,000 in Canada spending the night either in a homeless shelter or else in some place not normally meant for human habitation (in their car, or under a bridge, in an encampment, or on the street). Of course, some people are homeless only for a short time, which means that the number of people who experience these forms of homelessness over the course of a year is significantly higher: 235,000 in Canada, and something like 2.5 million in the United States.[11] That should be a shocking number: between two of the richest countries ever to have existed in the history of the world, almost 3 million people—something like the population of Toronto or Chicago—experienced homelessness last year.[12] Like many others, I think these figures are nothing short of disgraceful and that they demand a response. But in order to understand

[10] I was inspired to use "prestige" in this magic-related sense by a remark of Fred Wilmot-Smith's. The usage comes from a film, also called "The Prestige," which is well worth your time.

[11] The single night (or "point in time") numbers are, in the United States, from the HUD 2017 AHAR Part 1 and, in Canada, from the State of Homelessness in Canada 2016. The Canadian yearly total is from the same source. The US yearly total I had to estimate: I started with HUD's report that about 1.42 million Americans used a shelter bed in 2016 and extrapolated (conservatively) based on the Canadian yearly percentage of sheltered versus unsheltered homeless (136k vs 100k). If we extrapolate instead using the point in time proportions from the US data (where two thirds are sheltered and one third unsheltered), the number is closer to 3 million. These numbers vary over time, of course, so what I include here should be taken for illustrative purposes only and with a grain of salt.

[12] And in fact things are worse than that: if we count, as I'll argue that we should, people who have no home of their own but are instead staying with friends or family—the "hidden homeless"—we should probably add another million or more to our total.

why homelessness is wrongful and what response it requires, we need first to get a clearer understanding of what homelessness is.

What then, is it for a person to be homeless?[13] We can see pretty quickly that it is not a matter of their empirical circumstances. The category of the homeless is generally agreed to include people in a wide range of rather different empirical circumstances, from those who sleep rough, through those who stay in emergency homeless shelters, to the "hidden homeless," those who spend their nights with friends or family as guests, without being tenants.[14] This last class of people, the hidden homeless, helps to illustrate how homelessness cannot be understood empirically in a different way: someone who is homeless but staying with a friend or family member could quite plausibly have a life which, day to day, is relatively indistinguishable from the life of their host, the person at whose home they are staying. They could both come and go with the same frequency, perhaps each have their own key, each do "their own thing" at home (watch TV, read, have a bath). And yet, looking at the case from a different angle, we can see a crucial difference between the two cases. And at this point, it should be obvious what this difference is grounded on: the host has property in the space whereas the guest does not.[15] What others, including the guest, may do in the space is up to the host. Which means that the homeless guest is able to do all the things that they do in the host's home only because the host lets them do so. And we can generalize from this case to the others: the homeless, whether sleeping rough, or in a shelter,[16] or doubled up, are homeless in virtue of the fact that they are never in a space that is their own, a space over which they have property. When they are in

[13] For more detailed articulation of the arguments in this paragraph, see my "Property and Homelessness" 44 Philosophy & Public Affairs 266 (2016); "What Makes a Home: A Reply" 41 Law & Philosophy 469 (2022); and "Homelessness as a Legal Phenomenon" in Nicole Graham, Margaret Davies, and Lee Godden, eds, The Routledge Handbook of Law, Property, and Society 137 (2022).

[14] For some representative treatments of who counts as homeless, see the Canadian Definition of Homelessness §§2.1 (those in shelters), 3.2 (the hidden homeless) and the European Typology of Homelessness and Housing Exclusion (ETHOS) §§2.1, 8.1. For a different view of the hidden homeless, see Robert Ellickson, "The Homelessness Muddle" 99 Public Interest 45 (1990). A related set of ideas seems to be implicit in the UN definition of the Right to Housing, which provides, in part, "The right to housing should not be interpreted in a narrow or restrictive sense which equates it with, for example, the shelter provided by merely having a roof over one's head or views shelter exclusively as a commodity. Rather it should be seen as the right to live somewhere in security, peace and dignity." See Committee on Economic, Social and Cultural Rights, General Comment No 4 (1991), para 7.

[15] An Ontario court described, precisely and accurately, someone in this position as "no more than an especially privileged guest." See *R v Edwards* (1994), 19 OR (3d) 329 (CA), aff'd [1996] 1 SCR 128.

[16] You might think that the operators of a shelter would be disposed to allow their clients to continue staying on, but, that would be a paradigmatic instance of the kind of subordination that law is meant to address: the capacity of the homeless to stay in the shelter would depend entirely on the inclinations of the shelter operator rather than any legal rights. In some cases, a person in a shelter or staying with friends might have a contract with their host. But (as we saw across §§4.1, 4.6, and 5.3) a contractual licence is not a property right: it provides no protection against third parties.

private space they are always in space that is someone else's,[17] so that it is always up to someone else what they may do.

This account of homelessness should help to further clarify the claim that I made in §3.1 about homelessness and structural subordination. That claim arose out of a kind of paradox based on two apparently conflicting claims. To be homeless, as I said, is to lack any property in a space of one's own. That means that whenever a homeless person is in private space, what they do there is up to another. But that's also true of the propertied: when I am at your house, what I do there is up to you. The bare fact that when I am in the property of another person, what I do there is up to them, is not on its own a reason to say that I am subordinated to them. Quite the contrary: the relation between host and guest is actually an egalitarian relation, because it is grounded in the institution of property, the law of yours and mine. When you invite me over to your home (or not) and I accept (or not), we treat each other as equals by recognizing our mutual capacity to govern ourselves according to the terms of the law of property, recognizing that we are mutually related as the sort of beings that can interact in this way. To return to a point I made in §1.4, I can try to coax a racoon into or out of my yard, but I can neither invite it nor exclude it; the racoon and I will always only ever be able to settle the terms of our encounters through our relative strength.

So host and guest relate as equals, even when the guest is homeless. But to understand homelessness we need to take a broader look at the situation. From the point of view of the individual interaction, the egalitarian relation between host and guest is not (and cannot be) affected by the question of what property the guest does or does not own. The impersonal nature of property makes this clear: the institution creates egalitarian host-guest relations in part by ensuring that those relations are independent of the particular features of the particular

[17] You might object here that the homeless can go onto public space, and that we can and should address homelessness by making this easier or more legally permissible. (This is part of the argument in Jeremy Waldron, "Homelessness and the Issue of Freedom" 32 UCLA Law Review 295 (1991).) But this is a mistake, for two reasons. First, as we will see in chapter 7, it misunderstands the nature and value of public space. Second, it misconstrues the nature of homelessness: allowing the homeless to use public space to perform basic human functions (as Waldron advocates) fails to address the structural subordination with respect to the idea of yours and mine that is, I'm arguing, the core problem of homelessness. Waldron's proposal, although it is framed in terms of a certain characterization of freedom, is really about what Rainer Forst calls a "humanist" concern, namely, a concern about the distribution of basic goods to the worst off. Thus it obscures the way that homelessness raises a distinctive concern that sounds in *justice*, and is about the relationships between the homeless and the propertied rather than merely about what the homeless have or do not have. In my view, this is why we need to think about homelessness in terms of subordination, so that we can properly see that homelessness is not (merely) something bad that happens but is instead something that some people do to others (not directly but structurally, through the creation of institutions) and that its wrongness must be understood from that point of view. (Waldron sees this fact about homelessness, and to his great credit emphasizes it repeatedly in his work, but his philosophical commitments, as I've argued, make it impossible for him to properly account for it.) For the distinction between humanitarian and justice arguments in this context, see Rainer Forst, "Law, Morality, and Power in the Global Context," in The Right to Justification (Flynn trans. 2007/2012 in English) 241.

people who happen to be occupying the positions of host and guest. To think otherwise would be to think that an individual propertied person commits a wrong by refusing to invite the homeless onto their property.[18] But that strikes me as the wrong result: I doubt many of us take ourselves to be (legally) obligated to open our homes to the homeless in this way. Indeed, I think my reaction to someone coming to my door to ask for an invitation should be the same regardless of who they are, and no fact about them (barring certain emergency cases of imminent bodily danger that we can leave to one side) should compel me to allow them entrance. To think otherwise would be to efface the very possibility of having space as yours or mine.

The upshot, or the problem, is that if this is true for each person in my position—that is, each of the propertied—then the homeless will be left, as we saw that they are, without any space that they are permitted to enter. When they are in this position, their capacity to participate in the wide variety of activities and relations that take place in space—indeed, their capacity to be somewhere or even, in a way, to *be* at all[19]—turns out to lie entirely under the control of others.[20] So it seems odd to say that they can participate in those activities on terms of equality with the propertied. But crucially it does not lie under the control of any *particular* other. There is no individual private person about whom it is possible to say that they determine how any or all of the homeless may act, at least, any more than they determine how anyone else may act. For each private person who holds property, there is nothing (legally) wrongful in their denying the homeless person entry into their home, because there is nothing wrongful in denying any other private person entry into one's home at any time.[21]

Hence we arrive at the apparent paradox I mentioned. On the one hand, no private person subordinates a homeless person as such by denying them entry; the denial is instead to be understood as, on its own terms, egalitarian. On the other hand, the homeless are quite straightforwardly comprehensible as subordinated, since their capacity to do those things that happen in space is determined by others. This paradox—the homeless are subordinated even though

[18] It's important to be clear here. The claim isn't that it is not wrong for any one of the propertied to exclude the homeless because we are entitled to assume that someone else will invite them in. There are no grounds for such an assumption: it's not just that it is empirically highly implausible, it's also juridically unavailable.

[19] As Waldron puts it, "everything that is done has to be done somewhere." Waldron, "Homelessness and the Issue of Freedom" at 296.

[20] Nothing about this account of homelessness means that there's anything wrong (in political morality) with *choosing* to be homeless. Those who voluntarily choose not to have a home (like Jack Reacher or the #vanlife folks) clearly are missing out on the activities and relations constituted by a home, but they are free to choose to do so in pursuit of whatever other activities or relations they believe to be accessible through their choices. The claim will turn out to be about what the state must be obligated to provide its members, not what those members must do with it.

[21] I don't deny that there may be some moral wrongs here: telling an adult child or elderly parent that they need to leave one's home might be a moral wrong of some sort, but it is not a legal wrong.

nobody subordinates them—is resolved by the idea of structural subordination. No private person should be said to commit a wrong just in virtue of the fact that there are homeless members of their society. And it is this very fact that explains what is so difficult about homelessness: it is precisely that no private person has a duty to any particular homeless person that allows the homeless to continue to be homeless. Speaking loosely, we want to say that it is "the system" that makes homelessness a reality. At the same time, the system is not some depersonalized omnipresence. It is us. The institution of property that gives rise to homelessness is the very institution that we created to fulfill our requirement to solve the Problem of Yours and Mine, and the rights that the propertied exercise under that institution are omnilateral, so exercised in a way that can be said to have the endorsement of each of us. So while none of us in particular commits a wrong in virtue of the existence of homelessness, all of us—in general—are collectively committing a very serious wrong. So measures to address homelessness should be considered to be regulation of property in the sense I articulated in §6.1, namely, constraints on the exercise of private property rights grounded on justificatory considerations internal to the institution of property.

This account of homelessness suggests the correct account of what is required as a solution to it. Since homelessness is the result of no particular person's commission of a wrong but is caused structurally by an institution of which everyone is a (required, constitutive) participant, it requires a solution that can be said to be provided by everyone, acting omnilaterally.[22] As we saw in chapter 3, this omnilateral solution falls under the overarching abstract ideal of the community of yours and mine: part of the idea of an institution of property is that it must strive for the closest possible adherence to this ideal.

One well-known judicial articulation of such a right makes this structure clear. The South African Constitutional Court, in its decision in *Grootboom*, says that the state must

> establish a coherent public housing programme directed towards the progressive realisation of the right of access to adequate housing within the state's available means. The programme must be capable of facilitating the realisation of the right. The precise contours and content of the measures to be adopted are primarily a matter for the legislature and the executive. They must, however, ensure that the measures they adopt are reasonable.

[22] For what it's worth, this aspect of my claim is shared with Kant's. See Ernest J Weinrib, "Poverty and Property in Kant's System of Rights" 78 Notre Dame Law Review 795, 817 (2003): "the duty is incumbent on the people (and derivatively on the sovereign) rather than on any particular person. . . . The systemic difficulty that property poses . . . is resolved by the collective duty imposed on the people." The difference is that Kant takes the content of the duty to be one to support the poor rather than to provide them with property of their own.

At the same time, the Court recognizes the importance of what the South African constitution calls a requirement of "progressive realization":

> The term "progressive realisation" shows that it was contemplated that the right could not be realised immediately. But the goal of the Constitution is that the basic needs of all in our society be effectively met and the requirement of progressive realisation means that the state must take steps to achieve this goal. It means that accessibility should be progressively facilitated: legal, administrative, operational and financial hurdles should be examined and, where possible, lowered over time. Housing must be made more accessible not only to a larger number of people but to a wider range of people as time progresses.[23]

In the next sections, I will explore these ideas in more detail. The exploration of the idea of state provision of adequate homes to its members will have two parts. First, in §6.3, I will focus on *state provision* of adequate homes and second, in §6.4, I will focus on state provision of *adequate homes*. I will not say any more about the idea of progressive realization of the right. For one thing, I want to leave this more general question of public law theory to the experts. And for another, I take it that whether or not a state is fulfilling its duty to strive for compliance with the ideal of the community of yours and mine is an empirical matter that depends on particular social conditions, and so the question must be examined in detail with an eye to those conditions, along the lines of what the South African court says in *Grootboom*. So nothing more can be said in the abstract.

6.3 State Provision

Taking seriously the idea that each member of the society has a *right* against the state to adequate housing means that each person should be able to demand adequate housing from the state at any time, simply on the basis of that entitlement (i.e., as of right). A claim to housing might not justify its provision in any given case, since the person claiming housing might actually already have adequate housing, and an impartial legal process needs to be in place to resolve such cases. But in any case where someone does not have adequate housing—in any case where someone is homeless—they do have a claim to the provision of such housing as of right. And given the subordination involved in homelessness, such a claim seems to be one which needs to be provided immediately, or something close to it. In such a case, what should the state do as a matter of policy?

[23] *Government of the Republic of South Africa v Grootboom and Others*, [2000] ZACC 19, [41], [45].

Most contemporary states have picked from roughly two different models of provision of housing, and discussions of public provision of housing tend to divide most existing efforts between these two models. First there is what is known variously as public housing, social housing, project housing, and so on. On this model, it is the state itself that provides the housing, in the sense, roughly, of building it, operating it, and acting as landlord. The second model is the voucher model, which basically involves a state subsidizing the rent paid by beneficiaries of vouchers to private landlords. One introductory discussion sets the two models out as follows:

> Public housing and vouchers represent two distinctive forms of housing assistance. Public housing epitomizes a supply-side, project-based subsidy, whereby the subsidy is attached to a specific housing unit. Vouchers reflect a demand-side, tenant-based approach, whereby the subsidy is provided to an individual or family to help cover the rent for any eligible housing unit.[24]

Each of these forms of housing provision brings with it some form of constraint on rights understood purely within the private law of property. Voucher systems will involve some constraint on the choices that private owners can make with respect to who they will and will not grant a lease to (as they are typically legally disabled from refusing a tenant on the grounds that the tenant will pay by voucher); public housing systems will involve constraint on what property is available for private acquisition. Perhaps other constraints would exist as well. The point here is just that such constraints would be regulation in the sense articulated in §6.1, since they would be grounded on justificatory considerations internal to a system of property understood as the realization of the idea of yours and mine. But we can ask another important question. What, if anything, can the sorts of considerations that ground the right to housing tell us about these different options for the state to fulfill its correlative obligation?

One might begin by suggesting that since the obligation is held by the state, it must be the state that fulfills it, so that voucher programs are off the table as a matter of justice or the structure of the basic commitment. Some obligations are like this. When I promise to meet you for lunch, I do not successfully perform my promissory obligation by sending my spouse in my place. But not all are. I have an obligation to my children to ensure that they are well educated, but if my spouse is the one who turns out to manage their education, it is at least not obvious that I have not fulfilled my obligation. There might be some deep division in our obligations here. But we might instead just think that the

[24] Alex Schwartz, "Public Housing and Vouchers" in Daniel Béland, Christopher Morgan, and Kimberly Howard, eds, The Oxford Handbook of US Social Policy 413, 414 (2014).

distinction between these two cases can be explained by seeing the second obligation as something like an obligation to see to it that the kids are well educated, and then to understand the scope of "seeing-to" to include a relatively hands-off approach such as I may have taken by letting my spouse do all the work (while perhaps remaining ready to participate as needed). Within this frame, how should we understand the state's obligation in regard to housing? It seems that it is an obligation to see to it that each person is housed.[25] The state's role here seems to lie in its unique and constitutive capacity and obligation to see to such things as a matter of right, rather than in its ability to do things. After all, the state can only do things by getting persons to act for it. Many interesting questions arise in this area as to the conditions under which a private person's carrying out a public function can count as the rightful exercise of public power. But we need to answer those questions substantively, rather than to rule them out by fiat.[26]

These considerations also help us to see that the divide between the two models of housing provision is not as stark as it may have seemed a page ago. In any economy that is not completely run by the state—that is, in any economy that allows for at least some private market activity—one can imagine that a state might justifiably want at least some elements of its provision of public social housing to be realized through the participation of the private sector. Surely social housing which is constructed or cleaned or physically maintained by private persons (natural or corporate) who contract with the state to do this work still counts as social housing. And the same, presumably, goes for publicly owned and privately managed housing. In a case like that, the kinds of considerations I was adverting to in the last paragraph come directly to the surface: the superintendent of a building that is meant to count as public housing is surely bound by a set of public law norms requiring that the exercise of their public power be done consistently with its public source, for public purposes, and so on; and this is true whether or not their paycheck has the government's logo or the logo of some private subcontractor on it. So the two categories are in a way ideal types, and most systems will involve some blending between them—some participation by private actors and some work done by the state.

That all said, there does seem to be an important question at play here, about whether or not it is the state or the private market that determines how many units are available and at what cost. Under a pure voucher system, the state does not exercise any direct control over the supply of housing. It is true, of course, that in most economies the existence of a state subsidy provided to consumers

[25] I suspect, in fact, that this is how things are for a great many of the state's obligations. There are, of course, complexities in all such cases of, in effect, privatization.

[26] For recent discussion, see Chiara Cordelli, The Privatized State (2021).

of a good creates a significant incentive to increase production of that good, so the existence of a voucher program would tend to cause more housing to be made available. But this is a matter of the various contingent features of the housing economy at any given time, so the state cannot, through the provision of vouchers, have any direct control over the availability or cost of units. By contrast, the public housing model precisely involves the state creating (or at least directing the creation of) some set number of units. This difference between the systems suggests, I think, that creating or enabling or supporting a voucher-based system cannot on its own constitute a complete performance of the state's obligation to provide housing, since a voucher-based system does not provide any assurance that at all times there is some sufficient amount of vacancy to provide a unit on demand for anyone who needs one. To ensure it is able to respond to as of right demands for housing in a timely way, the state needs to maintain some sufficiently large stock of housing. And it seems that the only way that can be done is by the state maintaining public housing.[27]

By contrast, a voucher-based system does not seem to be a necessary part of a state's provision of housing pursuant to its obligation to ensure that each member of the society is adequately housed. One can imagine efficiency-based reasons for using a voucher system, but considerations of efficiency can only permissibly come into play in a context where the state ensures both that there is a sufficient supply of public housing to respond to demands for housing and that whatever housing is provided through a voucher system counts as *adequate* housing in the sense to be elaborated in §6.4. The actual voucher systems in place in many contemporary societies do not come close to meeting that last requirement. Many landlords do not accept vouchers (in violation of the law) and often those that do provide housing that is substandard in a variety of ways. For a system of vouchers to play any part in fulfilling the state's duty here, it must include systems to ensure that the housing that is being subsidized is adequate housing. Of course, the same is true for public housing.

The bottom line, I think, is that the idea of a right to adequate housing held against the state requires that the state ensure that such housing is available to all who qualify for it. Whether that is done entirely by public housing or in part by a system of vouchers is not a question that can be resolved in the abstract, and will fall to be determined by the social and historical conditions of particular societies. What is clear is that the state must strive to be, or to ensure the existence of, a provider of last resort, to ensure that homelessness is impossible.

[27] Even here, there might be a role for the private sector. The state could lease some number of units from a private owner on a long-term basis and sublease them to subsidized tenants, for instance. But the big-picture point here, familiar in other contexts, is that the state must be the provider of last resort.

6.4 An Adequate Home

An institution of property must aim for the closest possible adherence to the ideal of the community of yours and mine, through the progressive realization of a program to ensure that each of its members has an adequate home. Here we will concentrate on the factors that make a home adequate.

We do not need to spend a lot of time talking, in the abstract, just about the notion of a home. I will take for granted an understanding of the idea of a home as more than just a house, as something whose value seems in important ways deeper and more fundamental to our construction of ourselves in the social world.[28] Notably, while my particular examples and illustrations might seem perhaps rather closely tied to the particular sociocultural milieu that I happen to inhabit, the idea is a much broader one than that. For instance, the idea of a home plays a central role in the Odyssey, not just in the obvious way that Odysseus struggles to get back home, but also in the recurring centrality of the notions of home and hospitality that were in important ways constitutive of the social world of ancient Greece. At one point in the poem, Odysseus even says, "The worst thing humans suffer/is homelessness."[29] As Emily Wilson, a recent translator of the poem put it, "home" is "already a very loaded word in English . . . which means so much more than just house or place where you live. The Odyssey is fascinating in the ways that it defines home as something which involves both a living space, a particular kind of community, and a space where at least one member of the household has the choice about who to keep in, who to keep out."[30] Here Wilson indicates that, even in ancient Greece, we can discern at least two important elements of the notion of a home: the physical and the normative. A home is a physical space over which its owner has control.[31] An adequate home, then, is an adequate physical space over which its owner has adequate control. What does "adequate" mean? In the abstract, the question is easy to answer: a home is adequate if it is sufficient to ensure that its occupant is protected from the kind of structural subordination that constitutes homelessness. That is, the idea of adequacy is not external to the justification of the right but is located and understandable only from the inside of that justification; the right's content is determined partially by the right's role, by the problem it is meant to solve.

[28] For penetrating and subtle discussion, see Barbara Herman, The Moral Habitat ch 10 (2021). For wider ranging inquiries into the idea of a home, see Eula Biss, Having and Being Had (2020) and Witold Rybczynski, Home: A Short History of an Idea (1986).

[29] Book 15, ll 343–44, Emily Wilson trans.

[30] Emily Wilson, interview with Tyler Cowen, at https://medium.com/conversations-with-tyler/tyler-cowen-emily-wilson-literature-classics-4768b72d052c.

[31] You might claim it's more than just that, that a home requires loving relationships with others, or at least the possibility of them, or some such thing. I discuss that in "What Makes a Home: A Reply."

As I have indicated, we can helpfully think about adequacy in terms of two dimensions, physical and legal. The discussion so far showed that a home is about legal rights, not just a physical space. Someone who is inside a house but who has no rights to be there cannot call it a home. At the same time, a home is, in part, about physical space. A person who owned a square foot of space in fee simple would still be homeless.[32] So we need, in addition to a characterization of the legal rights, a characterization of the physical attributes that adequate housing has. Housing adequacy is not merely about a roof over one's head. But it is in part about that. Both elements of adequate housing should be understood through the lens of their role as constituents of adequate housing. Thus in both cases—the legal and the physical—we need to think about what would be required in order to ensure that the holder of this housing is not subordinated with respect to the activities and relations that take place in a home, in the manner that the homeless are. With respect to neither dimension is it easy to say very much that is concrete or determinate, because once again the correct approach depends to a very significant degree on the social circumstances in any given society. Still, I can make a few schematic remarks.

Start with the physical. These abstract ideas mean, in general terms, that the housing provided to each person should be of a character that would not reasonably generate shame on the part of those to whom it was provided; ideally, we would think here that public housing should be empirically indistinguishable from something like the median market-rate housing in a given locale. As a resident of public housing, I ought not to feel ashamed to bring others to my home as guests; ideally this would be explained by the fact that the physical quality of that housing would be such that nobody could know that my housing is publicly provided.[33] There are obvious examples in the real world of both sides of this ideal. On the one side, the best mixed-use housing developments arguably aim at this ideal, so that it is not at all obvious which buildings in them are market rate and which are subsidized. On the other, the phenomenon of the "poor door," where a building is divided into market-rate and subsidized units, the latter of which are accessibly only through a different, less attractive entrance, seems designed to communicate that the subsidized unit holders ought to be ashamed of where they live.[34]

[32] The Scotch whisky maker Laphroaig once had a promotion whereby participants could claim title (actually a life lease) over a square foot of space on the island of Islay, in Scotland.

[33] Here we might draw lessons from neo-Republican theory—e.g., the "eyeball test" from Philip Pettit, Just Freedom: A Moral Compass for a Complex World (2014)—or relational egalitarianism—e.g., the notion of "bowing and scraping" in Elizabeth Anderson, "What Is the Point of Equality?" 109 Ethics 287 (1999).

[34] See Hilary Osborne, "Poor Doors: The Segregation of London's Inner-City Flat Dwellers" The Guardian July 25, 2014 <https://www.theguardian.com/society/2014/jul/25/poor-doors-segregation-london-flats>'; Mireya Navarro, "Door for 'Poor' in Tower Opens a Housing Fight" New York Times August 27, 2014, at A1 <https://www.nytimes.com/2014/08/27/nyregion/separate-entryways-for-new-york-condo-buyers-and-renters-create-an-affordable-housing-dilemma.html>.

A different way to provide more content to the abstract idea is by reference to the various activities and relations that are constituted by the idea of yours and mine.[35] To fully vindicate the basic commitment, we must aim to ensure that each member of the society is provided with property that allows them to participate in a sufficiently wide set of these activities and relations: in short, it needs to be a dwelling which a person or family can reasonably call a home. That means that housing that is provided cannot be to allow only a place to sleep, eat, bathe, and so on. Rather it must be sufficient to allow for some significant amount of things like dinner parties, hosting guests or out-of-town relatives, creating lasting relations with neighbors, and so on. Some of these features are a matter of physical size, others of the security of tenure. There will be much more to say about these ideas in the context of a detailed consideration of an actual society, including its total wealth, its various social customs and norms, and so on. A richer society might be required to provide larger or more lavishly appointed premises than a poorer one (since in the latter case, it would take less for the inhabitants of the public housing to relate as equals to those in market housing). A society that had a norm of minor children sharing bedrooms would be permitted to ask that of the beneficiaries of the program, whereas a society in which each child is expected to have their own room would not.

An adequate home needs to be a place where children can play safely and where adults can work and rest, a place where everyone has some shelter from the elements as well as shelter from the world and from others. But all these ideas are at least in part indeterminate. The kinds of construction techniques and materials that are needed to make a home adequate in Canada are quite obviously different than those needed in Barbados. But that is not because the right to adequate housing directly requires that each person be comfortable with respect, say, to temperature at all times. Rather, it is because the social context in different societies gives rise to particular instantiations of the various forms of egalitarian relation that, as we have seen at length, are the particular forms of the abstract notion of relating as equals through the idea of yours and mine that property is meant to allow us to realize. From the point of view of property, each person is entitled to a home that is physically adequate not because of the good of physical adequacy as such, but rather because a physically adequate home is necessary to relate to others as an equal through the idea of yours and mine.[36] This grounding

[35] This move is meant to echo the way I used these activities and relations, as what I called a "concrete test" in §2.2 to discern whether or not some system counts as an institution of property in that it allows its subjects to relate as equals through the idea of yours and mine: there, the activities and relations are the familiar instantiations of such equal relations, so understanding if a particular system allows them is a guide to the abstract question.

[36] That's not to say that there might not be other grounds for some of these physical characteristics: each person should have a warm place to stay so that they don't freeze to death. But that doesn't explain why they should have a warm *home* to stay in.

of the idea of adequacy on the idea of equal relations is part of the explanation of the wide variability of what counts as adequate in a given social context.[37]

These considerations about physical adequacy of housing and equal relations will lead to a certain set of requirements in terms of both public housing and vouchers. The point is easier to see in the public housing context. Essentially, the thought must be that for public housing to count as adequate and so to count as a fulfillment of the state's duty to provide housing, the public housing must be of a sufficiently high quality and size to ensure that those inhabiting it are not thereby seen as second-class citizens.[38] (I noted some of the most obvious illustrations of the point three paragraphs ago.) The same basic considerations apply to voucher housing. The level of the voucher provided must be sufficient to ensure that someone who uses a voucher can afford housing in their jurisdiction that is not second class. The role of private landlords complicates things here, of course, since their incentives will always be to decrease their own costs by providing lower-quality housing. So a just system of vouchers requires significant oversight to protect against this kind of (all-too-literal) rent-seeking. Finally, the existence of a voucher system has the potential to create relations of subordination, in that a landlord might prefer not to rent to a voucher recipient because of various prejudices or stereotypes about recipients of government assistance. One solution to this problem might be to create a system of rent payment applying to *all* residential tenancies, subsidized and unsubsidized, that blinds the landlord to this information.[39]

There is a similar range of things to say about legal adequacy; indeed, I have said many of them already. The basic idea here is the one that is normally called "security of tenure": for a home to be adequate, one needs to be able to have control over one's home in a way that is legally secure—that provides rights against others' entrance—over some reasonably long time horizon. As we saw in §4.6, there are in most contemporary legal systems two forms in which someone can hold property in space: owning and renting. Owners have sufficient legal rights in their homes so as not to be homeless.[40] The more difficult case (as noted in the

[37] For discussion of these points in the context of housing size, see Olivia O'Connor, Shoshanna Saxe, Gabriel Eidelman, and Christopher Essert, "Minimum Adequate Housing Size as an Element of the Right to Housing" (ms).

[38] One of the many tragedies of neoliberalism is the denigration of the social housing form. From its origins in the late nineteenth century until something like the 1970s, social housing was often exemplary not just from the point of view of its role in addressing housing need but also from an aesthetic point of view. For an overview, see Miles Glendinning, Mass Housing: Modern Architecture and State Power—A Global History (2021).

[39] Think here about the introduction in the United States of electronic benefits transfer (EBT) as a replacement for food stamps in the late 1990s. Setting aside all questions of adequacy of the funds provided under this program, the move to EBT has the significant advantage of making it significantly more difficult for grocery stores and restaurants to know who is using EBT, since the consumer paying with EBT looks for the most part like a consumer paying with a debit or credit card.

[40] One objection here you might worry about is this: suppose I own a home that meets the physical adequacy requirements. But imagine that I suffer from some kind of mental health problem that

earlier discussion) is renting. The worry is that the position of the landlord vis-à-vis the tenant makes it impossible for the tenant to be able to use the space in a way that is sufficient to avoid the relevant form of subordination. But as we saw in that earlier examination of tenancy, during the course of a tenancy, the leased space is the tenant's space, a space about which the tenant can say "this is mine," and in which what others (including the landlord) may do is up to the tenant. The fact that the tenancy can end does not, on its own, vitiate this. Still, a worry lurks: can a tenant be secure in the space if they can be evicted at the end of the lease? I think so, but various legislative reforms dealing with a tenant's right to automatically renew a lease, for instance, are aimed at addressing this worry, and may often (or always) be called for. More on this point in the §6.5.

Finally, let me note how the idea of an adequate home here is, like the idea of yours and mine more generally, one that we ought to understand as a general structuring idea that allows us to think about particulars in the way that we have done. A home is not a cobbling-together of various particular uses, and we could never solve homelessness by providing the homeless access to places to sleep and places to eat and places to bathe and so on.[41] The state must provide a home, and those particular uses are relevant insofar as we can use them to think about whether what is provided is, in fact, a home.

6.5 Housing Rights and Regulation

In this section, I want to explore another set of issues relating to structural subordination and homes. An institution of property must strive for the closest possible adherence to the ideal of the community of yours and mine. This is the ground of the right to a home, but it can also be the ground for a variety of other regulations, which is to say public law rules that constrain the exercise of private property rights in furtherance of that ideal. There is a wide range of ways in which the accumulated effects of the exercise of private property rights can lead to forms of structural subordination: some of these are about the ability of those with homes to use them as homes; others are about various factors that make it harder to get a home or easier to lose one. Without any claim to being comprehensive, I will discuss noise bylaws, zoning, tenant-protection laws, mortgage financing and financialization more generally, and gentrification.

makes it difficult for me to live there unassisted. Am I homeless? In my view, no. I may have other problems, but homelessness is not one of them. The same goes for a case in which, while owning a home, I do not have money to buy food or clothing. That would be bad, but it would not be a case of homelessness. Homelessness is not the same as poverty.

[41] As suggested by Waldron: see my "Property and Homelessness" at 275–76.

Noise. Noise bylaws can be understood as a kind of land use regulation, a constraint on the use of property rights directed at protecting against structural subordination with respect to the idea of yours and mine. Although noise bylaws are not usually thought of as a pressing or exciting area of inquiry, they illustrate the idea of regulation very clearly and so are a helpful starting point. We can get the point easily if we set aside the law and imagine a cocktail party, where everyone is engaged in typical cocktail-party chatter. Suppose nobody is speaking unreasonably loudly—nobody is speaking loudly enough that, if it were just you and them speaking, your voice would be drowned out—but the accumulation of their voices generates such a din as to make your voice inaudible. Here it seems like you are literally silenced, but there is no particular person on whom we can pin your silencing. It seems somehow to be at the same time everyone's fault and no one's, and so an instance of structural subordination as I understand it.

If we return to the law, we can generate precisely this structure. Recall (from §4.2) that a nuisance is constituted by a defendant's using their land in such a way as to unreasonably interfere with a plaintiff's use and enjoyment of theirs. What counts as an unreasonable interference is indeterminate in the abstract, and will depend on all the relevant circumstances. One way in which this last point plays out is in the locality rule, according to which among those circumstances that are relevant is the character of the neighborhood in which the properties are located,[42] so that a level of noise that would constitute a nuisance in a quiet residential neighborhood might not constitute a nuisance in a busy commercial or industrial area.[43] This is the law's recognition of the fact that some areas are louder than others, and that there is nothing wrong with that as such. Just as with the cocktail party, in a loud commercial neighborhood, a plaintiff who wants quiet has no complaint against any particular neighbor, since no particular neighbor is, on their own, creating an amount of noise that, taking into account all the circumstances, unreasonably interferes with the plaintiff's use and enjoyment of their land. Nuisance is not about the harm that the plaintiff is suffering, but about the relationship between plaintiff and defendant, and therefore about whether or not it would be consistent with their equal standing ("reasonable") for the defendant to use their land as they are or for the plaintiff to have a right that the defendant stop.[44] To enjoin a defendant who is not emitting an amount

[42] For comprehensive and illuminating discussion, see S Steel, "The Locality Principle in Private Nuisance" 76 Cambridge Law Journal 145 (2017).

[43] The leading cases are *St Helens Smelting Company v Tipping* (1865) 11 ER 1483, *Walter v Selfe* (1851) 4 De G & S 315, and *Sturges v Bridgman* (1879) 11 Ch D 852.

[44] For a clear statement of the opposite, incorrect, view, see the obiter comments in *Lambton v Mellish*, [1894] 3 Ch 163, to the effect that two defendants, each of whom is emitting an amount of noise that would not on its own be a nuisance but the joint effects of which are loud enough such that a single defendant emitting such a noise would be creating a nuisance, are both liable in nuisance. This strikes me as clearly wrong for the reasons pointed to in the text. I find Steel's brief treatment of the case unconvincing, although I get the impression that his heart isn't really in it. Incidentally,

of noise that would on its own be unreasonable because others are also making a lot of noise would be to give the plaintiff a degree of control over what the defendant is able to do on their own land that could not be consistent with the parties' standing as equals, because, by hypothesis, the defendant is not emitting an amount of noise beyond what is consistent with that equality.

In such circumstances, it is too loud in some sense that is both everybody's fault and nobody's fault. We cannot solve the problem with nuisance. But we cannot leave it unsolved, since, in the housing context especially, noise left unchecked can quickly lead to a home's becoming unlivable. Because this is a problem of structural subordination, it must be solved with public law regulation, in the form of noise bylaws.[45] A noise bylaw has the public law structure of regulation: it constrains the capacity of individual owners to use what is theirs not to allow for equal relations between individual private persons but instead to ensure that the accumulation of nonsubordinating uses does not result in structural subordination. It does this, roughly, by just setting standards about what is too loud. Toronto's noise bylaw, for instance, identifies, in a couple of different ways, amounts of noise that are not permitted. There are specific rules about amplified sound, about animals, about construction, about motor vehicles, as well as a catch-all prohibition on "unreasonable noise and persistent noise."[46] These rules are not about specific wrongs to specific individuals. Rather, anyone who contravenes any of them "is guilty of an offence and on conviction is liable to a fine of no more than $100,000."[47]

Zoning. The idea that a kind of regulation acts as a response to an instance of structural subordination arising out of nuisance-like conditions will be familiar to some readers as one of the historical explanations of the state's power to engage in zoning. In the United States in particular, early discussions quite explicitly used this framing—"the need for zoning arises from the utter inadequacy of the law of nuisances to cope with the problems of municipal growth"[48]—and the Supreme Court's decision holding zoning to be constitutional adopts a similar

the Court in *Lambton* also relies on *Thorpe v Brumfitt* (1873), LR 8 Ch App 650, an earlier decision involving a right of way, according to which a group of people blocking a right of way (without acting jointly) can be jointly liable for a wrong—it is a nuisance to block an easement—even though none on their own would be creating a sufficient blockage to commit nuisance solely. But this is wrong. The easiest way to see this is with the equivalent situation in the tort of public nuisance. It's a wrong for one person to block the public street to make it impassible by members of the public. But when "a hundred do so [causing] a serious inconvenience," we do not call it a wrong. We call it "traffic."

[45] The municipal authority to impose noise bylaws is sometimes said to derive from a more general authority to regulate nuisance. See, for instance, *Montréal (City) v 2952-1366 Québec Inc*, 2005 SCC 62, [18]-[19].

[46] Toronto Municipal Code, Chapter 591, Noise, §§591-2.1, 591-2.2, 591-2.3, 591-2.5, 591-2.9.

[47] Toronto Municipal Code §591-4.1(A).

[48] Alfred Bettman, "Constitutionality of Zoning" 37 Harvard Law Review 834 (1924)

view of the subject.[49] The basic idea of zoning might be thought of along the lines of noise bylaws, but just broader: according to this view, zoning can solve problems about the accumulation of noise, but also about the accumulation of smoke, smells, and more.[50] However, zoning is much more complex than this briefest of sketches suggests; the analysis here may not so easily explain the idea of single-use zoning, since there is no obvious subordination-based reason to prevent someone from choosing to site their own residence in an industrial area. Zoning—as well as, indeed, noise bylaws—is probably better thought of as more of a hybrid between regulation and limitation in the senses defined in §6.1, since zoning can arguably be aimed at a wider range of public purposes than those grounded on the idea of yours and mine.

No discussion of zoning in a book about property in the society of equals would be complete without mention of exclusionary zoning. This is the name given to the phenomenon of, in various ways, using zoning to curtail or eliminate access to housing for identifiable classes of people (based on race or economic status or the like).[51] The (admittedly vague) suggestion that zoning might in some cases respond to a problem of structural subordination cannot justify contemporary forms of exclusionary zoning, like single-family zoning, which seems (very charitably construed) to privilege a single element of the right to a home (such as quiet) for some over the broader need for access to a home itself for others. Zoning that does that seems particularly pernicious, as it uses a tool that has the potential to further a system's adherence to the ideal of the community of yours and mine—a potential up to which at least some have aimed to live[52]—to precisely the opposite ends.[53]

[49] *Village of Euclid v Ambler Realty Co*, 272 US 365 (1926).

[50] It's common in discussions of the history of zoning to notice that, before comprehensive zoning became common, municipalities often passed ordinances directed at restraining particular noxious land uses, as in *In re Hang Kie*, 10 P 237 (Cal 1886). And a wide range of discussions of zoning see it, in broad strokes, as a response to various perceived inadequacies of private law forms of land use control such as nuisance and servitudes. See Thomas W Merrill and Henry E Smith, Property: Principles and Policies 1049-50 (2007); Robert C Ellickson and Vicki L Been, Land Use Controls: Cases and Materials 34–45 (3rd ed 2005), and the sources cited there.

[51] On racial land use controls, see Richard Rothstein, Color of Law: A Forgotten History of How Our Government Segregated America (2017). On class-based controls see Lawrence Gene Sager, "Tight Little Islands: Exclusionary Zoning, Equal Protection and the Indigent" 21 Stanford Law Review 767 (1968). On single-family zoning, the most prominent contemporary form of exclusionary zoning, see John Infranca, "Singling Out Single Family Zoning" 111 Georgetown Law Journal 659 (2023).

[52] *Southern Burlington County NAACP v Township of Mount Laurel*, 67 NJ 151 (1975).

[53] "The State controls the use of land, all of the land. In exercising that control it cannot favor rich over poor. It cannot legislatively set aside dilapidated housing in urban ghettos for the poor and decent housing elsewhere for everyone else. The government that controls this land represents everyone. While the State may not have the ability to eliminate poverty, it cannot use that condition as the basis for imposing further disadvantage." See *Southern Burlington County NAACP v Township of Mount Laurel (II)*, 92 NJ 158, 209 (1983).

Tenant Protection. In §4.6, I discussed some elements of landlord-tenant law, and argued that some important elements of the law are developments of the possibility of lessors and lessees relating as equals with respect to the leased premises, as well as ensuring that lessors have sufficient control over the leased premises to think of them through the idea of yours and mine and thus to relate to others as equals (*in rem*) in much the same way that owners do. I said that whereas a lease is a type of contract, the creation of a leasehold is also the creation of a kind of (artificial) res and so important elements of the relations that others have to the holder of that res should be understood using proprietary concepts. There is another important angle from which to think about this area of law: much of landlord-tenant law is regulatory, which is to say that it is public law in the sense we are here concerned with.[54] The main form of regulation here consists of rules constraining the bounds of permissible terms in lease agreements; this includes rules about rent control or stabilization, automatic renewal terms, subleasing and assignment, and so on.

The most familiar of these is rent control, so I will use it to illustrate.[55] Unlike the parts of landlord-tenant law discussed in §4.6, which relate parties within a private law form, rent control has the form of regulation. Your charging me rent, or increasing it upon the renewal of a lease, beyond a statutorily set amount does not straightforwardly seem to be an instance of your subordinating me: it is quite possible to think of cases in which I would freely and unproblematically agree to a rent that is above the regulatory limit. Nevertheless, rent control can be understood as a regulation that is designed to head off a kind of structural subordination in that unconstrained rental rates can, quite obviously, increase the market rate for rent in a way that can make it impossible for someone to afford to pay market rent in any available property. Such a person would not be wronged by any individual, but would seem to have a complaint against the system as a whole, a complaint of structural subordination, since they seem to be subordinated through the accumulation of others' nonsubordinating choices. The complaint here, it is important to emphasize, is not just about the availability of rental properties as such, or about increasing market supply in them. Rather it is about the fact that an individual person unable to afford a place to live can be seen as, in that respect, subordinated with respect to the idea of yours and mine by the structure of the institution of landlord-tenant law itself. Conversely, the landlord who attempts to raise the rent above the regulatory amount seems not to be

[54] For an earlier suggestion that much of landlord-tenant law is neither property law nor contract law, but regulation, see Mary Ann Glendon, "The Transformation of American Landlord-Tenant Law" 23 Boston College Law Review 503 (1982).

[55] For the classic discussion of rent control, see Margaret Jane Radin, "Residential Rent Control" 15 Philosophy and Public Affairs 350 (1986). Obviously, some of the interventions named at the end of the previous paragraph will need to work together: typical rent stabilization rules allow for unconstrained increases in rent upon new tenancies, so for the program to work some form of security of tenure is also required.

wronging the tenant (who might, as we are imagining, be happy to pay more), but is instead better seen as committing a public wrong by working to compromise the system and lead to structural subordination. That is why violations of such a regulation are public law offenses rather than private wrongs.[56]

Importantly, the role of these structural considerations in a particular actual society would turn on the degree to which housing is provided by the state: if someone who cannot afford market rent is provided with social housing, the structural subordination is addressed more directly. Moreover, the fundamental response to the structural subordination of tenants as a class—that is, the vulnerability to eviction and to failing to afford a home at market rent—must be the kind of right to housing that I discussed in the previous two sections. But rent control can surely play a role in some non-ideal circumstances.[57] And, indeed, it might be important even in a world with a right to housing. Suppose that a state instituted a right to adequate housing for those who needed it: we still might worry, in that world, about members of the society with high incomes who nevertheless wanted to rent, rather than own a home, and about the nature of the relations between this class of tenants and their landlords.

Housing Discrimination. A similar line of thinking can help us understand rules about housing discrimination. Private discrimination is a moral wrong and, according to a view to which I am sympathetic, it might also be a personal private law wrong (akin to battery) of its own distinctive sort.[58] But the paradigmatic wrong of housing discrimination is more insidious: it is the wrong of surreptitiously (or even unintentionally) denying housing to a person or class of persons on the basis

[56] See, for instance, the Ontario *Residential Tenancies Act*, SO 2006, c 17, s 234(x) (setting out the offense) with reference to ss. 111*ff* (setting out the rent control rules). Notice that the claim isn't just that these rules are regulatory because they are statutory. Rather, things are somewhat more complex. As I noted, tenant protection legislation takes many forms. While some have the full regulatory form I am here describing, others do not. For instance, the Ontario legislation contains a provision stating that "no pet" provisions are void. Here there isn't anything like a public law offense structure; rather the legislature here should be understood to have determined the terms of egalitarian relations between individual private persons in their capacity as landlords and tenants. Recall that in chapter 5 note 122, I indicated that equity might involve second-order problems of subordination grounded on existing private law institutions whose solutions themselves have a private law form. Some of the tenant protection rules about impermissible lease terms might partake of that same private-law-like form, which makes sense given the way that they seem to share some of the moral flavor of other equitable doctrines, perhaps including unconscionability in contract law.

[57] A further complicating factor is, I guess, macroeconomic, in that it's at least arguable that rent control decreases the supply of housing, and that therefore rent control and similar regulations disadvantage "low-income tenants as a class." See Thomas W Merrill and Henry E Smith, "The Property/Contract Interface" 101 Columbia Law Review 773, 821 (2001). But I set that aside here, because the full analysis would of course depend on a variety of specific facts in any actual case.

[58] For some considerations, see Sophia Moreau, Faces of Inequality: A Theory of Wrongful Discrimination (2020). There is also an application of the familiar idea of a public accommodation, that property that is held open to the public—in the sense to be developed in §7.4—cannot be held open selectively. An advertisement for rental housing that explicitly discriminates would be in violation of that requirement.

of some protected characteristic. As I said, this is morally wrong and may be a private wrong against a personal right. But it is hard to see it as a wrong as a matter of the private law of property: as we saw in the case of homelessness, an owner's capacity to exclude others from their land is very broad and can be recognized as required by the egalitarian form of the idea of yours and mine. The problem, of course, is that if everyone were free to discriminate against identifiable classes of people with respect to housing, those people would be unable to procure housing for themselves. And the right to housing would not solve this, since this problem could replicate itself at a place in the market far above the level at which the more basic right to housing operates: that is, rich members of a protected class could be left unable to buy housing on the market at a price that they would be willing and able to pay.[59] Again, though, it seems hard to say that an individual owner's choice not to rent or not to sell can itself be a wrong as such. The problem here is better seen as one of structural subordination, which means that housing discrimination law is a part of public law. Its structure bears that out: housing discrimination is viewed as a regulatory offense more than as a private wrong.[60] This is not to deny that there may be a distinctive moral or even legal wrong of discrimination and that the presence of that moral wrong might make housing discrimination worse than other kinds of structural subordination. It is just to locate the specific form of the problem within public rather than private law.

Gentrification and Financialization. It is probably worth my saying something about other, more diffuse processes and phenomena that might be at least partly understood through the lens of structural subordination with respect to the idea of yours and mine. I have in mind various manifestations of an unconstrained free market in real property, like gentrification or the even more general and diffuse phenomenon that is sometimes called "financialization." Gentrification, the process of a neighborhood's residential composition changing from (typically) lower income to (typically) higher income and from (often) racialized to (often) not is quite clearly predicated as a causal matter on some of the same ideas considered already. Landlord-tenant laws without tenant protections are clearly part of what makes gentrification possible in the now-familiar structural

[59] The structural problem is still formal in the sense that it is about the possibility that, if everyone were permitted to discriminate, some might not be able to find a home. There is no requirement that everyone actually does so.

[60] The structure of the American Fair Housing Act, 42 USC 3601 et seq, for instance, clearly seems to make housing discrimination an offense pursuable by administrative means rather than a private wrong. Things here are often complex. The Ontario *Human Rights Code*, RSO 1990 c H-19, s 2(1) does provide that everyone has a "right to equal treatment" with respect to services. But it's at least arguable that this is a right against the state. And it's also possible that, as I gesture toward in the text, particular instances of discrimination infringe multiple rights, so that housing discrimination involves both a private law wrong, infringing a right not to be discriminated against in any context, and a public law wrong as described in the text.

way. The phenomenon is meant to be understood as distinctive vis-à-vis more general concerns about tenants' rights insofar as it identifies harms located at the level of the neighborhood, so to speak, such as harms to those residents who are not displaced, which they suffer when, for instance, enough of their neighbors are displaced and local shops change or start to offer more expensive or different goods, or, more generally, when the neighborhood starts to change in a way that it no longer feels like "home." It seems plausible to suppose that at least some of these harms would be addressed by more robust tenants' rights protections of the sorts discussed already. Put really crudely, gentrification might be epiphenomenal to more basic problems about housing rights. There may be more to say about a broader conception of the harms that gentrification causes—a sufficiently broad conception might, I should say, move policies addressing it to the realm of limitation rather than regulation—but this is not the place to do so.[61]

An even more diffuse form of structural subordination might be encapsulated by the idea of financialization, by which I mean the increasing tendency to treat real property as a source of wealth rather than as the site of any of the other activities and relations that we need an institution of property to engage in on terms of equality.[62] To be clear, in principle the idea that property can be used to generate income, through leasing or as security for a loan, is not itself objectionable, and the development of these facilities surely counts as among the kinds of exercises of moral creativity that require property and, in turn, show us why it is an essential component of a society of equals. But various forms of financialization are merely one among that myriad of activities and relations that rest on property, and should not be allowed to grow so large as to engulf the others. (Sloganistically, one hears things like that a residential property should be a home first and an investment second.) And yet that seems to be precisely what has happened in many wealthy modern nations as land is treated merely as a tool for investment, leaving many homes unoccupied while others are homeless.[63] Another illustration arises out of the securitization of mortgages. While the details are complex and, like the rest of mortgage law, vary across jurisdictions, it seems relatively clear that securitization played a major structural role in the financial crisis in the first decade of this century that precipitated many people losing their homes.[64] I will not go into any detail about that, save to say that any kind of financialization process surely should be delimited and regulated by the requirement that it not generate structural subordination of the sort I am concerned with here.

[61] For some helpful recent discussions, see Tyler Zimmer, "Gentrification as Injustice: A Relational Egalitarian Approach to Housing" 31 Public Affairs Quarterly 51 (2017); Daniel Putnam, "Gentrification and Domination" 29 Journal of Political Philosophy 167 (2021).

[62] David Madden and Peter Marcuse, In Defense of Housing (2016).

[63] See, for instance, Samuel Stein, Capital City: Gentrification and the Real Estate State (2019).

[64] I don't want to be taken to be saying that subprime mortgages were not objectionable from the point of view of the private law idea of equal relations. Arguably they were, but I take no position on the point here.

7
Public Property

7.1 An Idea of Everyone's

In this chapter I will consider a range of questions about public property. By seeing the nature of public property and its role in a society of equals, we will gain not only an understanding of an important social institution but also a new and valuable perspective on private property.

Public property is an essential constituent of a society of equals, because many activities and relations that are necessary elements of such a society can only take place in space that is held by the public, rather than by any private person. We can call these "public activities." There is no need here to construct an exhaustive list of them—and we can set aside disagreements about the elements on such a list—but the category plausibly includes many familiar features of any democratic society: the operation of the legal system, including courts, legislatures, and governmental organizations; public education; coming and going along public rights of way, including streets and sidewalks, and in forms of public transportation like subways and trains; the operation of public utilities (power plants, landfills, water filtration systems); associating with others, engaging in political speech, protest, and labor picketing; and the diverse activities that take place in parks, community centers, libraries, and perhaps museums or art galleries. In this chapter, I will develop an account of the role of public property in a society of equals as formally parallel to the role of private property: in both cases, a specific form of rightful relation is needed in order to allow us to participate as equals in an important set of activities and relations. The core difference between the two cases is in the form of the relation and the associated set of activities of which it is a constituent.

The argument in Chapter 1 of this book showed that we could not relate as equals with respect to spaces and objects in the negative community. The argument for public property builds on that earlier argument, because when it comes to the sorts of public activities just noted, equal relations are also not possible in a world with only private property. As we have seen, what happens in private property is always up to its owner, which means that a world in which there was only private property would be a world in which whether or not these public activities took place (as well as, *a fortiori*, the terms on which they could take place) would always be up to some private owner or other. But the nature of public activities

Property Law in the Society of Equals. Christopher Essert, Oxford University Press. © Oxford University Press 2024.
DOI: 10.1093/oso/9780197768952.003.0008

and the role that they play within a society of equals are such that, were they to take place on private property, the relevant form of egalitarian relation would be unavailable. The public nature of these public activities means that they have to take place within space that is the public's space, rather than privately owned by any private person.

Consider some of the examples enumerated two paragraphs ago. First take public highways (streets, pedestrian paths, waterways, etc.): as Arthur Ripstein has persuasively argued, we need public highways to allow us to get from one place to another without the possibility of doing so being up to others. If there were no public highways, I would need the permission of everyone between my home and yours to get to the dinner party you are hosting; the public way is one that I can take without needing anyone else's leave.[1] Public roads, then, uniquely allow us to get from one place to another as equals. Another type of important public activities includes the exercise of expressive rights, association, protest, and the like. A long line of cases in common-law systems about the notion of a public forum emphasizes how some public property is needed for the effective realization of these rights.[2] Finally we can see a similar dynamic in thinking about the premises on which the events that make up the legal system "happen": if judicial or legislative proceedings could only take place on private space, subject to the will of that space's owner, that owner would have control over the law itself in a way that would obviously be inconsistent with the basic commitment.

For these public activities to happen in a way that is consistent with the basic commitment, then, they need to happen in space (and using objects[3]) that is not yours or mine (or anyone's); instead, as I will now argue, they need to happen in space that is everyone's, in a quite specific sense.

We can develop the thought by focusing on a particular kind of public property.[4] So consider a public park, with whatever variety of activities you take to be paradigmatic of such a space: people sitting or walking, birdwatching or reading, playing impromptu or organized games of chess or baseball, picnicking, handing out leaflets or demonstrating, and so on.[5] Part of the nature and value of such a place is precisely that the park is not anyone's private property. That means that there is no other private person who can claim that it is up to them whether or on what terms you use the park. In other words, you do not need anyone's

[1] See Arthur Ripstein, Force and Freedom: Kant's Legal and Political Philosophy 243–52 (2009).

[2] For one example see *Committee for the Commonwealth of Canada v Canada*, [1991] 1 SCR 139.

[3] Everything I say in this chapter should apply, *mutatis mutandis*, to objects, but I will mostly concentrate on public space.

[4] Throughout this chapter, the understanding of property as public or private will turn on who has control over the space rather than on legal title. So a building held by the government but leased to a private company is private whereas a privately owned office leased to the government is public.

[5] For more on parks and public space (and the arguments in this chapter) see my "The Nature and Value of Public Space (with Some Lessons from the Pandemic)" 50 Fordham Urban Law Journal 61 (2022).

permission to visit or use the space. Now, that might make you wonder if the park is a negative community in the sense we considered in §1.3. It is not. Recall that a negative community is something not far from a vacuum of rights with respect to spaces and objects: in a negative community, nothing is anyone's, so everyone is free to do what they want with any object or space that they come upon or hold. The situation in a park is different. We each have rights to use the park, in the sense that I would wrong you by destroying a part of the park—by digging up the baseball diamond or setting fire to the bench—or attempting to control your ability to use the park, by doing something like standing at the gate and barring or conditioning your entry. In a negative community, there would be nothing wrong with these actions.[6] At the same time, the fact that each of us is able to use the park also means that each of us can non-wrongfully prevent others from doing so when the prevention is merely factual: there is nothing wrong with my preventing you from sitting on the bench or playing on the diamond if and because I am doing these very same things.

The tort of public nuisance has long encoded these ideas into the law. The gist of public nuisance lies in the interference by the defendant with the use of some public property, normally the public highway.[7] But as the discussion indicates, it is clear that not every such interference can be a wrong, since of course if I am walking or driving here, you will need to walk or drive somewhere else. As one court put it, everyone has "a right to the free and uninterrupted use of a public way," but (therefore) equally a "right for a proper purpose to impede and obstruct the convenient access of the public through and along the same."[8] Indeed, it seems obvious that whatever rights you have against me to the use of the park or street are rights that I need to have against you. Thus, as a later case put it, the "law relating to the user of highways is in truth the law of give and take," such that interferences that are "only obtainable by disregarding" the equal right of others are wrongs. The law squares this circle by understanding the notion of disregarding the equal right of others to mean acting as though one is entitled to determine how those others may act, thus claiming a kind of superiority over them. That is, the wrong lies, in effect, in appropriating the public space for private purposes: "A permanent obstruction erected in a highway without lawful authority is necessarily wrongful and constitutes a public nuisance at common law, as it in fact operates as a withdrawal of part of the highway from the public."[9] There is no wrong in my sitting on the bench or playing on the diamond since,

[6] This shows in yet another way the problem with the negative community: it is a world in which there is only might and no right.

[7] For illuminating discussion, see Jason Neyers, "Reconceptualizing the Tort of Public Nuisance" 76 Cambridge Law Journal 87 (2017).

[8] *Herring v Metropolitan Works* (1865), 19 CB (NS) 510, 525.

[9] *Harper v GN Haden and Sons, Ltd*, [1933] Ch 298, 308, 320.

in so doing, I claim no entitlement to determine your rights to do so, but rather seem simply to be taking my turn or sharing them with you; by contrast, in purporting to dig up the diamond or decide who may come and go from the park, I am acting as though the use of these spaces is up to me precisely in the sense that it would be were they my private property. Difficult questions will arise as to whether or not a particular use of public property counts as the permissible kind of use that merely factually interferes with the use of others or instead as the wrongful kind of use that amounts to (mis)appropriation. But the formal distinction between categories is relatively clear.[10]

A Canadian case illustrates the point. A group of protesters took over a park in downtown Toronto, building semipermanent structures and, in effect, living there. The court's reasoning, in finding that the City of Toronto was within its rights to remove the protesters, notwithstanding that their occupation amounted to a kind of protected expression, which is itself an important public activity, echoes the analysis here. Private permanent structures exclude other members of the public from the park in a way that does not amount to the kind of give and take consistent with the equal right of all members of the public to use the park. Rather, as the court put it, the protesters were claiming a "monopoly over the use of the Park," and had "appropriated public land to their exclusive, private use."[11] This suggests that an important element in our understanding of public property is the way that public property contrasts with private property: crucially, public property is property over which nobody can claim the kind of right to determine how others may act that is constitutive of the idea of yours and mine (and thus of private property). The same line of thought also shows how public property is not like a negative community. In public property, unlike in the negative community, we do have rights that others not act in certain ways—ways that amount to private appropriation—with respect to the spaces and objects as such.

What starts to emerge here is the notion that we share public property, in the sense that none of us can take it for ourselves (for our own private use). This suggests that public property might be a positive community. Of course it is not a

[10] It may be helpful to recall the distinction between having and holding from §1.1 and the arguments about the positive community in §1.3: the claim in the text is that holding public property is permissible and non-wrongful, but claiming to have it is a wrong.

[11] *Batty v City of Toronto*, 2011 ONSC 6862, [97], [108]. Kohn critiques the decision as relying on a notion that the sovereign gets to decide how to use public space so that "erecting a tent in a park is a form of privatization because it violates ordinances that prohibit camping. This is true even if the tent is a large yurt that houses a library and has a sign inviting anyone to come in, read a book and talk about political issues." See Margaret Kohn, "Privatization and Protest: Occupy Wall Street, Occupy Toronto, and the Occupation of Public Space in a Democracy" 11 Perspectives on Politics 99, 103 (2013). In my view, the erection of the tent is a form of privatization not because of an ordinance but because it amounts to a claim to an entitlement to decide how the space on which it sits will be used. Those who erected the tent purport to invite others in, but, as we know from §1.5, inviting someone into a space is only something you can do if you have the power to exclude them.

pure positive community, since, as we saw in §1.3, there we need the unanimous consent of each other member of the community to make any use of any space or object, and we do not need others' consent to walk down the street or enter the park. But there is something plausible in the suggestion. From at least as far back as Locke, treatments of positive community have seen a requirement of universal consent to any individual use as unworkable.[12] This suggests that the members of the community need to settle on, as G A Cohen puts it, some "appropriate procedure" to determine permissible uses.[13]

What would an appropriate procedure look like? We need to remember where we started. Public property is property for public activities. For public activities to take place in a way that is consistent with the basic commitment, they need to take place on space where no private person can decide the terms on which others can participate. Thus public activities need to take place in space that is genuinely everyone's space. And in such a space, an appropriate procedure is one that treats everyone as an equal participant, where the decision as to how the space will be used is one that can be said to be everyone's decision on terms of equality. We have a name for that kind of procedure. We call it "democracy."

7.2 Public Property as Public Law

We can thus understand public property as the property that is held by the public—that is, by everyone—and decisions about the use of which need to be made democratically, in a way that is consistent with the underlying idea that public property is the public's property. We can see how elaborating this understanding of public property generates a range of helpful legal ideas. But we should begin with the connections between public property and public law.

I should first note how the account of public property here fits into the more general understanding of public law that I introduced in §6.1. I said there, roughly, that public law is the solution to a problem of subordination that arises structurally through the cumulative operation of the rules of private law. The version of that thought applicable here should now be easy enough to see. In a world with only private property, it would not be possible for public activities to take place in a way that is consistent with the basic commitment. Unlike the sorts of activities and relations that, as we saw in Chapters 1 and 2, are constituted by the idea of yours and mine, the nature and value of public activities—their role in a society of equals—rests precisely on the fact that they need to take place in property where no private person is in charge. Passing and repassing (i.e. getting

[12] John Locke, Two Treatises of Government II.5, §28 (1690).

[13] G A Cohen, Self-Ownership, Freedom, and Equality 84 (1995).

from one place to another) requires public roads over which no private person has control; participating in the sorts of activities that are distinctive of a park requires parks that are not private; the mechanics of the judiciary and other branches of the government requires space where what happens is not up to any private person. Public property can be understood as a solution to a problem that would arise in a world with only private property and thus as a part of the public law of property.

It may be helpful at this point to emphasize the abstract similarities and differences between public and private property. According to this account, both forms of property are required to allow for certain kinds of important activities and relations to take place on terms of equality, consistent with the basic commitment. So both private and public property are essential constituents of a society of equals. The difference between them lies in the form of the relations for which they are required. Roughly, private property is required for a range of private activities and relations, which is to say those we engage in on our own and with others but always in our capacity as private persons. Public property, by contrast, is about public activities, activities that are realizations of the idea of the public, the organization of all the members of the society as such. Where equality in the first case requires that it be up to me, rather than you, to decide what you can do with what is mine, equality in the second case requires something like the opposite, such that it is up to everyone to decide what happens with what is everyone's. These are entirely different forms of egalitarian relation. This difference may be helpful in noticing a certain dynamic raised by those concerned about privatization of public spaces and property. The thought is that because public property is constitutive of a certain distinctive way of relating as equals (i.e. as equal members of the public), privatization is destructive of that important and distinctive political value. A private space is, in this way, nothing like the public version of the same space because of the fundamental difference between the nature of the relations between members of the society of equals available in and appropriate for each.[14]

According to that sort of view—whatever the extension of its application turns out to be in the best theory of essential public activities, a question I continue to leave open here—the choice between public property and private property is nothing at all like an instrumentalist question about efficiency, as some have suggested.[15] Rather, it is a question about the very possibility of pursuing the

[14] For some expressions of concern see Brett Christophers, The New Enclosures: The Appropriation of Public Land in Neoliberal Britain (2018); Kathleen Sharp, "It's Your Beach. Don't Let Them Hog It" New York Times July 21, 2018, at A21; Nellie Bowles, "Court Opts Out of Ambivalent Billionaire's Surfer Fight" New York Times October 2, 2018, at B5; Kohn, Privatization and Protest; Andrew W Kahrl, "Free the Beach" Boston Review, May 21, 2018.

[15] Richard Epstein, "On the Optimal Mix of Private and Common Property" 11 Social Philosophy and Policy 17 (1994).

relevant public activities and thus about the very possibility of our relating as equals consistent with the basic commitment. While it might be cheaper to have only private roads, we could not do so consistent with our standing as equals, as the owners of private roads would be in a position that renders everyone else inferior, as everyone else would need these owners' permission to go anywhere at all. Although it might be more efficient to have privately owned courthouses, we could not have them consistent with our standing as equals as the very possibility of access to justice would in such a world depend on the will of those who owned them. I declared in the very first sentence of this book that private property is an essential constituent of a society of equals. The argument here suggests that public property is, too.

Another connection between public property and public law is slightly more complicated. To explore it, we can begin with an important contrast between public activities and the relations and activities that are partly constituted by the idea of yours and mine. The contrast is this: whereas the idea of yours and mine involves a certain kind of formal openness, in that when something is mine it is up to me to decide how it can be used in an open-ended sort of way,[16] public activities are more strictly delineated. Put differently, we might say that there is not really any such thing as public activity just as such, in the abstract: rather, there is a set of specific public activities—passing and repassing, legislating, deciding cases, being in the park—whose commonality is their publicness. This ties in quite neatly with a common understanding of the difference between public law and private law, according to which, in private law, for private persons, anything that is not prohibited is permitted, whereas in public law, for public authorities, anything that is not permitted is prohibited.[17]

The specificity of public property is actually easy to see in our thinking about the wider application of these ideas. The idea that public property is everyone's means, we saw, that each of us is entitled to use public property in a way that is consistent with its status as everyone's, which is to say consistent with others making like use of it. But that idea is very abstract, and to realize it, we need to provide it with content, in particular, an understanding of the specific purpose or activity to which a particular piece of public property is directed. Sitting down in the grass is a perfectly permissible use of the park, but sitting down in the middle of the road is a public nuisance; riding a bike in the street is permitted but riding a bike in the courtroom is prohibited. And so on. The nature of each particular piece of public property, along with the permitted

[16] See the text accompanying Chapter 1, note 50.

[17] In Canada, this idea is associated with F R Scott. See W S Tarnopolsky, "Frank Scott—Civil Libertarian" 27 McGill Law Journal 15, 25 (1981). For a judicial statement of the idea, see *R v Somerset CC, ex parte Fewings*, [1995] 1 All ER 513, 524 (CA).

uses of it, is determined by the public activity for which the property has been provided.[18]

This determination happens, in law, in a variety of ways. The most common is the application of the idea that concluded §7.1, namely, that we (the public) decide collectively what public property we will have and what it will be for through familiar democratic processes. In other words, we have laws, bylaws, regulations, ordinances, and other actions carried out by public authorities dedicated to determining what public property we have and what can happen in it. This includes the actual built environment: public authorities build courthouses and legislatures, parks and roads, and any number of other pieces of public property. The built nature of these spaces and the purposes that they are given are partly determinative of what kinds of uses members of the public may make of them: this is a road for coming and going, this is the courthouse for judicial proceedings. Of course, laws about public property also work in the "normal" way, in the sense that they set out, in varying degrees of specificity, what kinds of uses of a given piece of public property are prohibited or permitted. We have (lots of) rules about what is permitted and where and when on public streets.[19] Sometimes the legal structure involves discretion granted to public officials, like the bylaw officer in the park or bailiff at the courthouse. Other times, we have laws involving a kind of a power-conferring structure, as in the case of systems of issuing permits, whereby one can reserve a baseball diamond or a parking spot for a limited period of time. There are other kinds of examples, too.

In all these cases, to ensure that specific ordinances are consistent with the idea of public property, they need to be enacted in a way that allows us to understand them as instances of democratic decision-making about the use of public property. This idea has two aspects. The first is that the ordinances need to be cognizable as instances of *democratic decision-making* about the use of public property. When it comes to private space, the idea that this space is mine entails that what happens on it and under what conditions is up to me. And so, in parallel, when it comes to public space, the idea that that space is the public's must entail that rules about what happens on it and under what conditions are up to the public. And the way that the public decides questions like that is through its democratic processes, so that, when a rule says that I am not permitted in

[18] In note 4, *supra*, I introduced the complication of mixed public-private leases. I take it that the question of whether or not leasing out some public property to private persons is permissible or not is a version of the questions I am here considering, as to whether such a lease could be consistent with treating the space as public; the answer seems intuitively to depend on the nature of the space and the nature of the lease. Leasing of public property to residential tenants in public housing is uncontroversially permitted; leasing a public park to a private organization which will then have the power to exclude from that space seems harder to justify.

[19] An annotated copy of the Ontario *Highway Traffic Act* and its associated regulations runs to well over 1,500 pages.

the park after midnight, I can understand it as is a rule that I coauthored as a member of the public. Democratic decision-making is the mode of decision-making appropriate here since it is just the mode of decision-making that treats the members of the democratic public as equals.[20] At the same time, the democratic decision-making is not unconstrained: the second aspect of the idea is that these ordinances and rules need to be cognizable as democratic decisions about *the use of public property*.[21] As such, any positive law rules about public property must treat all the members of the public as equals, must not exclude particular persons from public property, must not amount to treating public property as anyone's private property, and so on.

I said that the specificity of the specific legal rules that apply to individual pieces of public property varies, in that sometimes we need quite specific and precise rules whereas other times the rules are more indeterminate. This indeterminacy, it is worth noting, can sometimes itself generate important forms of egalitarian relations among members of the public, since the abstraction of the positive law requires that members of the public themselves engage in a project of further specification on the ground (literally and figuratively), through what might be characterized as a kind of democratic negotiation to resolve particular interactions in a way that regards the parties to them as equals. You and I cannot both sit on this spot on this bench, or play both baseball and soccer on this field, at the same time. So we need to work it out: you reached the bench first today so you get to sit there; I cut short my time on the field in recognition of the fact that you are waiting for a turn. We might understand such apparently mundane interactions as small-scale acts of democratic politics, where we engage in acts of "collective self-determination by means of open discussion among equals," in our status as members of the public, to decide how we ought to govern ourselves in public space.[22]

[20] Seana Valentine Shiffrin, Democratic Law (2021), Niko Kolodny, "Rule Over None II: Social Equality and the Justification of Democracy" 42 Philosophy & Public Affairs 287 (2014).

[21] For the rest of this section, I will continue to talk loosely about the "use of public property," in a way that is meant to cross the boundary between trespass-like and nuisance-like applications of the abstract ideas. That is, both rules about when a private person can be excluded from public property and rules about when a private person's activities can be restrained when they interfere with others' use of public property are, for present purposes, the same.

[22] Elizabeth Anderson, "What Is the Point of Equality?" 109 Ethics 287, 313 (1999). On a longer time scale, sometimes this process works to change the nature of particular spaces, or even classes of space, and thus to change what can count as appropriate use. The common law's view of the nature and proper public use of roads, for example, has shifted over time with less, then more, and now perhaps again less emphasis on passing and repassing as opposed to a wider range of public activities. For more on this, see my "Nature and Value of Public Space" at 80. Something similar seems to be going on in public libraries: see Eric Klinenberg, Palaces for the People: How Social Infrastructure Can Help Fight Inequality, Polarization, and the Decline of Civic Life 31 (2018); Lisa M Freeman and Nick Blomley, "Enacting Property: Making Space for the Public in the Municipal Library" 37 EPC: Politics and Space 199 (2018).

7.3 Using Public (and Quasi-Public) Property

The idea that public property is the public's property and that the public determines how it may be used through democratic decision-making can help us to understand some important questions about the rights that individual members of the public have to use public property. This set of ideas suggests, I think correctly, that the default position for public property is that members of the public are permitted to enter it. But that default is in a way too abstract, since, as we saw, particular parcels of public property are directed at particular public activities. This means that both the use that may be made of some piece of public property and the limits on that use will be determined in light of the activity for which it is intended. For instance, when it comes to public roads, we are all generally permitted to use them for passing and repassing (and more), but we are prohibited from using them in ways that make it impossible (or unreasonably difficult) for others to do the same. Some of those prohibitions are encoded in statutory rules (about speed limits, stoplights, and the like) and others in the common law of public nuisance. In other spaces, the nature of the public activity circumscribes permitted use much more tightly: members of the public are generally permitted to enter courtrooms during judicial proceedings, but they must respect the dignity of the room, keep noise down, and the like, and more specific limitations on access may arise in the context of particularly sensitive disputes.[23] In some cases, the nature of the public activity might mean that members of the public are generally prohibited from entry: the offices of government ministers and judge's chambers have this character. And, of course, as the last two examples suggest, much public property involves a spectrum of rules along these dimensions: the courthouse lobby is generally open, the courthouse itself is open subject to rules about conduct, and the judge's chambers are generally closed to the public and reserved for the judge's use.[24]

Notice that, even in this last sort of case, the nature and justification of the prohibition on entry by members of the public is quite different than it would be in the context of a facially similar piece of private property. In private property, it is up to the owner of the space to make a determination for essentially any reason at all as to who may enter and under what conditions. But that is not how it is in public property, where legal rules about particular spaces must be tied to the nature of the public activity in question and the public officials charged with administering such spaces must only exercise their authority over the space in a way that can be justified on that basis. A slightly different way to

[23] See, e.g., Canada's *Criminal Code* s 486.5.

[24] Even here, though, notice that the judge's control over their own chambers is not limitless, and the judge cannot use the chambers for a birthday party or to run a business, but must instead limit their own use for the relevant judicial purposes.

see this is to note that trespass, which we saw in §4.1 to be the basic form of the realization of the idea of yours and mine, is about the egalitarian relation between owner and other. But the public officials administering public space do not relate to members of the public as equals when they exercise their public authority. Quite the contrary: the relationship between individual private persons and public authorities is marked by inequality, by the "juridical superiority of one party to the other."[25] The egalitarian nature of democracy and its associated processes for the enactment of public rules, creation of public authority, and empowerment of public officials lurks in the background here, so that the entire apparatus of public property maintains its egalitarian justificatory structure. But it is a different structure, and so the idea of trespass that is appropriate to relations between private persons through the idea of yours and mine is entirely inappropriate in the context of public property.

Another way to make the point I am developing here is to say that each act of exclusion from public property must be understood as an instance of an exercise of a public law power, and so must be justified, as any exercise of public law power must, on the basis of relevant public purposes. Sometimes, as in the case of the judge's chambers, the relevant public purposes, properly understood, will justify a scope of exclusion that will be quite close, extensionally, to what the parallel private law trespassory right would provide.[26] Other times, as in the case of streets and parks, the scope of permissible exclusion is much narrower. But the justification of the exclusion is the same: someone can be excluded only on the basis of reasons, only on the basis that their presence or use is inconsistent with the nature or purpose of the particular piece of public property in question. And, consistent with a familiar public law idea, this also means that, in a marked contrast to the private law case, the exclusion should be reviewable on public law reasonableness grounds. When a public authority claims, as some do, to have the near-absolute power to exclude members of the public from an otherwise

[25] Ernest J Weinrib, Reciprocal Freedom: Private Law, and Public Right 119 (2022).

[26] Two points here. First, the extensional overlap explains why, in many cases, we experience the public law restrictions on use of public property in much the same way as we experience private law restrictions: I understand that public property is not mine in the yours-and-mine sense, and so I understand that I must respect someone else's decisions about how it may be used, in the way that James Penner has emphasized (see J E Penner, The Idea of Property in Law 75–77 (1997)). The difference is just that in the one case that "someone else" is a private person whereas in the other it's the public as a whole. Second, this extensional overlap may tempt you to say, what's the difference, why not talk in terms of trespass. My view is that the egalitarian character of the idea of yours and mine helps to show why this is a mistake: I get to exclude you from what is mine because that is what is required for you and me to be able to relate as equals. But if we apply that thought to the control that public authorities have over public property, we can see the mistake right away: public authorities and private persons do not—cannot—relate to one another in the way that the basic commitment requires of private persons. A public authority is a fundamentally different kind of entity than a private person and relations between private persons and public authorities in contexts that resemble private law relations are merely resemblances.

open public space, like a park or square, on the grounds that the law of trespass applies and that the public authority is in a position akin to—or even that it is—the owner of the space, the state's authority is being abused in a way that is deeply inconsistent with the public nature of that public property.[27]

In fact, as I write this, Toronto's municipal government has been clearing, with a visible show of force, homeless encampments in a prominent city park. The encampments arose there—as they did elsewhere—primarily in the early stages of the COVID-19 pandemic, as many underhoused individuals decided, quite reasonably, that staying in a tent in a park was safer than staying in a shelter given the relative risks of infection. The question of the presence of semipermanent residential structures in public spaces is a difficult one. On the one hand, a semipermanent structure seems on its face to be at odds with the nature of public space, as it amounts to a kind of appropriation of the space as against other members of the public whose shared space it is; generally facially neutral rules prohibiting the erection of permanent structures in public parks are straightforwardly understandable as an application of these ideas. On the other hand, homelessness is a pressing social problem, and the state's duty to respond to it is among the central concerns of this book. The difficulty here arises because of the conflict between the form of equality appropriate to public property, where none may appropriate the space for themselves as against others, and the form of equality appropriate to private property, which calls for the state to ensure that none is homeless to ensure that none is subordinated (structurally) with respect to the idea of yours and mine. The presence of homelessness means that the state is failing to fulfill its duties in that latter respect. The question, though, is whether that failure means that it is unreasonable for municipalities to enforce parks bylaws prohibiting such structures in the face of homelessness. Many courts dealing with this issue have determined that the issue turns on the degree to which the state has provided alternative living spaces: where sufficient shelter spaces are available, staying in the park seems not to be permissible, whereas if there is literally nowhere for the homeless to stay except public property, it seems that the state's failure on the private property front might justify this otherwise impermissible use of public property.[28]

In the remainder of this section, I want to examine a set of cases that might make it seem like the contrast I have just drawn between public property (where

[27] In Canada, at least, there are provincial trespass statutes that provide remedies against trespass and that are taken to apply equally to private and public property. (The *Batty* case is on the surface about the constitutionality of the application of the Ontario statute to the facts of the case.) According to the view in the text, this statutory setup is at best imprecise. But I leave fuller treatment of that question to a later date.

[28] See, e.g., *Victoria (City) v Adams*, 2009 BCCA 563. In the *Batty* case, by contrast, the expressive activity of the claimants was held by the court not to be sufficient to find that it was not unreasonable of the city to enforce the bylaw prohibiting their structures.

control must be justified on public law reasonableness grounds) and private property (where control is close to absolute) is reductive and confused. I will do so through one of the most famous of such cases (which was, incidentally, the first case I read in law school), *Harrison v Carswell*.[29] The case is commonly used as the introduction to a property course in Canada, because its two judgments illustrate a range of important parts of the common-law process, including the conflict between precedent and principle, the relation between private rights and public policy, and so on. The facts are familiar from a range of similar cases: the defendant was said to be trespassing by engaging in a labor picket at a shopping mall where she worked. The Court had to decide if the relevant trespass statute applied to the case. The majority held that it did, that the mall was privately owned space and so its owner could eject the defendant as a routine matter. The dissenting judgment, written by Chief Justice Laskin, reaches a different, and for our purposes, more interesting, result.[30]

There are a couple of different lines of thought in the judgment, but the most interesting for our purposes is the idea that a mall is "open for use by members of the public."[31] Here Laskin seems to be invoking the very old common-law idea of a public accommodation. This is the idea that, in certain circumstances, private persons can engage in (typically) commercial activity in a way that generates a distinctive set of legal ideas about the relation between them and members of the public. Familiar examples of public accommodations are inns, taverns ("public houses"), restaurants, and stores. In these cases, the common law has long held that the proprietor of the business must offer their services to any member of the public who can pay the fee.[32] Again, we do not need here to set out a comprehensive account of what should and should not count as a public accommodation. But the traditional explanation for the phenomenon, along with a brief historical

[29] [1976] 2 SCR 200.

[30] Another explanation of the result in the case invokes what is usually called the principle of horizontality, the idea that fundamental (constitutional) rights should somehow apply to at least some private law interactions. The idea is broad in that, at least in principle, it applies to cases far beyond the quasi-public space of a mall, as when it is invoked in support of an argument that a private organization like a condominium corporation cannot prevent certain uses of land if such prevention would interfere with the exercise of fundamental rights. But it is also narrow in that, as stated, it applies only to uses of property that invoke fundamental rights, and so might not cover all the cases of interest in the quasi-public space context, since some such cases involve a more diffuse sense that a mall, say, is public space and so should be open for something like wandering around aimlessly, which seems not obviously to be protected by a fundamental right. As I said, though, this explanation is external to my view in that it invokes this broader notion of horizontality, a notion that is itself deeply complex and contested and certainly applies beyond the law of property. For further discussion see Weinrib, Reciprocal Freedom, Ch 6.

[31] *Harrison* at 203.

[32] *White's Case*, 73 Eng Rep 343 (1558). For a general discussion, see Charles K Burdick, "The Origin of the Peculiar Duties of Public Service Companies, Part I" 11 Columbia Law Review 514 (1911); Joseph William Singer, "No Right to Exclude: Public Accommodations and Private Property" 90 Northwestern University Law Review 1283 (1996); Aravind Ganesh, "*Wirtbarkeit*: Cosmopolitan Right and Innkeeping" 24 Legal Theory 159 (2018).

sketch, can suggest the outlines of one that will be sufficient for our purposes. The history usually referred to here involves inns in late medieval England, a land apparently beset by highwaymen and other criminals. In this context, it came to be recognized that inns generally available to travellers were essential for long-distance travel to be possible; but these difficult circumstances quite obviously generated a problem of potential exploitation by innkeepers of unsuspecting travelers, so that a large body of law developed ensuring that travelers could access rooms on fair terms. This, and related doctrines about similarly important services, came to be understood in terms of the idea that operators of these public accommodations are carrying on a business "of a quasi-public character," or occupying "as it were a public office."[33] The discussion of public property provides the means to offer a particular version of this idea. I want to suggest that, in the context of public accommodations involving real spaces that are opened to the public, we ought to focus on the nature of the space in which the public accommodation operates. The suggestion will be that, in a public accommodation, private property is held out as and thus should be treated as if it were public property in the sense developed in this chapter. On that basis, members of the public in general are permitted to enter the space and to engage in the form of public activity that is appropriate to it.

We have seen how individual parcels of public property and the rights of the public to use them are constituted by the specific substantive public activity for which they exist. In each case, the nature of the public activity generates both the rights of the public to use the property and the limits on those rights. These limits, in particular, mean that anyone who purports to be entitled to use the property for a purpose inconsistent with the carrying out by members of the public of the relevant public activity may be prohibited from doing so: you may not set up a picnic in the middle of the highway or sell guacamole in the courtroom (and if you do you will be removed). Any use that is within the limits set by the nature of the public activity—consistent with the laws specifying that nature and decisions of public officials tasked with interpreting and applying them—is rightful, so that members of the public are generally entitled to do it and cannot be excluded for doing so. The idea of a public accommodation can be understood using this set of concepts. A private owner who holds their space out as open to the public for a specific purpose is, in effect, making their space available as a space for engaging in some form of public activity. In such circumstances, members of the public are entitled to use the space for the relevant activity and the private owner of the space is no longer empowered to exclude individual members of the public from using the space in the relevant way. While held open to the public, the space is (as

[33] *De Wolf v Ford*, 86 NE 527, 529 (1908); *Ansell v Waterhouse* (1817) 2 Chit R 1. To the same effect, see *R v Ivens* (1835) 7 C & P 213, 219.

it is said) quasi-public, in the precise sense that the public and owner must treat it as if it were actually public space. This does not mean, of course, that such spaces are free-for-alls: the nature of the space provides the grounds for limits. We can rely on the decision of the owner to dedicate the space to a particular public activity to specify the uses which members of the public may and may not make of it: if I open my space as an inn, members of the public may come to sleep there but not to operate nightclubs inside; if I open my space as a restaurant, members of the public may come to eat and drink but not play baseball.

Notice that thinking about the phenomenon in these terms allows us to avoid the difficult question of what, if anything, must count as a public accommodation. For the most part, public accommodations count as such simply in virtue of the fact that they are actually held open to the public by their owners.[34] Crucially, we need to remember that this is an objective notion, not a question of the subjective intentions of the owner. Whether or not property is open to the public is determined by the communicative content of the owner's use of their property, including its physical set up, signage, and so on. Stores, restaurants, malls, and the like are spaces that a reasonable person understands as being open to the public because, here and now, that is how such spaces are treated. There may be some historical or social circumstances in which certain business must be understood as public accommodations—my historical handwaving about inns might be like this—but for present purposes a more positivistic account is sufficient.[35]

Again, as in the case of genuine public property, the owner of quasi-public property may further specify the nature of the public activity that may take place in the space by enacting and posting specific rules: no shirt, no shoes, no service. Because these rules themselves will have a quasi-public character, they must adhere to familiar rule of law principles of publicity, nonretroactivity, and the like. And because they are rules about quasi-public property, they must meet the desiderata appropriate to genuine public policy, in that they must be rules that could have been enacted by a democratic public authority in a genuinely public version of the same space. Similarly, an owner may exercise discretion in particular cases to remove disorderly customers if, again, the customer's behavior is inconsistent with the nature of the activity to which the property is dedicated.[36] In other words, as in the case of genuine public property, the owner of a public

[34] This is also Singer's view: "No Right to Exclude" at 1330–31.

[35] Carol Rose, drawing on Adam Smith, notices that public space is necessary for the kind of "truck, barter, and exchange" that makes up much commercial activity. Carol Rose, "The Comedy of the Commons: Custom, Commerce, and Inherently Public Property" 53 University of Chicago Law Review 711, 774 (1986). Kant had a similar thought about public markets. Treating stores as public accommodations accomplishes the same end.

[36] *Fraser v McGibbon*, 10 OWR 54 (1907).

accommodation may not exclude members of the public "at his whim," but must instead have a "proper reason . . . to justify the order to leave."[37]

It is important to see here how this account of quasi-public property maintains the *quasi*-public character of the property, in the sense that it does preserve the basically private nature of the private owner's property. This is true in two ways. As I briefly noted, the idea that operators of public accommodations are quasi-public officials strikes some as implausible, partly because they are entitled, in their capacity as private owners, to act for private purposes (like profit maximization) that would be inappropriate for genuine public officials. Treating the space as quasi-public avoids this worry. It permits the owner's pursuit of private purposes but constrains the means with which they may be pursued, by saying that they must be pursued in a way that is consistent with the dedication of the space to the relevant public activity. (So the innkeeper can charge any fee the market will bear as long as the inn is open to anyone who can pay.) Second, the private owner retains ultimate control over the property in that they are always uncontroversially able to end its status as quasi-public: the inn can be converted to a private home, the restaurant can be torn down. The quasi-public character of the property and the public's rights to enter it are all conditioned upon the owner's (private) choice to hold the property open to the public.[38]

In light of all of this, Chief Justice Laskin's reasoning in *Harrison v Carswell* is easy to understand. The public activity to which a shopping mall is dedicated is something like that of a public square or pedestrian street. As Laskin says, a mall is "closer in character to public roads and sidewalks than to a private dwelling,"[39] and as another court said, when it comes to a mall, "access to the public is the very reason for its existence."[40] The public is invited not merely to shop but to do quite a bit more—wander the common spaces, hang out, drink coffee, walk for exercise or to soothe a crying baby. In effect, to treat the common spaces of the mall like they are a public street or square.[41] So the owner of the mall is not entitled to eject those patrons whose use of the space is consistent with that

[37] *Harrison* at 207.

[38] Not all publicly accessible privately owned space is like that. A prominent phenomenon in many urban centers is the so-called Privately Owned Public Space (POPS), such as the squares in and around office buildings and condominiums, which are created by private developers either as part of a quid pro quo with a state agency, according to which the developer is allowed to build beyond the default planning requirements of a location in exchange for setting some land aside that is open to the public, or more directly as a condition of any building in certain areas. (For an example of the former, see New York City, New York Zoning Resolution, Article 3, Chapter 7, §37-70; for an example of the latter, see San Francisco Planning Code, §138.) The analysis in the text applies to these spaces with the only difference being that they are nonrevocably held open to the public.

[39] *Harrison* at 207.

[40] *Schwartz-Torrance Investment Corp v Bakery and Confectionary Workers' Union, Local No 31*, 394 P2d 921, 924 (Cal 1964). *See also Robins v Pruneyard Shopping Center*, 592 P2d 341 (Cal 1979).

[41] To the same effect, *see New Jersey Coalition against War in the Middle East v JMB Realty Corporation*, 650 A2d 757, 761, 772–73 (NJ 1994).

activity. Following this line of thought, the owner of the mall may set terms for its use—"no skateboarding," "no smoking"—that can be understood as consistent with the purpose and may exercise discretion to eject those who engage in what Chief Justice Laskin calls "misbehaviour."[42] But as we saw, there are limits to the power that can be exercised by a private owner once they have chosen to hold their property open to the public. In the context of a mall, the reasonable interpretation of the built environment suggests, as I said, that the space is to be treated as if it were a public square or pedestrian street. And genuine versions of such spaces are spaces in which the activity that Carswell—the defendant in the case—was engaged in is within the scope of the public's right to engage in public activity. Labor picketing is an activity that, to play the role it needs to play in a society of equals, must be permissible in public property that is reasonably proximate to the employer's private property. In other words, just as a public street is open to the public for labor picketing (and other similar expressive activity), a mall—a quasi-public street—is, too.[43] Since the picket in question was peaceful and not disruptive and did not interfere with the ability of other members of the public to enter the mall, it was wrong for the mall owner to exclude the claimant for engaging in it.

7.4 Public or Private

Now that we have this picture of public property in place, we can return to a question that occupied us much earlier in this book. Recall, briefly, the dialectic that was at play in Chapter 2. In §2.2, I defended the claim that, in a system of (private) property, individuals relate to one another through the idea of yours and mine and thus relate as equals with respect to property's sphere. In §2.3, I defended the claim that *only* under such a system of property can we relate as equals with respect to the relevant subject matter. I considered a few obvious putative alternatives to property and showed how either they reduced into or

[42] *Harrison* at 208.

[43] In *Ralphs Grocery Co v United Food & Commercial Workers Union Local 8*, 290 P3d 1116 (Cal 2016), the court declined to extend the rule about expressive activity in malls, in part by noting that a grocery store differs from a mall in precisely this respect. This point could be developed further to vindicate the thought that a sort of private business including (but not limited to) cafés and bars counts as a kind of public space, as suggested by elements of Habermas' theory of the public sphere (see Jürgen Habermas, The Structural Transformation of the Public Sphere: An Inquiry into a Category of Bourgeois Society (1962)) or the sociological idea of a "third place" (see Ray Oldenburg, The Great Good Place: Coffee Shops, Bookstores, Bars, Hair Salons, and Other Hangouts and the Heart of a Community (1989)). These sorts of spaces are, we could say, held open to the public to use for a certain set of public activities, in particular various forms of discussion and debate. The argument here would suggest that patrons of such establishments should have a wide latitude to engage in even unpopular forms of speech, while nevertheless being prohibited from, say, playing basketball.

depended on a system of property or else how they failed to allow their subjects to relate as equals. But I left one system to be discussed later, a system of, roughly, public control of everything. The basic proposal is that we could meet our obligation under the basic commitment to relate as equals with respect to objects, spaces, and so on by, instead of realizing the idea of yours and mine, realizing something like the idea that underlies the notion of public property.

One helpful way to think about the issues here is by thinking about how we could sort the wide range of activities and relations that constitute our social world into private and public in a way that is consistent with the basic commitment. As I indicated, the nature of public activities means that they must take place in public property in order for them to take place consistent with the basic commitment. (Echoing the point to come, I said in §7.1 that we could set aside the question of just what needs to count as a public activity.) At the same time—this was, essentially, the argument of Part I—there are some things—things that paradigmatically take place in a home, like sleeping or intimate activities or bathing—that, if we are to relate as equals, we need space to do them in over which we have the kind of control over others' access that is grounded on the idea of yours and mine. And then there seems to be a third category, a category of cases that could go either way. Take baseball: a world in which we could only play baseball in private space or a world in which we could only play baseball in public space or a world in which we could do either all seem like worlds in which we could relate as equals. What we might call a given society's public-private property balance is determined by the way it sorts the activities and relations that fall into this third box. There is obviously an enormous range of permissibility here: some places might encourage picnicking in public space where others ask that dining take place in private; some might provide generous public sports fields where others prefer sports to take place in private space; one might provide public bicycles where in another everyone would own their own bike.

The theoretical question we are concerned with here—the question that I held over from Chapter 2—is this: could we relate as equals in a society in which everything is put into the first box, a society in which every activity and relation involving spaces and objects was governed according to the model of public property?[44] This really would be a world without property, as it would be a world in which nothing could be thought of in terms of the idea of yours and mine. I doubt that, in such a world, we could actually relate as equals. My imagination is limited,[45] but note the basic outline: everything that happens in such a world would happen along the model of a park or street. Take sleeping, or any of the

[44] I won't give any space to the absurd libertarian fantasy that all property should be private: we saw earlier in the chapter how, at the least, roads and the sites of the legal system need to be public.

[45] For a description of a world that is said to be one without property from an imagination exponentially less limited than mine, see Ursula K LeGuin, The Dispossessed (1974).

other activities that make up a home: you would be able to sleep only if there was a public bed available for you to sleep in. But there would be no guarantee that there would be a bed, no guarantee that you would be able to find a place to sleep. This lack of a guarantee is not just practical, it is normative, in this sense: there would be nothing wrong, in this world, with others preventing you from finding a place to sleep by acting to always beat you to the closest bed, so that you were never in a position actually to get into a bed. I think this would be a problem.

Contrast the case of an actual park, where every time you show up, there is already someone playing baseball, so that you can never actually play. This seems like a drag, sure, but baseball seems optional in a way that sleeping does not. So a world in which your ability to find a place to sleep was dependent on the actions and goodwill of others would be one in which you were not able to relate to them as equals with respect to something unavoidable and so, I think, not able to relate to them as equals at all. Essentially the problem here is an instance of a more general problem about majoritarian control in a democratic society. I take it that it is consistent with the underlying egalitarian justification of democracy that some matters of policy are determined by the will of the majority, but not all are, and that this is why a complete account of a democratic society must include an account of the role of fundamental rights within it.[46] And so in this case, the thought is that the very core of the idea of yours and mine is something that needs protection in a similar way and cannot simply be left to the general will. Without developing the thought, roughly what I am saying here is that if you wanted to think about all property as the public's, you would need, in order to meet the basic commitment, to ensure that there was some rights-based protection not subject to the general will for at least some limited set of activities and relations to take place in space governed on an individual basis. But that would just be to ensure—in a roundabout sort of way—that there was some property governed according to the idea of yours and mine.

It is at this point in the argument where a common objection arises, roughly to the effect that some non-Western or, in particular, Indigenous forms of resource allocation present an alternative to a system of property that satisfies the basic commitment. The objection says that many Indigenous cultures seem not to have property and yet seem to be egalitarian, indeed, more egalitarian than Western societies. But it is far from clear that the facts bear this out. We can focus on the Indigenous societies in what is now called North America. While there is significant variation across different groups, there seems to be something close to a consensus that many, if not all, of these groups have or had at least some form of property in at least some resources. Some groups practiced farming in a

[46] For one statement of this broadly shared idea, see Ronald Dworkin, Freedom's Law: The Moral Reading of the American Constitution 15*ff* (1996).

way that involved something close to ownership of land; others held most land in common but realized the idea of yours and mine in other kinds of objects. So we might better think of these societies as ones in which only a limited set of activities and relations are governed through an idea of yours and mine, where the others are governed according to a norm more like that which applies to public spaces in common-law systems. If that is right, then the objection falls away, and we see here, rather than a genuine alternative, a variety of different systems of property, some of which, to be sure, might be preferable to the ones realized in common-law systems.[47]

It is important to see the implications of the general line of thought here. It might turn out that the set of activities and relations that must take place on private property turns out to be relatively narrow. Perhaps we each need to have nothing more than a small home for ourselves or our family in which to sleep and to participate in small-scale intimacies with our loved ones. And then perhaps it would be that so much of what we do now in private could happen in public: dinner parties, reading, karaoke, cooking, and so on would all be available on the model of a park, perhaps involving permits or perhaps available simply on a first-come, first-served model. Surely there would be diverse advantages and disadvantages to doing this with respect to various particular activities and relations, and the kinds of considerations that often seem prominent in Humean-influenced discussions of property would be among these: considerations of efficiency and free-riding and so on might be part of why a society would choose

[47] I'm grateful to John Borrows for helpful discussion of the issues raised in this paragraph, as well as related questions. (I have set aside another reason he suggested to doubt the premise of the objection, namely, that many Indigenous societies are rigidly hierarchical rather than egalitarian.) For a wide-ranging and legally informed discussion of Indigenous forms of property, see Kenneth H Bobroff, "Retelling Allotment: Indian Property Rights and the Myth of Common Ownership" 54 Vanderbilt Law Review 1557 (2001). And to similar effect, see Allan Greer, Property and Dispossession: Natives, Empires and Land in Early Modern North America 27–64 (2018). In the more centrally anthropological literature, there is at least some debate about the question of which societies have property, although many of those who argue for the negative answer turn out to deny a narrower proposition, namely, that not all societies have property in what I called in chapter 2 the full liberal sense. But as I have emphasized, that is not the only possible form of property. For discussions that explicitly endorse a more encompassing account of property consistent with the claim I make in this paragraph, see several essays in C M Hann, ed, Property Relations: Renewing the Anthropological Tradition (1998), including in particular, C M Hann, "Introduction: The Embeddedness of Property," James Woodburn, "'Sharing Is Not a Form of Exchange': An Analysis of Property Sharing in Immediate-Return Hunter-Gatherer Societies," and James G Carrier, "Property and Social Relations in Melanesian Anthropology"; Robert H Lowie, Primitive Society 205–56 (1920). For a more critical take, see Adrian Tanner, "The New Hunting Territory Debate: An Introduction to Some Unresolved Issues" 28 Anthropologica (NS) 19 (1986). For good general discussion, see Paul Nadasdy, "'Property' and Aboriginal Land Claims in the Canadian Subarctic: Some Theoretical Considerations" 104 American Anthropologist 247 (2002); Colin Scott, "Property, Practice and Aboriginal Rights among Quebec Cree Hunters" in Tim Ingold, David Riches, and James Woodburn, eds, Hunters and Gatherers, Vol 2: Property, Power and Ideology 35; and A Irving Hallowell, "The Nature and Function of Property as a Social Institution" 1 Journal of Legal and Political Sociology 115 (1942).

for some things to happen in private space and others in public space. Similarly, notice that the familiar content of discussions around something like "public ownership of the means of production," which I mentioned in §2.2, fit into this same abstract framework: perhaps a society would be more equal in terms of wealth or political control if the means of production were owned publicly rather than privately. I will not say much about any of this, or about the common set of suggestions that our societies would be better, healthier, more egalitarian, and so on, were we to move away from a model that focuses too heavily on private property at the expense of public governance. I tend to agree with many of those suggestions, but more in a personal than professional capacity. The point is that the range of permissibility here in terms of the basic commitment is really quite wide, but the permissible options do all require at least *some* form of (private) property. A world in which literally every space and object was public property would be a world so unlike ours that, it seems to me, we cannot realistically envision it as an alternative to our own in a way that is consistent with the basic commitment.

Conclusion

When I started writing this book, I thought it was going to be a book about the way that institutions of property are justified in the context of an egalitarian democratic society. As it turns out, I wrote something . . . different. As often employed these days in social philosophy, talk of justification tends to be associated with some notion of being favored by the balance of reasons or something along those lines. But that idea of justification seems to me to be too unstructured to guide our thinking about an institution as enormous and pervasive and important as property. So let me conclude by saying three things about the argument of this book and the question of justification.

First, I think the central argument of the first part of this book shows something quite a bit stronger than that property is justified in the sense just adverted to. Again: an idea of justification, at least when it is associated with reasons-talk, can be an idea that sets a pretty low bar, an idea that can apply in really small-stakes situations. We can ask if I am justified in choosing the guacamole over the avocado toast, if I am justified in watching this show or reading that book, by asking if I have reasons that favor one over the other. But that idea of justification is not in the same register as the claims I made here. If I am right that property is the only possible solution to the Problem of Yours and Mine, and that the Problem is one that needs solving for us to satisfy the mandatory moral demand that is embedded in the basic commitment, then property is not merely justified in the sense that it is okay to have it. Rather, the argument is that property is *required* by our most basic moral commitments, or, if talk of justification is necessary, that it would *not* be morally justifiable *not* to have an institution of property. That is the core of the claim that property is an essential constituent of a society of equals. Property is not merely something we can have, an institution we can create. Property is something we are required to have, an institution that we are morally obligated to create. That makes it justified, in a way. But talk of justification there seems not quite sufficient to get the central point across.

Second, the second half of the argument of this book, that our institutions of property are deeply defective, that they are bad versions of their kind, that they require deep and significant change in order to approach the ideal to which they ought to aim, is also not one that is easily put in terms of justification. The ideal of the community of yours and mine gives us reason to radically revise our institutions, and we ought to do everything we can to make that happen. But

Property Law in the Society of Equals. Christopher Essert, Oxford University Press. © Oxford University Press 2024.
DOI: 10.1093/oso/9780197768952.003.0009

the fact that our institutions are defective does not mean that they are unjustified. And this is true in two ways. First, as I have stressed throughout, we cannot solve the problems of structural subordination that property can generate by eliminating property. That would be a mistake: as I just said, the argument about property's essential role in a society of equals can be understood as an argument that it would not be justified not to have property. We cannot go backward in the sequence of ideas presented here, only forward. A second way that the defectiveness of our institutions does not affect their justification is, as I argued at a few points, their defectiveness does not, at least in the case of structural subordination, undermine the obligatory nature of the private law relations that are the basic form of the realization of the idea of yours and mine. In other words, the fact that there is homelessness does not mean that it is wrong to enforce private property rights: it means that the state has a public law obligation to solve homelessness. It is not impossible to say all of what I have said here just using concepts of justification and reasons, but again it seems like the common way of using those concepts obscures the sequencing and structure of the ideas I have presented.

Third, some people have pressed me to say whether or not, even if the entire argument of this book is right, property is justified *all things considered*. Here the worry seems to be that, beyond everything said here, property creates what we might loosely call externalities that do not sound in the key of equal relations. It might be that property is a central cause of climate change or of mass extinctions or so on. Here, I must confess, my arguments run out. Remember the central claim: property is an essential constituent of a society of equals. And remember that the notion of a society of equals here is embedded in what I called the basic commitment, namely, an idea in political morality that seems to me to be the fundamental motivating notion of the entire idea of our legal and political systems. Perhaps someone wants to argue that we ought not to relate as equals, that there are values beyond our relations to each other that are so important that respect for them will require us to subordinate one another. I hope that is not true. But I cannot argue the point here: I have to stop (or start) somewhere, and a basic commitment to equality seems to me about as good a place to do so as I can imagine.

Appendix: An Inescapable Feature of the Social World

During the course of writing this book, I had an appendectomy. Like, the real thing, the medical procedure. So I now have what you might call an "internal connection" to the idea that an appendix is something superfluous. Anyways . . . what follows here under the title "Appendix" is superfluous, strictly speaking: you do not need to read it. But there is a point about which some readers might have questions, and I felt that answering those questions when they came up would have disrupted the flow of the book. So I have displaced them until here.

The questions are about the idea that we need to solve the Problem of Yours and Mine in order to meet the basic commitment because the idea of yours and mine is constitutive of a wide range of activities and relations that are so central that it is, as I put it, difficult to conceive of a social world without them for creatures like us. The suggestion is that because it makes these things possible, property is a morally inescapable feature of our social world. But there is a fair amount of ambiguity in that sentence: what does it mean for property to be "morally inescapable" or "difficult to conceive" of a world without it? What exactly is "*our* social world"?

To explore these questions, I will assume in this Appendix that the basic argument of the book is correct. That is, I will assume that it is impossible for us to participate in the wide range of activities and relations involving spaces and objects that we are familiar with in a way that is consistent with the basic commitment without property. Taking this for granted, the form of the question that we will explore here is, Are we sure this is something we should care about? Think about it in terms of this comparison: assume that we could not play baseball consistent with the basic commitment absent the rules of baseball as we understand them. Now suppose that there are various social costs associated with baseball—wasted youth, misuse of park space, overproduction of sunflower seeds—and that these costs are sufficient to make us question whether or not we should abandon baseball. Would that be okay? It seems like it would, it seems like a social world without baseball is one that is perfectly imaginable and that raises no problems in the realm of political morality: it might be bad in a specific way, but it would be consistent with the basic commitment or whatever other underlying moral ideals we might have. How is the case for property different? Answering that question turns on the differences between property and baseball and on the specific interpretations of the elements in the phrase under consideration.

We can think about this on a kind of a scale. At one end we understand the idea that property is necessary to our social world as meaning that it is necessary for the actual currently existing social world, "in a landscape vandalized by increasingly inane and powerful flows of capital."[1] Saying that property is necessary for this seems utterly uncontroversial, but it also seems unsatisfying, especially given the way in which the account of property I am offering here is meant as a sort of emancipatory project, in which careful attention to the nature and relations between our social concepts can lead us to a more just world. That is, I do not want the account to be merely a Panglossian just-so story about what we now have. You might move slightly away from this endpoint of the scale while maintaining its basic contingency, and say that our social world is one in which people are mostly selfish with some limited altruism, and that property is an institution for that social world—you would be Hume, basically—and then suggest that we could reshape those aspects of our social world, and that if we did, we would not need property. But I think I have shown that property is more deeply embedded than this picture suggests, that it is not about selfishness or possessive individualism. We need property for a wide range of forms of generosity and sharing, for important forms of communal living, and so on.

On the other end of the scale, we would understand my claim as an instance of robust Kantianism or perhaps of the kind of neo-Kantianism present in P F Strawson's work. In "Freedom and Resentment," for instance, Strawson argues that our interpersonal reactive attitudes are, in a way, inescapable. Asking if we could imagine a world in which we never had these attitudes, he says:

> I suppose we must say that it is not absolutely inconceivable that it should happen. But I am strongly inclined to think that it is, for us as we are, practically inconceivable. The human commitment to participation in ordinary inter-personal relationships is, I think, too thoroughgoing and deeply rooted for us to take seriously the thought that a general theoretical conviction might so change our world that, in it, there were no longer any such things as inter-personal relationships as we normally understand them; and being involved in inter-personal relationships as we normally understand them precisely is being exposed to the range of reactive attitudes and feelings that is in question.[2]

[1] This evocative phrase is from Willy Staley, "This Thing of Ours. What 'The Sopranos' Knew about America That We Didn't—Yet," which appeared in the *New York Times Magazine* on October 3, 2021, and which, as the title probably suggests, is not otherwise related to this book's subject matter. Also, see, more generally, Mark Fisher, Capitalist Realism: Is There No Alternative (2008).

[2] P F Strawson, Freedom and Resentment and Other Essays 12 (2008). Elsewhere Strawson offers an abstract characterization of this way of thinking about things: "It is possible to imagine kinds of worlds very different from the world as we know it. It is possible to describe types of experience very

A fair amount of what I have said here fits well with this. We cannot imagine life without being able to use and access spaces and objects, and interacting with spaces and objects in important ways requires the idea of yours and mine. Still, you might continue to object that my imagination is too impoverished, that there are forms of life that are both different enough from our own that they would not involve the idea of yours and mine and at the same time close enough to our own that we could actually conceive of living in them in a way that is consistent with the basic commitment. Sometimes, I am inclined to refer to my central claim in terms like this, as being about something like the moral impossibility of a world without property, or about such a world being morally unimaginable.[3] But, as I have said at least once, my own imagination might be limited. I tried, in §2.3, to show schematically that the obvious candidates for such an imagined world turn out not to work. But maybe you want to come up with others.

It is also important to notice there might be something in the middle of these two extremes. The crucial claim is that an egalitarian (i.e., basic commitment-compliant) social world—a society of equals—without the idea of yours and mine is inconceivable for us. And it might be that there is an interpretation of "us" that is not on the one end merely equivalent to "inhabitants of 21st century capitalist so-called democracies" while on the other end not requiring the sort of elaborate metaphysical commitments that Strawson wants to embrace. Here the idea would be to embrace a kind of Peircean pragmatism, and say that the depth and breadth of the embeddedness of the idea of yours and mine is too great to allow us to abandon it without remaking our social world to a degree which is in some sense beyond us. (This picture might also resonate with certain Rousseauian ideas on which there was or might once have been a kind of Golden

different from the experience we actually have. But not any purported and grammatically permissible description of a possible kind of experience would be a truly intelligible description. There are limits to what we can conceive of, or make intelligible to ourselves." P F Strawson, The Bounds of Sense 3 (1966).

[3] In this respect, this book has been deeply influenced by Seana Shiffrin's treatment of promising. Shiffrin opposes her account of promising to familiar conventionalist accounts, like Hume's, on which promising is a tool that we create to solve a problem that is comprehensible independent of any ideas of promising, that is, a "a more convenient way to do what could be done" without it, and so a tool all of whose features are up for grabs. Shiffrin instead argues that promising is "unique and indispensable," because it allows for a certain kind of morally essential relation that could not be achieved in any other way; one interpretation of Shiffrin's view is that the moral need for promising makes the creation of an institution of promising non-optional and also sets important constraints on the rules of that institution. Shiffrin at one point describes her argument as transcendental, in the sense that she begins with the claim that we need to do certain things, then argues that we need promising to do those things, and so concludes that we need promising. At this point, it will be clear how the structure of my argument here echoes a lot of what Shiffrin says, and so how one interpretation of my argument—the one that really emphasizes the parallel with Strawson—might make it look transcendental in the same way. For Shiffrin's argument, see Seana Valentine Shiffrin, "Promising, Intimate Relationships, and Conventionalism" 117 Philosophical Review 481 (2008).

Age in which we lived without yours and mine, but which, given human psychological and social development, we cannot return to.[4]) The transformation of human life and human societies that would be necessitated by the abandonment of that idea is too great to realistically contemplate, especially given the fact (herein established) that property is an egalitarian institution. In other words, we have an institution that allows us to relate to one another as equals with respect to spaces and objects (and so on), and this institution is clearly a basic and indispensable part of our social world and a wide variety of social worlds that are "nearby in conceptual space." As I have argued, the idea of yours and mine is realized not only in societies of possessive individualism (including those grounded on the common law) but also in more communitarian societies, societies (real or imagined) in which the means of production are collectively held, societies in which wealth is spread more evenly, and non-Western and Indigenous societies in which certain resources (notably land) are held communally. Are there other potential social worlds out there? Perhaps. Do we want to move to them? I have no way of knowing the answer to that question. The world we have now is a world in which property, by realizing the idea of yours and mine, allows us to meet the basic commitment to equality with respect to a hugely important part of our lives. And that seems good enough.

[4] There are also echoes here of the suggestion that non-Western or Indigenous forms of resource allocation might provide an alternative to property, which suggestion I discussed in §7.4.

Index

For the benefit of digital users, indexed terms that span two pages (e.g., 52–53) may, on occasion, appear on only one of those pages.